WHEN WOMEN STOP HATING THEIR BODIES

Also by the Authors

OVERCOMING OVEREATING

PREVENTING CHILDHOOD EATING PROBLEMS
(Jane R. Hirschmann and Lela Zaphiropoulos)

WHEN WOMEN STOP HATING THEIR BODIES

Freeing Yourself from Food and Weight Obsession

JANE R. HIRSCHMANN and CAROL H. MUNTER

FAWCETT COLUMBINE
New York

A Fawcett Columbine Book
Published by Ballantine Books

Published in the United States by Ballantine Books,
a division of Random House, Inc., New York, and simultaneously in Canada
by Random House of Canada Limited, Toronto.

Library of Congress Cataloging-in-Publication Data
Hirschmann, Jane R., 1946-
When women stop hating their bodies : freeing yourself from food
and weight obsession / Jane R. Hirschmann and Carol H. Munter.
p. cm.
ISBN 0-449-90680-9
1. Compulsive eating—Treatment. 2. Reducing—Psychological
aspects. I. Munter, Carol H. II. Title.
RC552.C65H54 1995
616.85′26—dc20 *94-27851*
CIP

Text design by Ruth Kolbert

Manufactured in the United States of America

First Edition: March 1995

10 9 8 7 6 5 4 3 2 1

In memory of Gertrud Rosenthal Hirschmann
In honor of Naomi Roth Munter
And to the next wave—
Kate, Nell, and Leta Hirschmann-Levy

Contents

Part Three

RECLAIMING YOURSELF

Preface

IT WAS CLEAR BY 1992—THE YEAR OF THE WOMAN—THAT FEMINIST ACtivity, somewhat stalled during the backlash of the eighties, had revived. Growing numbers of women launched campaigns across the country to end sexual abuse and harassment both on the job and at home. More women than ever entered government, and calls for "equal pay for equal work" and "reproductive freedom" were heard once more with renewed vigor.

Women, again, were on the move.

Ironically, despite the fact that women's power and position in the world have changed dramatically, millions of women—of all shapes and sizes—still wake up every morning, look at themselves in the mirror, and say, "Yuck." The purpose of this book is to explore that contradiction.

We have worked with thousands of women with compulsive eating problems for more than two decades and we are convinced that hatred of one's own body, a syndrome we have named "Bad Body Fever," is central to women's oppression. It is, in fact, explicit evidence of the ongoing oppression of women. To be sure, the position of women has changed, but Bad Body Fever—the malaise women contract as a result of living in a culture that devalues them—is still as rampant and contagious as ever.

Bad Body Fever propels women to diet and to spend their lives in the futile quest for power through physical transformation. Bad Body Fever causes women to focus on their bodies at the expense of their lives. And it is Bad Body Fever that makes women resist the incontrovertible evidence that dieting is futile and dangerous. In our view, until every woman can look at herself in the mirror and smile with pleasure at her reflection—*just the way she is*—women's struggle for equality is far from over.

The Birth of a Nondiet Approach

In April of 1970 a handful of women in New York City joined forces to tackle the ubiquitous problem of compulsive eating and self-image. Carol Munter started this particular group because, as a large woman, she felt different from the others in her conscious-raising group. She understood their complaints about being objectified as sex objects, but felt she had not had the social experiences that her friends were so eager to put behind them. Naturally thin as a child, she knew that the way women were viewed and treated was part of the reason she had gained weight as an adolescent. Yet Carol, like most women, also longed to feel desired.

Carol and the women in that first group came to recognize the extent to which they had internalized the attitudes of a culture that treats women as inferior and presumes to tell them what shape they must take. The climate of the 1970s, in which radical thoughts among women flourished, gave the women in this group permission to question some of their long-held assumptions.

"What's wrong with being fat?"

"Why should we diet?"

"Why is it that even though we've been *good* girls and done exactly what we've been told to do about our weight, we're fatter than ever?"

"Is there something inherently wrong with us that makes it impossible for us to stay on diets—or is the problem with the diets themselves?"

"Who are these people who have told us what to eat and how to look?"

"Why are *they* entitled to wield so much power over us?"

Finally, the women in the group made a revolutionary decision.

"We are not dieting anymore. Whatever happens to our weight, we will never deprive ourselves of food again."

Critical to the success of this resolution was the support the women in the group offered each other. They came to recognize that the diet/binge cycle was symptomatic of a deeper self-revulsion and together they managed to block out the vision of a harsh, disapproving culture and replace it with a kinder vision of their own. They took photographs of each other, and studied them, and eventually transformed their disgust into self-acceptance. They drew pictures of themselves. They shopped for food and for clothes, and when the clothing did not fit, they sewed their own.

These women talked endlessly about the pain of compulsive eating, and they also talked about their families and their lives. They became astute detectives, asking questions and searching for clues as to why they used food the way they did. "Why after not needing to lean on food for weeks, did I suddenly crave brownies when I wasn't the least bit hungry?" someone would ask. "What were you feeling at the time?" someone else would inquire, and the discussion would begin. Ultimately, the women in this group relearned how to feed themselves.

In 1974, Jane Hirschmann used this nondiet approach to cure her own eating problem. The experience affected her life profoundly, and she introduced these concepts in the public health settings where she worked. Years later, as a new mother, she became interested in how this approach could be used to prevent and to cure eating problems in children. In 1985 she co-authored *Preventing Childhood Eating Problems* (originally titled *Are You Hungry?*) with Lela Zaphiropoulos.

Over the years, through their teaching and in their work with clients, Carol and Jane expanded and distilled this nondiet perspective on eating problems. Their efforts culminated in the writing of *Overcoming Overeating,* published in 1988. *Overcoming Overeating* appeared at a time when the inefficacy of diets was becoming evident. In recent years, myriad research projects have demonstrated unequivocally that diets do not work. Of those people who go on diets, ninety-five to ninety-eight percent regain their weight, plus some. Diets make us fatter. Diets turn us into compulsive eaters. Diets make us sick!

Why do we keep engaging in an activity that both harms us and fails us time and again? Why do we continue to cling to the promise of diets despite documentation that the more we restrict food, the more desperate we become, and the more desperate we become, the more we eat? Why on earth haven't women put the diet industry out of business?

"Ahaa!" might cry Sherlock Holmes or Nancy Drew in observing this most puzzling case of self-deception and self-destruction. "Here is a mystery worthy of the world's greatest detectives!" They would be right. On the surface, the reality is completely confounding.

Diets are based on women's dislike of their bodies. Why, after all their advances, do women continue to feel compelled to change the very essence of who they are in an effort to comply with a standard that is rooted in sexism?

A mystery indeed!

But do not despair. There are answers to be found in the social and personal dynamic of the oppression itself. Follow the clues with us. It will take some work, we admit, to assemble a clear and accurate picture. But, for all who have suffered the agony of food obsession and body hatred, this is a case well worth solving.

Acknowledgments

The ideas in this book developed from our dialogues with the women who attend our New York weekly workshops. Although the cast of characters changes from week to week, different women, at different times, form a consistent core. In the years since we wrote *Overcoming Overeating*, these women have been our respectful challengers, a focus group for our new ideas and, most important, our inspiration. They push us to formulate ideas we did not know were waiting in the wings, and they show us each week that with courage, persistence, gentleness and imagination, it is possible to overcome body hatred and compulsive eating. We are joyfully in their debt and hope that we have done justice to their remarkable efforts.

We thank and acknowledge Karen Levine for once again giving clarity, grace, and shape to our work.

Our gratitude to our editor, Ginny Faber, for her ongoing support of our work, her editorial talent, and her willingness to hang in there with us. Thanks, too, to Margaret Ryan for her insightful and skillful work on the manuscript.

Our sincere appreciation to the people at Ballantine—Matthew, Carol, Jane, Sally, and Beth—for taking up the challenge and making it happen.

Special thanks to our agent, Ellen Levine, and to her associate, Diana Finch, for all their efforts on our behalf.

My heartfelt and deepest thanks to Bert Wainer for his loving, unflagging support of me and of this project.

To Richard Levy whose love, support, good cooking, and humor afford me the freedom to pursue my life's work. I thank you.

For their helpful comments on the manuscript we thank Alan Gelb, Adrienne Queller, Lucille Spira, Joan Stein, and Vicki Zoldessy.

For their dedication, risk-taking, and ability to get the word out, we are grateful to Jill Donovan and Jill Hroneck of Jade Publishing. Our special thanks to Mark Wagner for his firm belief in this work.

For their initiative in our collaboration and their contributions to the development of these ideas, we thank Carol Coven Grannick and Judith Matz, directors of the Chicago Center for Overcoming Overeating.

Introduction

When Women Stop Hating Their Bodies is a complete handbook for women who want to free themselves from body hatred and from the dieting it spawns. More precisely, it is a guide to overcoming the formidable opposition a woman encounters when she resolves to tackle the problem of Bad Body Fever.

For a woman to say "No more diets!" "No more self-contempt!" "No more efforts to make myself over in his (or anyone else's) image!" is nothing short of revolutionary. Her "No mores" are declarations of independence. They inevitably trigger reactions from the world around her, and unsettle her own equilibrium as well.

In *Overcoming Overeating*, we urged women to stop renovating their bodies and to move into them with love and respect, precisely as they are. We explained how compulsive eating, a problem that plagues millions of women, is the inevitable legacy of dieting and we prescribed "demand feeding" and abundance as the cure.

Many thousands of women have adopted our approach. They have stocked their homes with all kinds of food, including the most "forbidden," and they have begun feeding themselves when, what, and how much their bodies need. They have joined existing Overcoming Overeating support groups, formed groups of their own, or simply found the strength within themselves to say "No more." They have replaced self-reproach and body hatred with self-care and self-acceptance. They have abandoned their scales and bought clothes that they love—clothes that actually fit.

These women, whose names we have changed but whose stories we recount throughout this book, report extraordinary changes in themselves and in their lives. They no longer feel obsessed with food. They no longer hate their bodies. They no longer feel driven to eat when they are not hungry. And many of them have lost weight as a by-product of demand feeding.

These women also report that the struggle to free themselves from dieting and body hatred has been more difficult then they ever could have imagined. They had understood at the beginning that giving up dieting was a revolutionary act, but they had not understood the extent to which they had used dieting and body hatred to cope with the central issues of their lives.

Unfortunately, we live in a culture that accepts body hatred and dieting as normal components of femininity. Women are encouraged to expend enormous amounts of energy shaping their bodies rather than their lives. When a woman declares an end to dieting and body hatred she is breaking rules, rules that have formed her sense of herself. She may feel exhilarated at her first taste of freedom, but as a dweller in this culture, she cannot help but worry about the consequences of her actions. Although Bad Body Fever causes a woman great pain, this pain has become an integral part of her entire emotional and psychological makeup; any attempt to heal it causes an inner reshuffling and understandable protest.

When women first hear that we recommend saying "No more" to diets, they smile with pleasure or giggle nervously. Very soon, however, they say, "I think you're absolutely correct, but . . ." These "yes, buts" are expressions of resistance. They are a way women have of saying, "We want to free ourselves from body hatred and dieting, but who will we be without them?"

When Women Stop Hating Their Bodies is a response to your "yes, buts." Each and every concern you have about abandoning body hatred and dieting deserves exploration. Each "yes, but" reveals something about how you have internalized the rules of the culture.

Although dieting and body hatred have made women miserable, they have also worked for us in a number of ways. For example, dieting and body hatred keep us in good standing as female citizens. We have done everything we have been told to do about eating and maintaining—or striving for—the "right" weight. When we think about saying "No more," we worry about standing apart from the cultural norm. We may love the idea of freedom, but hesitate to jeopardize our "good girl" status.

We also worry about what we ourselves will think or feel if we are not directing so much energy toward condemning and fixing our bodies. Dieting and body hatred have distracted most of us from some of the central issues in our lives. Thinking about our problems rather than eating them into temporary oblivion is liberating but takes some getting used to. If instead of saying, "I feel fat," we tell the truth about what is bothering us, what will happen?

Finally, we wonder what will replace all the rules about food and the negative attention we have focused on ourselves. If we no longer live with the belief that, once we are thin, everything in our lives will fall into place, then we must start attending to our own needs very differently. We have no role models to follow in this area. We have not seen many women who take care of themselves and their bodies with love and respect. Many of us may never have known even one woman who could look in the mirror and say, "I'm fine just the way I am"—and truly mean it.

When Women Stop Hating Their Bodies explores all of the problems women encounter as they try to free themselves from body hatred and dieting. We suggest that you read the book through first. We have included a detailed index so that you can refer back to the book each time you are troubled by a particular "yes, but." Remember that giving up dieting and curing Bad Body Fever are revolutionary acts that require ongoing attention.

A Note to Men

We recognize that many men also suffer from the problem of body hatred and compulsive eating, and our approach works as well for men as it does for women. We have made a decision, however, to write about this problem from a woman's perspective. We did this for two reasons.

First, women are still very much defined by how they look and what they eat. The culture we live in continues to afford men more latitude when it comes to appetite and body size.

Second, it is clear to us that our culture's hatred of fat is inextricably linked to our cultural ambivalence about female strength and power. A woman's body hatred is her internalized version of cultural misogyny. She tells herself each and every day that her body is wrong and that she takes up too much space in the world.

In a society in which fat is associated with being female, a fat man is considered less male. When a man chastises himself for his large belly, for example, he is actually berating himself for not living up to the cultural standard of manliness. Men, too, must challenge the rules of the culture by asking such questions as "Who says that my body is not okay just the way it is?"

Many men experience enormous pain around the issues of body size and compulsive eating. Although our book is written about women, we believe that men can work well with this approach, applying it to their specific needs.

The Process

When Women Stop Hating Their Bodies is divided into three parts: Reclaiming Your Body, Reclaiming Your Appetite, and Reclaiming Yourself.

In Part 1, Reclaiming Your Body, we describe Bad Body Fever, explore its unwanted resilience, and outline its cure. Much of this cure rests on your ability to challenge ideas you have taken for granted. For example, you must learn to ask "Who says that flat stomachs are the most attractive?" "Who says that we should all be thin?" We also explore our contention that a "bad body thought" is never about your body and teach you how to use your bad body thoughts as clues to your emotional life. In Part 2, Reclaiming Your Appetite, we review our proposal to replace dieting with demand feeding and explore the difficulties, both external and internal, that come into play as you attempt to become attuned to your body's needs.

In Part 3, Reclaiming Yourself, we describe "mouth hunger," or psychological hunger, and discuss the steps you must take in order to get to a point where you can think about your problems rather than eat about them. What qualities do you need to develop in order to sit with your feelings and work them through?

The voices in this book come from the women who have attended our workshops in New York City and across the country. We are certain, however, that they echo the thoughts and feelings of the many women who have been working with the Overcoming Overeating approach on their own. These voices represent countless courageous women who have given up dieting and are well on their way to curing their Bad Body Fever. They are an inspiration to us, and we trust that they will be an inspiration to you, our readers, as well. Each of us is waging a private struggle, but there is great comfort in knowing that others are engaged in that same effort.

We believe that the time has come for women to tackle Bad Body Fever—a pivotal, deep manifestation of the problem of inequality between men and women. We hope to convince you that the time has come for you, personally, to reclaim your appetite, your body, and yourself.

Part One

Reclaiming Your Body

Chapter 1

BAD BODY FEVER

YOU WAKE UP IN THE MORNING AND MAKE YOUR WAY INTO THE BATHroom to shower. Groggy with sleep, you turn on the water and take off your nightgown. As you are about to get in the shower, you see yourself in the full-length mirror. "Yuck!" you say. "I feel so fat."

You are not alone. Every moment of every hour of every day millions of women of varying shapes and sizes utter some variation of the phrase "I feel fat." You might be fully clothed when the bad body thought strikes. You might catch a glimpse of yourself reflected in a shop window and gasp, "God! My stomach is huge." You might be daydreaming while waiting for an appointment only to find yourself thinking that your thighs are disgusting. Or you might be walking to your car when you suddenly feel huge.

If this kind of self-loathing were experienced by only a small number of women, we would be justified in attempting to understand it in terms of the individual's psychopathology. The fact is, however, that fat feelings—or bad body feelings—occupy the minds and hearts of the vast majority of women. Bad Body Fever is neither viral nor bacterial, but it *is* epidemic.

How does Bad Body Fever affect you? Take a pen and a sheet of paper and review the last twenty-four hours of your life. Think about getting out of bed in the morning, taking your shower, getting dressed, and heading out the door to work or do errands. Think about specific interactions with friends, family, and acquaintances. Think about buying, preparing, and eating food.

As you recall each activity, ask yourself what accompanying thoughts you had about your body and the way you looked. Write down the thoughts as you recall them, making certain to use the same phrases you used during the day.

When the women at our workshops do this exercise, their lists include such phrases as:

"I look monstrous/gross/revolting/disgusting."

"I'm weak/self-indulgent/out of control/a pig."

"I have no business leaving my house."

"Nothing fits me."

"Everyone is looking at me."

"I feel so fat, I want to die."

What does it mean when a woman says, in one way or another, "I feel fat"? Although *feeling fat* is a relatively recent addition to our language of feelings, unfortunately it is a feeling that most women understand. Because we live in a society in which fatness is denigrated, each time a woman says, "I feel fat," she is saying, "There is something wrong with me." Each time a woman feels fat, she is feeling self-hatred and self-disgust. The disturbing truth is that our culture fosters and supports this kind of self-denigration in women.

How can we rid ourselves of Bad Body Fever? First, we must investigate the environmental conditions that foster its growth. In order to understand an ailment like Bad Body Fever, which is so clearly gender-related, we must stop thinking only in terms of our individual psyches and begin thinking in terms of the collective position of women in our society. After all, Bad Body Fever has not always been around; it is a phenomenon of our current culture. Once we understand Bad Body Fever as a social ill, we must look deeply within ourselves in order to discern the particular ways in which our psyches have been shaped by our culture, leaving us vulnerable to Bad Body Fever in the first place.

What Makes Bad Body Fever Flourish?

Turn on the TV and pay particular attention to the commercials. Actually study them. What do you see? What do you hear? What are you being told about your female body? The message of commercials requires no deciphering when the product is a diet pill or an exercise machine. But look at the commercials that have nothing to do with body altering. Who is selling the product? Do you look like her? Does anyone you know look like her? Probably not.

More often than not, the actresses and models we see on television have bodies they did not come by naturally. It is likely that the body of the woman who is selling the car has been altered surgically and masked cosmetically; in addition, she has endured endless hours of workouts and many years of deprivation. When you open your favorite magazine and see a photograph of the same smiling woman with the same beautiful car, you can be sure that the photo has been retouched and airbrushed to achieve an even higher degree of blemish-free perfection. The image before you is a creation, not a reproduction.

Commercials and ads like the one just described convey a dual message. The first message is "Buy this car." The second message, which is subliminal, says in essence, "If you look like me, people will pay attention to you and you might get nice things like this car." After hearing these messages over time, both women and men come to believe that all women *should* look like models.

Of course, Bad Body Fever takes time to develop. You did not start out life feeling that your body was deficient. Hopefully, your infant body was loved and cuddled and cared for. As a baby and toddler, when you were told how adorable you were, you actually felt adorable. You enjoyed your body and its functioning. You also enjoyed your mother's body. She felt warm, soft, cozy, and safe.

Julia, a participant in our New York workshop, described her discovery that things were not as they appeared to her child's eyes. "When I was very young, I thought that my mother was beautiful," she recounted. "Then one day, I saw her look in the mirror and grimace at her reflection. I was confused. I asked her what was the matter and she said she looked 'ghastly' without her makeup. I also remember her complaining that she had nothing to wear even though I thought her wardrobe was vast and magical. By the time I was six or seven, I realized that my beautiful mother did not think she was beautiful at all. That made me sad—and it made me sad to see her not eating in order to get thinner.

"I remember wondering why someone as beautiful as my mother would think that she was ugly. And then why did she tell me I was so pretty? What did it mean to be pretty? Was *I* pretty enough to look in the mirror and like what I see?"

Little girls learn a great deal about what is valued by how their mothers did or did not value themselves. As girls approach adolescence, the same eyes that once looked at them so adoringly suddenly become more critical as mothers feel the need to ensure their daughters' safety and success. "You know," says the mother of a thirteen-year-old, "you have to change before you go out. That top is too revealing." Or, "You know, dear, you're developing a little belly. You'd better start watching what you eat." As that belly and those buttocks and breasts begin to develop, mothers begin to watch their daughters more closely, fathers begin to avert their eyes, and the world of men begins to take notice.

There is no question that teenage girls feel a great deal of ambivalence about the shape of their bodies. On the one hand, they want to look good enough to be noticed. On the other hand, they don't want to be noticed at all. "Look beautiful," they are told by their mothers, by every TV program they watch, and by every fashion magazine they read, "but be careful." Young girls learn that it is good to be beautiful, but it is not good to elicit a certain type of attention. Seek to be desired and chosen, but fear it, too. In the end, most young girls learn to *wish* more than they fear: They wish for smaller noses, curlier or straighter hair, larger or smaller breasts, fuller or thinner bodies. As Susie Orbach writes in *Fat Is a Feminist Issue II,* "selling body insecurity to women (and increasingly to men too) is a vicious phenomenon. It relies on the social practices that shape a girl's growing up to make her receptive."

Our culture is deeply ambivalent about women and their bodies. Women are idealized and denigrated, protected and abused, encouraged and discriminated against. Each decade promulgates a new shape for the female form. By the time most girls become women, they have confused and conflicting feelings about their place in the world. This confusion manifests itself in a dissatisfaction with their bodies and their appearance. Before long, their confused and conflicting feelings boil down to one issue: Fat. In our culture, fat has come to represent flesh, female, and undesirable. For most girls, "fat talk" becomes their mother tongue.

Fat Talk—The Language of Bad Body Fever

Susan, a teacher, told us that she was waiting in the wings with a group of eleven-year-old girls on the opening night of a play they had been rehearsing for weeks. "As they were listening nervously to the overture, I heard one of them say to a friend, 'I feel so fat.' 'No,' her friend responded. 'You look great, but look how big my stomach is.' They were terribly anxious and I realized that they've already learned to do what all of us do: They talk about their bodies instead of their anxiety."

Susan was telling us that these girls have already learned to speak in code. What precisely were they anxious about that night? Most likely they were afraid they would not measure up; that, in some critical way, they would be found lacking. This concern about inadequacy translated into "Something is wrong with my body." They may also have had conflicting feelings about being in the spotlight, wishing to be stars but uncomfortable about their right to have such a wish. Rather than indulge their fantasies of stealing the show, they thought about their "bad" body fat. Very soon, many of these eleven-year-olds who secretly wish to be in the spotlight will go on diets and attempt to make themselves smaller. "Look at me"/"Don't look at me": the paradox of young girlhood.

The statement "I feel fat" is never really about fat, even if you are a fat person. Each time a woman looks at her thighs and says, "Yuck," she is really saying, "There's something wrong with me or with what I'm feeling." We turn our bodies into metaphors for all of our bad feelings—and we find confirmation for doing so everywhere we look.

Fat Was Not Always Bad

Why is it that when we want to berate ourselves, we call ourselves fat, rather than short, or tall, or blue-eyed, or brown-eyed? We are all so accustomed to thinking of the word *fat* as a slur that it is hard to imagine a time when it was anything other than that. The fact is, until fairly recently, *fat* was not a dirty word. A quick review of other languages tells us much about the history of the word.

According to *Webster's* dictionary, the Latin word for fat is related to the word *optimus*, which means "fertile" or "copious." In Greek, the word for fat is related to the words *pidyein* and *pidax*, which mean "to gush forth." In Sanskrit, the word for fat, *pivan*, means "robust." English definitions include "well filled out," "of sizable proportions," "thick" (as in a fat letter or volume of verse), and "unusually large, substantial and impressive" (as in a fat bank account, a fat fee, or a fat part in a play). The list of positive definitions continues with "productive," "fertile," and "fruitful." Only at the bottom of the list of definitions do we find negative connotations like "coarse," "gross," or "slow-witted."

It is very hard for women today to imagine a world in which people were not repelled by fat, but we urge you to do just that. Plan an excursion to a museum and look at paintings of large women. Try to find one with a body like yours. If the museum gift shop has a postcard of that particular painting, buy two of them. Put one on your refrigerator door and see how much more relaxed you feel in the kitchen. Put the other in your purse. Each time you have a bad body thought, take out the postcard and think about what life was like for the woman who modeled for the painting. She may have had her problems, but her size was not one of them. She was not assaulted with electronic and print images of what her body should look like. She sewed her own clothes or had them made to fit her body. There were no standardized sizes for women's clothing until the late nineteenth century. Imagine never being asked your size.

We said earlier that every time a woman says, "I'm fat," she is really saying, "I'm not good enough" or "I'm bad." Now we would like you to consider the possibility that when a woman says disgustedly that she feels fat, she is really saying that she feels she is too large—larger than any woman is supposed to be in a man's world.

How much space is a woman supposed to occupy? How fertile and substantial is a woman supposed to be? Is it possible that women feel fat when they think their ideas, wishes, and feelings are out of line or unladylike? We believe that when women suspect they have overstepped some boundary, they attack themselves for the transgression by calling themselves fat. In this way, women keep their ideas, feelings, and forbidden ambitions in check.

Does this sound too far-fetched to you? Consider Mary's story. Mary received a long-overdue promotion at work. She was delighted. Then her supervisor called to tell her that a photographer would be there the next morning to take her picture for the company newsletter. From that point on, all Mary could think about was how fat she felt and how much she did not want her picture taken. That night she slept fitfully. Each time she woke up she saw herself looming large in the photograph. The joy she felt about her promotion was completely eclipsed by her concern about being too fat, too big, too successful.

Megan told us that she had recently completed an intense self-defense class for women. "I didn't recognize myself—fighting back in the class the way I did. But ever since, I haven't been able to stop thinking about my body. I feel huge," she said. Like Mary, Megan felt that she had overstepped some boundary.

Before Fat Was a Bad Word

Bad Body Fever is an outgrowth of a culture that makes women feel inferior. Women feel that their bodies are deficient because they are born female into a world in which men hold the power. Women are, in fact, treated as if they are not good enough.

Although it has shown itself differently in different cultures, women have been treated as inferiors for as long as men have held power. In some primitive societies, menstruating women, isolated from the tribe, were feared and shunned. Some variation of this practice still goes on today in more than one religion, where women continue to be regarded as unclean or unworthy of performing sacred tasks. Clitoridectomy, the ultimate measure by which men control women's sexuality, is still a common practice in parts of the world today. In *Possessing the Secret of Joy*, Alice Walker reports, "It is estimated that from ninety to one hundred million women and girls living today in Africa, Far Eastern and Middle Eastern countries have been genitally mutilated."

Although women have been oppressed throughout recorded history, the particular result of that oppression that concerns us—body hatred—is of recent vintage. According to the historian Roberta Seid, women's bodies were not regarded as "packaging" until the eighteenth century, when women began to compete on the marriage market. Before that, fashion was regarded as part of upper-class life for both men and women. Even when fashion became a female concern rather than an upper-class one, the emphasis was on clothing and decoration, not on diet, exercise, and body shaping. If women wanted to emphasize their buttocks, they wore bustles—they did not try to build up their actual muscles.

Naomi Wolf argues convincingly that the hatred of fat per se did not emerge until women began to join forces and reject their inferior status. "Soft rounded hips and thighs and bellies were perceived as desirable and sensual without question, until women got the vote," she writes in *The Beauty Myth.* It appears that the more powerful women become, the more pressure there is for us to get rid of the padding and curves that make our bodies so different from the bodies of men. When we loathe ourselves for being fat, we are succumbing to this pressure. When we lash out at our stomachs, our thighs, our hips, our backsides, our breasts, and our cellulite, we are hating our femaleness. We live in a culture that demonstrates its ambivalence toward women in the violence of its pornography and in the prevalence of rape and battering. When we hate our bodies, we are turning against ourselves.

What do you think would happen if all women stopped hating their bodies? We routinely ask this question of workshop participants. Their answers are always strikingly similar and demonstrate what we have been saying about the inhibiting effect of Bad Body Fever. "Our energy would be astounding," said one workshop participant. "No question about it," said another, almost giddy with pleasure. "We would take over the world!"

Shape our bodies or shape the world? It is a choice that men do not have to consider. Yet, by the time we reach womanhood, each of us has internalized the pressure to make ourselves less than we are, to take up less room in the world. Our bad body thoughts preoccupy us, constrain us, and control us.

Dissecting Bad Body Fever

It is important to recognize the intensity with which the vast majority of women evaluate their bodies. We *hate* our bodies with a passion. And, as is the case with all passionate hatred, there is more to our response than meets the eye.

Generally, passionate hatred disguises some other story: We hate what we fear; we hate what we envy; we hate the people and things that frustrate our needs and desires. But our focus on hating, like our focus on fat, keeps our real feelings at bay. Think about the intensity with which people hate minority groups or foreigners. Such hatred is fueled by a fear—which is the real feeling—that something strange and unknown about these groups will threaten the values and power structure of the dominant culture.

Fear, envy, and frustration underlie hatred on a more personal level as well. For example, have you ever felt that you hated a coworker who always insisted on having things her way, when, in fact, what you really felt was envy of her ability to assert herself and frustration at your inability? Or did you ever hate a friend's self-involvement, realizing that, underneath your attentiveness to others lurked an equally pervasive self-absorption? Or perhaps you hate your ex-husband, when what you really hate is the fact that he did not love you the way you loved him.

What is the story behind our hatred of our bodies? We have already talked about the fact that our bodies reveal our femaleness. Now we must go one step further and explore the fear, envy, and frustration that underlie the hatred with which we regard our female flesh. After all, social ideas must be endorsed by each one of us in order to be effective without the use of coercion or violence. We endorse ideas willingly only if they correspond to our needs. Our intensely negative feelings about our female bodies take hold in part because they are rooted in our very earliest experiences.

The Ambivalence of Dependency

In her book *The Mermaid and the Minotaur*, Dorothy Dinnerstein suggests that nothing fundamental will change in the relationships between men and women until child care is shared equally. She believes that as long as women are in charge of caring for children, both boys and girls will continue to turn to women for nurturance and then blame them when they feel deprived. All of the ambivalence that children feel about being dependent and not getting everything they want exactly when they want it is directed toward their mothers, who are both the recipients of their love and the targets of their rage.

Dinnerstein maintains that we continue to act out our love and rage toward our mothers throughout our lives. Men act it out directly when they exert power over women, and women act it out indirectly when they acquiesce to men. In other words, when we either allow ourselves to be demeaned or demean ourselves, we are—by identifying ourselves with her—reaping revenge on the mother who frustrated us, and whom we both loved and feared.

For all of us, fat represents the large, nurturing, and feared bodies of our mothers. Our culture's current ambivalence toward female bodies, which is expressed in the ideal of thinness, is able to flourish because it echoes the deep feelings we each hold about our early dependency on our mothers. It was our mothers' bodies with which we fiercely wished to merge, and it was their bodies from which we fiercely wished to separate. It was our mothers who enforced the restrictions we resented yet who gave us enormous pleasure. We approach our own womanhood with both sets of feelings: loving our mothers/their bodies and hating our mothers/their bodies. As Kim Chernin states in her eloquent book *The Obsession: Reflections on the Tyranny of Slenderness*, "When we attempt to determine the size and shape of a woman's body, instructing it to avoid its largeness and softness and roundness and girth, we are driven by the desire to expunge the memory of the primordial mother who ruled over our childhood with her inscrutable power over life and death."

At some point in our development, we realize that our mothers, who had so much power in relation to us as children, have a lot less power in the "real" world. For us as young women, this realization is met with ambivalence: On the one hand, it means our mothers are far less threatening; on the other, it also means our mothers have little power with which to endow us for our own adulthood. Either way, we lose.

The Real Weight Large Women Carry

As a gender-related condition, Bad Body Fever infects women regardless of their actual body size. However, while Bad Body Fever runs a similar course for thin *and* fat women, the virulence of it is considerably more painful for large women—the really big mothers of our world.

There is a great difference between being fat and feeling fat. When thin women feel and talk fat, the world responds by telling them how thin they are. But the world is eager to join in the lamentations of a large woman who censures herself—after all, hasn't she broken all the rules? Being female in a male-dominated world engenders the self-hatred that leads to Bad Body Fever. Living large in a supposed-to-be-thin world is an added hell.

You go to the doctor and the gown covers only half your body; the blood pressure cuff barely makes it around your arm. The doctor lectures you "in your best interest" about the need to lose weight for health reasons—as if you had not spent a lifetime dedicated to this very task.

You get on the bus and the half seat next to you is the last to be taken. You ask the airline hostess for a seat-belt extender and the people around you stare as she says she'll see if she can find one. You go shopping and find a great T-shirt that is marked "one size fits all." You don't know whether to laugh, cry, or scream.

You compose a personal ad. How to say it? Carefully you choose your words: "Full-bodied woman would like to meet. . . ." You have some nice chats on the phone, but when your prospective friend asks, "How will I recognize you?" you want to die.

You interview for a job. The interview goes well. As you are leaving, you notice that the next woman in line is a size ten. If everything else is almost equal, guess who will get the job?

You wonder what people think as you walk down the street. Many of them actually speak up. Those who do not may well be thinking just what you think they are thinking. It is what your mother thinks, your aunt thinks, your cousins think, and you think: "She'd be so pretty, if only . . . How can she do that to herself?"

If you are truly larger than most, you are the visible manifestation of what we have all learned to hate and, as a consequence, you suffer real punishments and daily humiliations. In addition, it is likely that you suffer from a virulent case of Bad Body Fever.

The Consequences of Bad Body Fever

Bad body thoughts and fat talk are the first symptoms of Bad Body Fever. They trigger a predictable chain of events.

First, Bad Body Fever leads most of its sufferers into dieting. The logic behind the so-called antidote goes, if you feel too fat, simply set about losing weight and that will solve your "problem." We know, however, that the problem we attempt to solve by dieting is not a fat problem but is, instead, the way we feel about ourselves *as women*. Therefore, no matter how thin we get, we still feel fat—larger than we consider appropriate.

As we all know, as dieters we inevitably become trapped in the diet/binge cycle. Not only do we end up fatter than had we never set eyes on a single diet, worse still, we become lifelong compulsive eaters in the process. When Bad Body Fever becomes truly unbearable, its sufferers try such drastic measures as gastric stapling and liposuction.

These painful and unproductive "solutions" succeed only at keeping women focused on the single issue of their physical imperfections, but there is an illusion of comfort in this insular focus. A new diet, exercise program, or surgical procedure creates a kind of temporarily comforting distraction from the issues in our lives that need our undivided attention. "I felt so energized by the possibilities," said one woman in a workshop. "As long as there was some new pill or program to buy or try, I had hope. Nothing was too expensive or painful. I actually felt noble in my willingness to sacrifice for the sake of losing weight."

However, self-contempt never inspires lasting change. After a while, the enthusiasm for each new approach fades. We stop going to the gym; we binge out of our diet; we miss the weigh-in at our local diet center. The initial zeal, which is actually part of the Bad Body Fever syndrome, is gone, and in its place is a deep sense of failure and fatigue. Chronic Bad Body Fever is exhausting and exacts a heavy toll from us, its sufferers. Not only do we lack energy, but as a result of turning so much anger against ourselves, we feel depressed and even despairing.

Is there a way out of this despair? Is there a way to break the diet/binge cycle, free ourselves from body hatred and emerge energized to tackle the real issues that weigh us down? The cure for Bad Body Fever is part of the overall cure for compulsive eating. Ironically, our prescription for ending body hatred meets with strong resistance.

Chapter

2

Resisting the Cure

How can you cure yourself of Bad Body Fever? If you accept the idea that Bad Body Fever develops as a result of the inequities between men and women, its cure then becomes part of the larger struggle for women's liberation. As a result of this struggle during the past twenty-five years, the general condition of women has improved considerably. Despite these improvements, however, Bad Body Fever lingers and is more virulent than ever. It is time to address this ailment seriously, to ask ourselves why we have such difficulty recovering from it, and to explore specific remedies.

Legalize Your Body

The cure for Bad Body Fever involves a liberation from all cultural views on body size. To cure Bad Body Fever you must *legalize your body*. In other words, you must stop trying to lose weight and accept your body precisely as it is, regardless of size. Understandably, this suggestion inspires fear and disbelief in most women. Stop trying to lose weight in a culture like ours?

This task is an extremely difficult one. Accepting your body regardless of its size requires a great deal of self-nurturing, an ability to free yourself from cultural beliefs, and a willingness to finally get to know yourself. You will discover how much you rely on the negative thoughts you have about your body—your bad body thoughts—to mask other important issues in your life. You would not be so focused on your body if you felt comfortable acknowledging your thoughts and feelings more openly. Shedding that mask and confronting those issues head on can be a frightening prospect, which we will discuss in the following chapter.

Along with ridding yourself of bad body thoughts, you need to *inhabit your body*, as it is, with genuine love and understanding. This kind of self-affirmation leaves no room for the negative judgments of the culture in which we live. We will be dealing with this issue of befriending your body in Chapter 4.

In *The Beauty Myth* Naomi Wolf writes, "A man's right to confer judgment on any woman's beauty while remaining himself unjudged . . . is the last unexamined right remaining intact from the old list of masculine privilege . . . that it was universally believed that God or nature or another absolute authority bestowed upon all men to exert over all women." For most women, the notion of challenging such longstanding authority by loving and accepting their bodies, regardless of their size, feels about as possible as the notion of defying gravity. The fact is, however, that you can learn to love and accept your body without altering it in any way. To get an idea of what that might feel like, we suggest you try an exercise that some of you may remember from our last book.

Suspend your disbelief for the moment and imagine that the atmosphere is about to be infused with a strange and powerful substance—a substance that will make it impossible for anyone to ever gain or lose another pound. Your body and the bodies of everyone you know will remain exactly at their current weight.

How would you lead your life in this new atmosphere? What would you wear once you were no longer waiting to change size? Would you take that trip to the beach you have been postponing until you lose weight? And how about the exercise regime you were planning to begin? Are you still interested, even though you know it will not have any impact on your size?

Before you answer these questions, consider this one final piece of information. This strange and powerful substance that you are now inhaling with every breath has an additional quality: It creates an environment in which no one's body is considered more beautiful than any other, an environment in which bad body thoughts no longer exist, in your mind or in anyone else's, and all bodies are regarded as lovely and interesting.

How would you feel living in a world in which the size and shape of your body were regarded without any judgment? How would you feel walking down the street, sitting on a bus, buying your groceries, and eating your lunch in a world in which you knew that your body's size and shape were just fine?

Right now, such a world is only a fantasy. Regardless of what is happening in the world around you, however, you can create the kind of acceptance we are talking about *within yourself.* You can create a world in which you see your body *as it is* and enjoy it. You can challenge all of the ideas you have unconsciously internalized about how bodies should look. You can take your bad body thoughts and put them aside. You can dress yourself in ways that please you. And you can begin to live the kind of life you have put on hold "until I lose weight."

The power to create an environment of self-acceptance is within you. We know, however, that you will react to our proposal to create that environment with a great deal of ambivalence.

Your Objections to Legalizing Your Body

Women generally agree that Bad Body Fever is extremely debilitating. After some exploration, the women in our groups usually recognize bad body thoughts as a reflection of the woman-hating in the culture around us and realize that they use these thoughts to police themselves.

"I got a great response to a presentation I made at work and was feeling really good about myself," one woman said, "and then I passed a store window, looked at my reflection, and was overwhelmed by this powerful feeling of self-disgust. My hips looked enormous. I'm beginning to see how much hate is contained in these thoughts. It makes me sad that I do this to myself."

Ask any woman how she would feel if she did not look at herself with disgust—if she did not say, "Yuck!" every time she caught her reflection in a shop window—and her face will light up. "I can't believe how free I would feel," one participant in a Texas workshop said. Yet when we tell women that the cure for Bad Body Fever and compulsive eating rests on doing just that—on giving up bad body thoughts and accepting their bodies regardless of size—they object quickly and vigorously.

"Stop trying to lose weight? I'll never accept myself at this size!"

"I have bad body thoughts because I'm fat and I hate it. How can I learn to like something that I hate so intensely?"

"You've got to be kidding! I'd have to be a Martian to live in this world and not have bad body thoughts. Come to the cafeteria at work with me and listen to what goes on. Diets and bodies. Diets and bodies. It's all anyone talks about."

"Maybe I'll give up bad body thoughts and dieting after I've lost some weight."

"What you're really saying is that I should just throw in the towel and quit."

The idea that giving up body hatred and dieting is an admission of defeat is a common one. Although many people begin with that idea, once they actually stop trying to lose weight, they discover that they do not feel at all defeated.

"When I got rid of all the clothes that didn't fit and bought comfortable outfits that I really liked," said one experienced nondieter, "I actually felt great. I thought I'd feel like I had given up, but what I really felt was that I had given into the reality of what my body was. I still feel sad sometimes that my body doesn't look right in the clothing I admire on thinner women, but then I remind myself that the real problem is that clothing is designed for their thin bodies rather than for mine. The more I challenge the idea that there is only one acceptable body type, the more I'm able to appreciate the body I have."

The distinction that this woman makes between *giving up* and *giving into* the reality of her body is a critical one. Every body has its own unique shape. When you decide that you are willing to embrace the possibility of living at your current size for the rest of your life, the only thing you are guilty of giving up on is a culture that attempts to stamp out individual differences and squeeze us all into one mold. Once you are able to say, "I will not play this game anymore," you open the possibility of looking at yourself in a fresh, new way.

"I couldn't believe myself," said Sarah one evening in our New York workshop. "There's a new ice cream store in my neighborhood and I went in and ordered a soda. The woman who owns the store said, 'Oh, we have Slimfast shakes, if you'd prefer.' I said, 'No,' very calmly and repeated that I wanted an ice cream soda. In the past, I would have died of humiliation. This time, I had a quick talk with myself that went like this: She may think that I'm too fat to be eating ice cream, but that's her opinion and it's no longer mine. And besides, she's having plenty of anxiety about whether her store is going to make it. Focusing on my weight is probably just her way of dealing with her own anxiety."

Does Sarah sound like a loser? We think not. She has dropped out of a cycle that always left her feeling bad and she has moved into a lifestyle that accords her dignity and confirmation about who she really is. Loser? No way! Like Sarah, when you promise to put an end to your bad body thoughts, you are granting yourself the acceptance that you have always sought from others.

The Importance of Self-Acceptance

When we stress the importance of accepting your body *as it is*, we are not saying that you will never lose weight. In fact, we are not addressing that issue. We are saying that in order to make any change in your eating or your weight, you need to stop focusing on your weight and start cultivating self-acceptance. After all, it is this very lack of self-acceptance—your body-bashing—that accounts for much of your overeating. Each time you berate yourself for your size, you head for the refrigerator. Each time you look at yourself with disgust and start to think about dieting, you begin to crave "forbidden" food. None of us react well to such affronts.

Self-acceptance is your birthright. The seeds for self-esteem should be planted in infancy and nurtured by your parents' unconditional love and acceptance. But not all parents are able to nurture those seeds, and not all women are able to continue nurturing their own seedlings when their parents' work is done.

Think about the teenage girl whose mother says, "You would be so pretty if only you would lose weight." Think about the college student who hears that a male friend who likes her a lot cannot think about her romantically because she is too fat. Think about the wife whose husband tells her he is no longer attracted to her because of her size.

We've all gotten these messages in one form or another and

they leave us trapped in a catch-22. When we diet to gain acceptance, we are buying into a system that says that we are unacceptable the way we are, that part of us is bad. Consequently, the acceptance we seek by losing the so-called bad part of ourselves does not really feel like acceptance. It feels like approval for *not* being ourselves. Invariably, we gain back the weight in the hope that someone, someday, will tell us that we are lovely and fine just the way we are.

How do you find your way out of this trap? Self-acceptance. You need to find a way to give yourself the unconditional love that you seek from others. And after you have done so, you will be able to cure your Bad Body Fever and compulsive eating.

What about losing weight? As we will discuss in the next section of the book, once you become an experienced demand feeder, no longer using food for reasons other than stomach hunger, you will return to what is a natural weight *for you.* Your natural weight is determined by your genetic heritage, your age, and the state of your metabolism after years of dieting and binging. Depending on these factors, some of you who use our demand feeding approach will lose weight and others will not. When you lose weight as a by-product of self-acceptance and demand feeding, your weight loss comes with no reproach attached. If your mother or anyone else says, "Oh, don't you look terrific now that you have lost some weight," you will not have to flinch from the implied criticism of how you looked in the past. You can say to yourself, "Yes, losing weight was a by-product of solving my obsession with food, but my body was okay with me long before I ever lost an ounce."

Size Acceptance: A National Movement and a Personal Goal

How is it possible to find the kind of self-acceptance we are talking about in a world that places such a tremendous emphasis on appearances? Confronting all of the obstacles in a culture as obsessed with body molding as ours can be a daunting prospect, particularly when you feel as if you are doing it alone.

Fortunately, you are *not* alone. A size-acceptance movement, the National Association to Advance Fat Acceptance (NAAFA), was organized in 1969. However, it is easy for many of us to disassociate ourselves from organizations for large people because, despite the fact that we seem large to ourselves, many of us do not look large to the rest of the world. Recognizing that size acceptance is an issue for all women—not just large women—would go a long way toward curing the cultural aspects of Bad Body Fever and solving our nationwide eating problems. After all, it is our cultural intolerance of certain body sizes that sends us to diets in the first place. And it is these diets that turn us into compulsive eaters.

We suggest that, for inspiration in cultivating your own revolutionary self-acceptance, you subscribe to a magazine like *Radiance*, which is in the vanguard of the size-acceptance movement. We also urge you to join NAAFA.

You also can extend your personal commitment to ending bad body talk by making others aware of how destructive this kind of talk is. Bethany, a woman in our New York workshop did precisely that.

"I had three friends at my apartment one day, and saw how much of the conversation was about diets, weight loss, and exercise," Bethany began. "I just couldn't stand it one more minute. They just went on and on about it until I finally said that I wanted to change the subject."

Before changing the subject, however, Bethany told her friends why she wanted it changed. "I'm a lot larger than any of them," she said, "and I told them that the way they were going on about how bad fat was made me very uncomfortable. I also told them that I was no longer willing to put up with body-bashing because all of this body hatred is incredibly sexist."

Bethany felt frightened when she confronted her friends. "They rushed to tell me that they thought I looked fine and that they had never intended to insult me," she said. "But I was firm. Women have to stop trashing themselves."

Did Bethany convince anyone? She was not really sure. She knew, however, that she felt better about having spoken up than she had ever felt about keeping quiet and, beyond that, she knew that her friends would not talk in the same way around her again.

The Internal Obstacles to Self-Acceptance

Unfortunately, as we struggle to overcome body hatred, external pressure is never our only hurdle. We are all products of our culture. The world that exists outside of us exists inside of us as well. As a citizen of a fat-phobic world, you have become your own worst critic. Before you can cure yourself of Bad Body Fever, you must learn to look honestly and openly at how you have been treating yourself and resolve to confront your own body hatred just as Bethany confronted the body hatred she heard among her friends.

In order to do that, however, you need to feel fed up and angry. You must be willing to confront what is obvious: that all of your bad body thoughts have never gotten you anywhere, that you have said the same hateful things to yourself thousands of times over the years, and that you have simply become more depressed—and larger. In addition, you need to recognize that the notion of thin being beautiful is a dangerous by-product of a cultural bias against women. In essence, you approach body hatred in the following way. First, you challenge conventional thinking on the subject and then you examine your own reluctance to move beyond those conventions.

You *can* cure Bad Body Fever, and in subsequent chapters we will offer many concrete suggestions for doing just that, but you can only approach the task effectively if you are fully acquainted with the stumbling blocks you are likely to encounter along the way. Given the suffering that goes with bad body thoughts, fat talk, and Bad Body Fever, it may seem difficult to understand why anyone but a masochist would want to hold onto them. Yet you will come to see that this painful and very familiar preoccupation with your body does indeed satisfy deep psychological needs. In fact, you will not be able to understand the persistence of your bad body thoughts until you understand the complex ways in which you have come to depend on Bad Body Fever.

The Losses That Come with the Cure

What is it that we lose when we give up our body hatred? We lose the false hope that weight loss is the solution to all our problems; we lose the focus that has camouflaged our real concerns and anxieties; we lose an easy outlet for the anger we feel about being a woman in a man's world; we lose a sense of camaraderie with other women; and we lose the bizarre satisfaction of feeling that we are being punished for our secret "crimes." Let's look at these losses one by one.

Giving Up False Hope

At the core of the body hatred/dieting/compulsive-eating pattern is the notion of perfection. For many years you have been dieting and exercising your way toward a more perfect body and what you hoped would be a more perfect life. When you stop thinking about attaining that perfect body, you lose the pleasure of the fantasy of perfection. There have been many times over the years when your focus on that fantasy made you feel hopeful in an otherwise hopeless moment. When you were feeling bad about something, the resolution to eat less, work out more, and lose weight inevitably made you feel better. This wish to attain an ideal body size—and the hopeful feelings attached to that wish—consumes the energy of many women and greatly distorts their perspective. After losing sixty-seven pounds on Optifast, Oprah Winfrey said it was the most significant achievement of her life, a staggering perspective for a woman who has accomplished so many extraordinary things.

Getting beyond body hatred requires that you live in the present rather than the future. It requires that you remind yourself time and time again that your body, *as it exists right now,* is just fine. The excitement of making plans to magically reconfigure yourself—and your future—is gone.

Mary addressed this loss of hope at a workshop in San Diego. "It used to be that each time I started a diet, I felt like I was wiping the slate clean," she said. "It was as if by going on a diet, I'd wipe away past sins and problems and could become whoever I wanted to be. Living in my body, just as it is, doesn't allow me to do that. My body, with all its lumps and bumps, is like a metaphor for me, with all my ups and downs. Letting go of the fantasy that I might undergo a magical transformation is difficult. I have to come to terms with who I am, rather than think about who I might become . . . and that can be very hard."

In our last book we talked about the game we call "Change Your Shape and Change Your Life," which Mary and countless other women play. For many of us, the idea that we must settle into our bodies rather than renovate them feels more like a death sentence than merely a loss of hope. To be deprived of the possibility of changing shape means that we are trapped in our female flesh with no possibility of redemption.

Suzanne, a participant in our New York workshop, cheered up everyone one evening when we were discussing how difficult it is to accept our bodies as they are, without thinking about losing weight. "I had an incredible experience several months ago," she said. "I was feeling lonely, which was not at all unusual. What was unusual was that I was fed up with feeling that way. I'd been feeling much better about myself and my size, but I really wanted company—romantic company, specifically! I sat down and composed a personal ad. I couldn't believe I was doing it, but I kept at it. 'Rubenesque' was the way I described myself. I got a lot of responses. What really surprised me, though, was that the body issue did not come up at all. I actually had the same experience that my thin friends have described—some losers on the phone, some disappointments when I met others, and some perfectly pleasant evenings. I feel incredibly lucky because I've found someone whom I really like. But it is crystal clear to me that none of this would have happened if I hadn't already come to very loving terms with my 'Rubenesque' body. I felt *entitled* to be out there."

At one workshop, we asked participants why they thought that declaring an end to body hatred is so difficult to do. One woman said, "It's like giving up on the truth." She went on to tell us that her weight and her body had been the focus of her family's disgust for as long as she could remember. It was very clear to her that every hateful thing she said to herself when she looked in the mirror had been told to her at one time or another by her mother or father. "For me to challenge those labels," she said, "is to challenge my parents and to give up the hope that they'll ever change their minds about me. It means moving on in my life with my own ideas about who I am. I can see that it's an exciting prospect, but at the moment, it feels mostly like a loss."

Many of us have internalized a general feeling that our female bodies are not all right. Others of us, like the woman above, have been the focus of raw disgust and ridicule for much of our lives. If you have such a history, giving up body hatred means not only turning away from the culture, but also turning away from your family's point of view. And even though your family may have been abusive, turning your back on their message can feel like a painful loss of hope, connection, and identity. It is no wonder that we cling to the painful self-definitions we have internalized. We are clinging to what is familiar.

"In my family," said Anne, "people didn't pick on my body per se, but appearance was all anyone talked about. I have two sisters and they and my parents are absolutely obsessed with thinness. I have an impossible time with bad body thoughts. I come to a workshop and for a few days I understand that such thoughts are a way of avoiding other issues. But the truth is that I feel so strange and empty without them. Before long, I get filled up with them again. If you could hear my family interact, you would see how the fat talk ties everyone together. It's our main topic of conversation. It sounds strange to say this, but without fat talk and bad body thoughts, I feel very lonely and unanchored."

What does it feel like to stop trying to fit into a culture—or a family—that views you, at best, with ambivalence? Most women report that when they finally let go of their efforts to fit in, they feel both loss and liberation. Perhaps this passage would be easier if we designed ceremonies to mourn the loss and celebrate the liberation.

One woman we know, Lily, did just that. She took her very favorite "thin" clothes and piled them all in the middle of her floor for weeks. From time to time, when she passed them by, she would choose one of the garments. She would sit with it, thinking about what her life had been like when she had worn it. She thought about what had given her pleasure then, what had not, and she tried to imagine reviving some of the pleasant experiences.

When she felt ready, Lily gave away the clothing to friends who were thinner. "By the time I gave something to a friend," she said, "I was ready to part with it. In the end, I had to give a lot of clothing to the daughters of my friends—they were the only people small enough! You can imagine how many years those things had been sitting in my closet, haunting me."

Indeed, the "thin" wardrobe Lily held onto had taunted her as well as haunted her. Every time she opened the closet door and saw that clothing hanging there, she was filled with bad body thoughts. It was not until she gave the clothing away that she began to rid herself of those thoughts.

Giving Up the Disguise

Bad Body Fever and all of its symptoms divert our attention from real concerns and anxieties. Another way of saying this is, "A bad body thought is never about your body." If you have doubts about this point, you are not alone. Many people disagree when we make this statement.

"When I'm feeling terrible about my body, there's no way you can convince me that all of my feelings aren't really about my body," said a woman at a California workshop. "At that moment, I really am convinced that I'm fat and disgusting and that my cellulite is the ugliest thing on earth. I've heard you make the point that, since we aren't always thinking about our bodies, it's important to think about what exactly is going on when we are suddenly gripped by cellulite anxiety. But it doesn't feel like that when it happens. When I get a cellulite anxiety attack, all I know is that I'm looking at my thighs in the mirror and they look absolutely disgusting."

This woman is correct about our point of view. We would maintain that, although she thinks that looking in the mirror is what makes her feel awful about her thighs, something else is happening within her at that moment, which she conceals from herself by focusing on her body in a negative way. This focus disguises the real problem.

Bad Body Fever involves a displacement. When you are having a bad body thought, you are attacking your body instead of allowing yourself to feel or think something else. Ultimately, when you have a negative body thought, you lose track of what you were feeling and become convinced that your problem is your fat. The nice part about believing that your fat is your problem is that it is a problem with a seemingly concrete solution: You can go on a diet and/or embark on an exercise routine. Unfortunately, real problems cannot be dieted away.

Most of us have become so accustomed to living with Bad Body Fever that we have a hard time believing that bad body thoughts are about anything other than our bodies. Long-term nondieters in our New York workshop enjoy bringing in examples of bad body thoughts that they think disprove our theory that such thoughts are a way that women have of speaking in code.

"This time I'm sure of it," said Laura in one of our advanced workshops. "I'm feeling fat and thinking fat because I am indeed fatter! Toward the end of my vacation, I ate a lot more than my body needed and I have expanded as a result. Given my enlarged waistline, my bad body thoughts seem pretty straightforward."

As we talked with Laura more, we stumbled upon the real feeling that her bad body thoughts were concealing. At some point in our discussion, Laura mentioned that, as the end of her vacation drew near, she began to dread going home because she was in the midst of expanding her business. There were many issues she would have to confront upon her return. She focused her anxiety on her waistline when, in fact, it was her expanding and enlarging career that concerned her. A bad body thought is never about your body!

At this point, it is important for you to understand that bad body thoughts are difficult to give up precisely because they are such an effective way to distance yourself from your real thoughts and feelings. As painful as body hatred is, it feels familiar and straightforward, less painful than the murky conflicts it masks.

Consider some other examples. One woman said, "I'm terrified about my business. One client called to cancel his contract earlier today and I noticed that, ever since, I've been feeling more and more disgusted with how I look. Every few hours I remember the call, but mostly I'm just feeling fat. I wonder if all women who are worried about the recession are feeling fat? I guess I felt angry at him for leaving and turned it against myself. I just couldn't accept the loss. I suppose I think that if I whip myself into a diet and lose weight, my client list will suddenly grow larger. Of course, I work mostly on the phone in my business, so this idea is particularly absurd!"

Another woman in a Houston workshop was visibly upset. She had been working with our approach to compulsive eating for several months. We discovered that, despite some heartening experiences when she first stopped dieting, she had been out of control and gaining weight for about three weeks. She was in a great deal of pain about her appearance and preoccupied about the dress she was planning to wear at her daughter's wedding ten days away.

"The dressmaker has already let it out once, and now she'll have to do it again," this woman said. "I'm delighted about the wedding, but I just can't stand the thought of how I'm going to look walking down the aisle. I've been dieting and binging for twenty-five years, but I just can't accept this fact. Look at these rolls! They're just not me."

It did not take long for us to discover the real source of this woman's pain. She was aware only of what she did not want others to see—her fat. In fact, she was intensely focused on her fat in order to avoid something that she herself did not want to look at. She had lost her first husband, the father of her soon-to-be-married daughter, when she was a very young woman. He had died suddenly and she had married again, had two more children, and lived a very full life. When her daughter announced her marriage plans, she said that she wanted to restore and wear her mother's bridal gown.

Although this woman was thrilled by her daughter's request, her feelings about the loss of her first husband were revived as the wedding day approached. Her whirlwind of eating and body hatred was an attempt to ward off these feelings. Although her sadness seemed somewhat relieved when she began to talk about it, she continued to try to return to the topic of her body. After twenty-five years, body hatred was a more familiar and comfortable way for her to experience her pain.

As long as we resist knowing the truth about ourselves and our lives, we will continue to focus our energy on bad body thoughts and fat talk, and our Bad Body Fever will continue to rage.

Giving Up Misdirected Anger

Many compulsive eaters discharge their angry feelings about being a woman in a man's world by berating their bodies. All of the body areas about which women obsess—stomachs, thighs, hips, breasts—are distinctly female areas. Each time we rage against these particular parts of our anatomy we are saying in essence, "I am not okay; girls are not okay; women are not okay." We express our rage at our second-class position in society by turning it against ourselves and aligning with the dominant cultural viewpoint. When we as women think about curing Bad

Body Fever, we must also contemplate losing this alignment with authority, and that can be frightening. After all, what would we do with all of that anger if we no longer dumped it on ourselves?

Donna Pittman, a psychotherapist in Houston (and, as she would say, "a woman of size"), told us an interesting story. She was at the checkout counter in a supermarket with a cart heaped with groceries. The man behind her asked if he could go ahead of her because he was buying only a few things. Donna, who had already waited in line for a long time, was on her way home from a long day's work and was tired. She said she was sorry, but that she was in a hurry herself.

Upon hearing her response, the man proceeded to talk very loudly about "the fat woman buying all this food." Donna turned to him and said, "I guess you find it difficult to have someone say no to you." He continued harassing her, and she asked the manager to intervene.

Donna did not for a moment feel fat or have bad body thoughts. She was absolutely clear that the issue had nothing to do with her size, but had everything to do with her sense of entitlement. It was up to her to say yes or no to this man's request. She owed him nothing, even though she was a woman and even though she was large. Indeed, the anger she might have dumped on herself found a productive outlet in her assertive behavior.

Another workshop participant reported a similar shift in herself. "Now that I'm no longer stuffing my feelings down with food," Lorraine said, "and no longer looking at my body with disgust every other minute, I'm just not as nice as I used to be. I feel like I'm taking up a lot more space. When someone says, 'Do you mind?' if I do, I say, '*Yes.*' I think a lot of the anger I dumped on my body was misdirected. I think I was afraid to notice the things around me that I didn't like. Now that I'm not so angry with myself, I notice that I'm not as deferential."

Giving Up Mother-Bashing

As we indicated in the previous chapter, each time we talk about our disgusting stomachs and breasts and hips and thighs, we are unconsciously expressing our ambivalence about our mother's female body. Each time we say that we are not okay the way we are, we are making a comment about her female body as well. When we give up hating our bodies, we also let our mothers off the hook; and when we do that, some of us come face-to-face with the underlying ambivalence of that relationship.

A woman named Nina noticed that she was suddenly upset about the size of her stomach in a way that she had not been in a very long time. It was the first thing she thought about every morning when she woke up. Finally, she realized that she had to confront whatever was really going on. It did not take long for her to figure things out.

The month before her stomach-hating frenzy had flared, Nina had learned that her mother was terminally ill. Her relationship with her mother had always been difficult. Her anger at her stomach was an indirect way of expressing her feelings about this very difficult, unresolved relationship and her anticipated loss. It was Nina's way of saying, "Mom, I know that you are going to die and I feel awful about that. But I feel even worse about the fact that we have had such a rocky relationship and that I have been angry at you for so many years for not being there for me. All of these feelings make it difficult for me to be sympathetic to your needs right now. I feel like a bad daughter for not being able to put my old conflicts aside and just attend to you lovingly. That's what I'm really saying when I look at my stomach and say, 'Yuck.' "

Giving Up the Sisterhood of Fat Talk

Unfortunately, Bad Body Fever also negatively connects us to women other than our mothers. Women everywhere spend an inordinate amount of time together talking about their bodies in a contemptuous way. "I can't imagine a group of women getting together with no mention of diets or fat," said one woman. "I mean, it's amazing to think about what the conversation might encompass."

Imagine liking your own body and taking pleasure in looking at other women's bodies. Imagine investing the same energy you currently spend in discussions of dieting and body improvement projects in discussions of art, politics, literature, and life in general. The prospect gives new dimension to the word *liberation.*

Giving Up Punishment for Secret Crimes

Many of us are stern disciplinarians when it comes to ourselves. Each time we wish for something that we consider "off-limits," for example, we crack a whip and tell ourselves that we are too big or too flabby. "Down girl," we say, like the lion tamer holding a chair in one hand and a whip in the other. "Don't want too much. Don't say too much. And, above all, don't ever make waves." Through continuous self-flagellation we punish ourselves for a wide variety of secret pleasures, "forbidden" feelings, wishes, and aspirations. It is a way that we keep ourselves in check.

Melissa, a woman in a New York workshop, kept close track of her bad body thoughts to try to uncover their source. "I kept a pad and pen with me at all times," she said, "and forced myself to write down all of my bad body thoughts for a few days. I couldn't believe what awful things I said to myself. When I went over the list, I realized that you must be right. All of this cruelty must be about something more profound than the shape of my body."

Melissa's bad body thoughts usually came too fast and furiously for her to trace, but at several points she noticed that a bad body thought followed a mean-spirited thought she had just had about someone else. "I have so much invested in being a nice girl," Melissa explained, "that when I have a mean or envious thought about someone else, I automatically cover it by punishing myself with a bad body thought. I must have some thoughts and feelings I consider very cruel, because I'm certainly extremely cruel to myself."

Sometimes the symptoms of Bad Body Fever flare up in a sudden way. You might be walking along the street and suddenly feel unhappy about your reflection in the shop windows. If, for example, you are a person who fears confrontation, you might discover that at the precise moment this flare-up of self-hatred struck, you were deeply involved in a fantasy argument with an old friend, telling her some of the things you've been wanting to say for years—how she neglects you, how she doesn't listen to you, or how insensitive she can be to your feelings. This fantasy showdown—a showdown you might never have the courage to initiate in reality—becomes fodder for a bad body thought: "Bad girl. How could you think such things? How dare you wish for more than you have?" You continue on your way feeling fat, or, as we would say, feeling punished for your thoughts. At the same time, however, you also feel safe. After all, as long as you keep yourself in line with those bad body thoughts, you don't have to worry about having your anger uncovered.

Kate, a participant in our Chicago workshop, told us that having good feelings about her body triggered her bad body thoughts.

"I've noticed that as soon as I feel any pleasure in my body, I start focusing on the parts of it I don't like. I spoil my pleasure before anyone else can be mad at me for enjoying my body."

Kate's parents were very strict and rigid; for them, it was paramount that everyone look and act "proper." Kate internalized their standards—and then some. "Whenever I feel good about my body, I make myself pay for it in bad body thoughts," she said. Nell, a participant in a California workshop, commented, "I think that the idea of women taking pleasure in their bodies is one of the strongest taboos we live with. We are supposed to be pleasing for others to look at and touch, but we are not supposed to enjoy our own bodies." Nell went on to say that the idea of loving rather than hating her own body made her feel extremely independent and powerful.

Women in workshops all over the country talk about the fact that we seem to feel that we should be nice to everyone except ourselves, and how that lifelong belief shifts when we recover from Bad Body Fever. But this new perspective can be intimidating. Many women talk about how much more comfortable they feel with self-abuse than with outer-directed anger. "I'm not used to feeling powerful in this way," one such woman said. "I've reached a point where I feel strange when I hear other women putting themselves down for the way they look. It's an odd sensation to begin noticing how badly so many women treat themselves. It actually makes me feel very, very sad."

Moving Beyond Loss

How do we move beyond our fears and our sense of loss to recover from Bad Body Fever? As with any challenge, it is important to feel motivated. For most women, that motivation comes from feeling sick and tired of years of self-abuse. "I finally realized how many years I have spent yelling at myself and looking at myself with disgust, and none of it has made a dent in my problem," said one woman. "When I realized how futile all the pain I suffered had been, I decided I'd had enough."

This realization that contempt never inspires change is an important one. All of the diets and exercise programs that evolve from self-hatred are doomed to failure. We recognize that it is almost impossible to completely eradicate the wish for a thin body in a culture that idealizes thinness, but given the diversity of our shapes and sizes, the fact that only one body type is considered attractive is outrageous. Millions of us are struggling to fit into one mold, and that is nothing less than tragic.

The anger you feel when you recognize the futility of your bad body thoughts, and the anger you feel when you realize that many of the women you know hate their bodies, can enable you to make a deep decision. In order to cure yourself of Bad Body Fever, you must resolve to end the war against your body. What that means in action is that you put an end to bad body thoughts and vow to treat yourself with kindness, even if the rest of the world does not.

Self-Care

How do you transform self-contempt into self-love and self-care? This transition is at the heart of curing Bad Body Fever and has many facets. In general, however, developing an independent point of view about your body requires an extensive internal system of support. You need to develop an ally or caretaking presence within yourself to help you challenge old beliefs and replace them with more life-enhancing values.

Our friend and colleague Robyn Posin, a psychologist in California, calls this process of developing internal support "creating the mommy within." Robyn learned our approach to eating many years ago and has applied the principles of self-acceptance and respect for internal cues to many aspects of her life and the lives of her clients. She teaches people how to create a nurturing mother within themselves in order to cope with the fears that accompany freeing yourself from ingrained attitudes that have been harmful. Robyn understands that it is one thing to learn about your inner child, but it is still another to foster that child's growth.

With courage, patience, and resolve, you can learn to care

for yourself unconditionally and give yourself the support you need to cure your Bad Body Fever. Are you going to clobber yourself or care for yourself? Each time you stop a bad body thought, you strike a blow for all women and take another step in the direction of self nurturance. As you gain experience confronting your thoughts and then treating yourself kindly, you will begin to notice that your bad body thoughts come less and less frequently. Be patient. It took time for you to accommodate yourself to the kind of self-abuse that we associate with womanhood, and it will take time for you to make new associations as well. With effort, you will slowly but surely begin to feel independent and strong.

Chapter

3

BAD BODY THOUGHTS

THE CURE FOR BAD BODY FEVER RESTS ON CLEARING YOUR MIND OF bad body thoughts. Such thoughts are your personal way of perpetuating a code of restrictions against women that caused the fever in the first place; they are the way you collude in female body-bashing.

Bad body thoughts are so interwoven into the fabric of women's lives that becoming cognizant of them is a formidable undertaking. Beginning to notice your bad body thoughts, however, is only a first step toward curing Bad Body Fever. Once you notice them, you have to know what to do with them.

ADDRESSING YOUR BAD BODY THOUGHTS

At our workshops, we encourage women to move through a four-step process each time they have a bad body thought: apologize, challenge, set the thought aside, and learn about yourself from it.

Step One: Apologize

You are walking down the street when, suddenly, you are struck by a bad body thought. Considering its impact, your thought might just as well have been a two-by-four. "I'm so gross," the thought goes. "My stomach is unbearably disgusting. I wish I could disappear."

In the past, you had this very same thought countless times without even breaking stride. Now, not only do you notice the thought, but, with the assistance of your new internal caretaker, you address it.

"Wait a minute. What just happened?" your caretaker asks. Even before the two of you figure it out, she asks you to apologize to yourself for having treated yourself so badly. Bad body thoughts, after all, are abusive. If, for even a moment, you doubt their sting, try keeping track of them on paper, as Melissa did in the previous chapter, and read them over from time to time. Would you ever have the nerve to talk to anyone else as callously as you talk to yourself? You have done nothing to deserve such abusive treatment and you deserve an apology.

In the past, rather than apologize to yourself, you may have used food as an anesthetic to lessen your pain. Now you are beginning to learn that kind words are much more effective.

Step Two: Challenge the Authority of Your Bad Body Thought

Once you have apologized to yourself for having been abusive, you need to challenge the belief behind your bad body thought. The phrase "Who says?" is a very important one.

Each time you think your stomach is "really disgusting," you are endorsing a cultural belief that there is such a thing as a perfect-looking stomach. We understand, of course, that you have been indoctrinated to believe that the only "right" stomach is a flat one. But now the time has come to ask why.

One workshop participant told the group about a day care center her son attended from the time he was an infant until he was three. "There were three day care providers," she said. "One of them was very large and the other two were quite thin. They were all terrific women, but it was clear after a while that the infants all gravitated to the large woman. It finally dawned on me one day, when she greeted me with a hug, that it felt really great to be held by her. Her body—her stomach and her breasts—felt soft and comfortable. I'm sure the babies felt the same way!"

Who says that a flat stomach or a small stomach is best? The flat, hard stomach is as arbitrary an ideal as is blonde hair. You have accepted that ideal for years, but you *can* cease to do so. Indeed, we believe that the longer you continue to accept the ideal, the larger and rounder your stomach will become, just as the longer you continue to deprive yourself of food, the more you will eat. Let's face it: You are a survivor; you fight back even if you do so in hidden ways.

Now you must openly challenge the beliefs and assumptions behind each and every bad body thought. Who says that my body should look like hers? Who says that my thighs are the wrong size and hers are the right size? Who says my butt's too big? Who thinks so? What's wrong with large butts?

People laugh nervously when we start questioning why one size thigh should be considered more attractive than another, or why a youthful body is regarded as more attractive than an aging one. Challenging these old beliefs may feel sacrilegious, but it's worth the risk. Think how astounding it would feel to take as much pleasure in a fleshy thigh as you would in a slender one, just as the babies took pleasure in the larger, softer body.

Your internal caretaker believes that every part of your body is pleasing simply because it is part of you, and she regards the notion that there is an ideal *anything* as rubbish. If you have not yet caught up with her perspective, now is the time to take heed and make the leap.

Step Three: Set the Thought Aside

After apologizing to yourself and challenging the validity of your bad body thought, the next thing to do is to actually put your bad body thought aside. In other words, dismiss it. When your bad body thought returns, simply refuse to entertain it.

Bad body thoughts, like dandelions, die hard. Step on them and they spring back. Pull them out and twice as many return. You will have to strive, on a daily basis, to free your mind from them. Remember that you have been translating your unnamed worries and concerns into bad body thoughts for most of your life. Your hatred of your body has become enmeshed with your psychic equilibrium. Now, you have to learn a different way of living in your body and a different way of dealing with your psyche.

You and your internal caretaker have a great deal of work ahead. But the fact that it is difficult to set bad body thoughts aside should not prevent you from making the effort. Each time a bad body thought resurfaces, simply repeat steps 1, 2, and 3. Remind yourself that thoughts are simply thoughts; whether you dwell on them or not, is ultimately up to you.

Step Four: Learn from Your Bad Body Thought

As you begin to have fewer and fewer bad body thoughts, you need to use the ones you have to your advantage. Once you learn to decode them, each bad body thought can become a springboard for self-exploration. After all, each time you have a bad body thought, it means that you are ambivalent about noticing something you are thinking or feeling. Becoming adept at decoding means addressing your real thoughts and feelings with compassion and understanding—and the more compassionately you treat yourself, the less need you will have for the camouflage that bad body thoughts provide.

Decoding a Bad Body Thought

Once you accept the premise that a bad body thought is never about your body, the obvious next step is to ask yourself what it really is about. In order to best answer that question, you will need to keep very close track of your bad body thoughts, even to the point of writing them down as they occur. Look closely at the words that comprise your bad body thoughts; the words themselves are clues. Look also at the context, both emotional and physical, in which your thoughts arise. What were you doing, feeling, or thinking when you first noticed the bad body thought? The more specific you can be, the more likely you will gain insight.

Mara: "I feel huge."

Mara, a thirty-two-year-old computer software designer in California, told our New York group about her detective work with one of her bad body thoughts. "I woke up one morning feeling huge. I tried to put my bad body thoughts aside, but they kept returning. I dressed comfortably so that there would be nothing concrete, like a tight waistband, to fuel my bad body thoughts, but throughout the morning, my fat feelings continued to come and go."

Each time she noticed her bad body thoughts, Mara attempted to go through the process we have just described. She asked herself what was going on, but nothing came to mind. She knew from past experience, however, that if she tuned into her random thoughts, she might get a general sense of what was disturbing her.

"As my workday progressed, I noticed that I kept flashing on last night's dinner engagement. At first, I was not aware of any specific thoughts, but I kept visualizing myself and my husband seated at a restaurant with another couple. The other man is an old friend of my husband's who has just moved back to the city with his new wife."

Mara noticed that she didn't really want to think about the scene in the restaurant. She kept focusing on how huge her stomach felt. "I kept thinking that I must have eaten a lot, but I knew I was having bad body thoughts. I was just having a lot of trouble getting beyond them. Then, at a certain point, I realized that I was no longer feeling as bad. From past experience I know that I always start to feel better when I acknowledge that there is a thought I'm trying to avoid. I also know that in order to feel completely comfortable in my body, sooner or later I'll have to go further in my thinking."

On the bus going home that evening, Mara tried to focus on the dinner. Comments the other woman made came to mind, and slowly Mara realized that she was angry with this woman who kept talking about her accomplishments and who made it a point to look at Charlie, Mara's husband, each time she spoke.

"I was upset to discover that I was still struggling with competitive and jealous feelings, but I also couldn't help but notice that as soon as I acknowledged these feelings, I stopped feeling fat." Like many women, Mara feels the need to punish herself for thoughts and feelings she considers to be unacceptable.

Mara had never explored her bad body thoughts until she became convinced of our premise one day, when it suddenly struck her that, despite the fact that her body weight remains fairly constant hour to hour, her bad body thoughts come and go. "That day, I was feeling perfectly fine in the morning about how I looked and then, suddenly, I started feeling fat and repulsive. I knew I looked the same on the outside as I did that morning, so I realized that I had to think about where those feelings were suddenly coming from."

Jill: "I look so big."

"I gave a speech at the annual dinner of an organization I'm involved with and I just saw the pictures someone took that evening," said Jill, a new mother and a professional fundraiser in Boston. "I kept looking at those photos and saying, 'Oh, I look so big.' I couldn't believe it. I thought I looked gigantic. I am, in fact, larger than all the other women who were there and I worried all evening that they were thinking, 'Jill has gained so much weight. She's just enormous.' When I saw the pictures, I was certain that that's what they were thinking."

It was difficult for Jill to understand that when she said with disgust, "I'm so big," she was actually referring to something other than her size. Clearly, she had been the center of attention during the evening in question. When we finally got the whole story from her, we learned that she had received endless compliments on her speech, and that all her life, she has gotten a great deal of attention for being so bright and articulate.

Jill's real concern was whether she had been "too big" in the sense of being too outstanding and possibly an object of envy. It was extremely embarrassing for her to acknowledge that she wanted the attention and was very pleased to stand out as she did. Instead, she turned her embarrassment into a bad body thought.

Leta: "I look disgusting in a bathing suit."

Of course, there are always those disbelievers who want to convince us that some bad body thoughts really are about their bodies. In one workshop, a young lawyer named Leta was certain she had found one. "The other day I was at my gym changing into my swimsuit. I caught a glimpse of myself in the mirror and had a bad body thought. I'm sure the thought was really about my body because it occurred when I looked in the mirror. I wouldn't have had the thought if I were at work."

We challenged Leta and repeated our belief that every bad body thought, no matter when it occurs, conceals some kind of personal concern that has nothing to do with the shape of one's body. To prove this, we asked Leta exactly what she had said to herself as she looked in the mirror.

"I looked in the mirror and said, 'Why do I even bother to get into a suit?' " Leta answered. We then asked her to describe what had happened from the time she arrived at the gym until she had the thought. Suddenly, Leta struck gold. "Oh, my God! I see what went on," she exclaimed. "I took my usual aerobics class before swimming. There's a very cute man in this class and I had been wondering if he would be there. Sometimes he and I make small talk. At the end of this particular class we again made contact. I'm always surprised that he bothers to talk to me because I automatically assume that he's not interested in me. I think the real message of my bad body thought was, 'Why bother going after him since, in the long run, he won't be interested?' Also," Leta added, "there may have been an element of punishment in my swimsuit remark for having had the nerve to want to pursue this man—or any man, for that matter."

Nancy: "If I fit into these, I must really be fat."

Nancy, a woman in this same workshop and the mother of twins, was inspired by these stories and remembered one of her own. "I was doing my laundry and taking the clothes out of the dryer to fold," she said, "when I was suddenly struck by how enormous my shorts were. I held them up and said, 'If these shorts fit me, I must really be fat.' Is that a bad body thought," Nancy asked, "or is it a simple statement of fact?"

We suggested that if Nancy were to take her statement at face value, she would miss out on an opportunity to explore what was really on her mind, so she decided to probe a bit and think about what might have prompted her remark. At first, Nancy could not think of anything in particular. Then she recalled a conversation with her husband the night before she had the bad body thought.

Nancy's husband had decided to go back to school, which meant that, for a while at least, Nancy would become the sole financial support for her family. The prospect of attempting to "fill his shoes" made Nancy uneasy. Was she "big enough" for the job? Could she "fill the space" he once did? Indeed, Nancy is ambivalent about her future, feeling both excited by the prospect and resentful about some of its implications. She wants—and does not want—to be big enough for her new role.

Ann: "I'm ugly."

Ann spoke up at a New York workshop and said that she had been attacking herself for being fat. When we asked what words she had been using in these attacks, she replied, "Ugly. I keep saying that I'm *ugly.*" When we asked her to think about what this word meant to her in a context other than her body, her face lit up. "Oh, boy," she said. "I never would have thought of it, but even as we speak, there are contractors renovating part of my house. Yesterday, they wanted to start doing something with the plumbing. I felt uneasy about it and said that I wanted my own plumber to come over and look at it. They gave me a hard time and were clearly angry about my refusal to let them do it, but I stood my ground and called the plumber. When I left the house after this incident, that's when the screaming began. I just couldn't stand how I looked. I see now that what I thought was ugly was the fact that I had stood up to them. I didn't just acquiesce. I wasn't a good girl. I guess I've bought the idea that assertive women are ugly women."

Patricia: "I shouldn't have bad body thoughts."

Patricia, who is quite sophisticated in this process of decoding, fell into an interesting trap. While riding uptown to our weekly meeting, she had a bad body thought and immediately responded with the following speech. "I know I shouldn't have this thought. It's really a comedown to be having bad body thoughts after all these years of work on size acceptance."

We asked her to think about why she had yelled at herself instead of apologizing to herself for having had her bad body thought. We suggested that she might find a clue in the words she had used when she scolded herself. Specifically, Patricia had said, "It's a comedown."

Patricia thought about what could have been bothering her and finally made a connection with the word *comedown.* "Today I received an insulting letter from a client, chastising me for the way I interacted with her at a meeting last week," she said. "I feel it's beneath my dignity to even respond. I think I'm still upset about that letter, but instead, I pinned my distress on having had bad body thoughts."

Diane: "I have rolls of fat that were not always there."

At a workshop one evening Diane told the group, "When my husband goes to touch me in bed, I tighten up because I think he'll feel the rolls of fat that were not always there." Diane insisted that she was embarrassed at these moments because she knows that her husband is unhappy about her weight. "He may not say it out loud, but I know he's turned off when he touches that part of me." We were intrigued by the phrase "were not always there" and curious to know more about the context in which she has these bad feelings about her midriff.

When we pressed Diane about the last time she'd had these feelings, she told us that she and her husband had had a long talk lying in bed. "He has not been in good spirits for a couple of years now," she said. "I think he's disappointed in how his work has evolved as well as in a number of other things. Maybe it's midlife crisis, but these long talks usually revolve around his feeling stuck and down on himself."

We asked Diane how she felt during these talks and she replied, "I always feel sad for him and come up with endless suggestions about how to make things better. But, to tell you the truth—and this is hard to acknowledge—I think I have some other feelings as well that I don't pay a lot of attention to. If I think about it, I often feel impatient during these discussions, but that's not what bothers me the most. It's more that I start feeling a little superior. In truth, I've done a lot more emotional work than he has in the past ten years and I'm reaping the rewards. I'm very happy at work, I get a lot of satisfaction from my kids, and I'm generally feeling pretty good about myself. I might even say that, as he's talking, I have a glimmer of feeling smug or triumphant, and that feels terrible to admit. How can I be feeling triumphant when he's so miserable?"

Diane's question is a good one. It does seem unkind to feel smug in the face of someone else's suffering. However, knowing that all behavior can be understood if it is explored without being judged, we continued to ask questions and brought up the phrase "the rolls that were not there before." "What's different now," we asked, "from the way things used to be for you?"

"Well," she said, "I guess that when it comes to my relationships with men, for a lot of my life I felt vulnerable and, I guess, inferior. What comes to my mind is my father, who was so big and so furious all the time. I remember wanting to be just as big as he was so I could scream back at him. Not to mention how I felt about my brother, who was considered everyone's great hope. I guess the rolls of fat that weren't there before refer to my increasing sense of power and my role as a woman."

Diane discovered that what seemed like a statement of fact about her fat and her husband's dislike of it actually referred to her own misgivings about her newfound strength and power. Was it feminine? Was it okay for her to feel good even though her husband was having a rough time? Diane was afraid to identify the feelings beneath her bad body thought because what was new about her—her sense of power—was linked in her mind to old, vengeful wishes she had had toward her father, her brother, and other men. Once decoded, Diane could look at her feelings, explore them with compassion, understand them, and move on.

Body-Part Exercise

To get accustomed to decoding your bad body thoughts, we suggest the following exercise. Think about a part of your body that you dislike and write down the precise words you use to describe it. Then, suspend your disbelief and trust us when we say that the words you use to describe your most hated body part actually are words you might use to describe some other aspect of yourself that disturbs you—specifically, some aspect of your personality or character.

It is not until you take the focus off your body that you can begin to explore what you *really* feel bad about. Perhaps you have feelings and desires that you think are wrong. Perhaps you have personality traits you consider undesirable. Perhaps you feel inadequate in one way or another.

In our workshops, this process of exploration is a collaborative one. We listen to each other, we bounce ideas off each other, and we move beyond our shared body hatred.

The best way to become convinced that a bad body thought is never about your body is to listen to other women as they try to discover precisely what their thoughts *are* about. To that end, we are going to recount women's responses to this exercise from workshops all across the country, first citing the bad body thought then the decoded version of it. We have grouped these thoughts according to body parts and have included a section on the more general bad body thoughts with which women torture themselves.

Stomach

"My stomach is flabby." *means* "To me, flabby is the same as needy and wimpy. I often feel that way."

"My stomach is huge (or gross)." *means* "I feel insatiable."

"My stomach protrudes." *means* "I think that I'm obtrusive and want too much attention. I keep fighting against that. It's about feeling that I want too much."

"My stomach sticks out." *means* "I shouldn't stand out."

"My stomach is like a balloon. I don't fit." *means* "Maybe I don't fit in my marriage."

"My stomach is just too much." *means* "I feel that my needs are too much."

"My stomach is soft and mushy." *means* "I'm always feeling like I have no backbone, that I give in all the time. I'm too wishy-washy. I can't seem to end this bad ten-year relationship."

"My stomach—I want to cut it off." *means* "I think I want to cut myself off from my family."

"My stomach is big and up front." *means* "I'm sticking myself out in the professional world, putting myself on the line, sticking my neck out."

"My stomach is fat. It's in the way." *means* "I stand in the way of my own success."

"My stomach makes me look pregnant." means "I feel shame at not having had any children. I *do* have a wish to have children, and I'm upset with myself for not having done so."

"My tummy is fat, chubby, gross." *means* "I feel like I'm not good enough. There's something wrong with me. I heard these messages as a child growing up with four brothers. It's no accident that I still use childlike words like *tummy* and *chubby* when I attack myself. I guess I'm making the same comments to myself that were made to me at a much earlier time."

"I hate the scar on my abdomen from my C-section. It makes me look deformed, scarred, and dead." *means* "I feel dead sexually. My older brother molested me when I was a child. My husband wants to have sex every night and each time he touches my abdomen I feel dead inside. I know I have work to do around the issue of the abuse."

"When I look at my stomach I feel like a gluttonous, piggish slob." *means* "I haven't figured out yet what I want to do with my life. I feel undisciplined and unfocused. I think I just don't want any responsibilities, and I condemn myself a lot for that."

"My stomach is bloated, weak, annoying, in the way." *means* "I feel out of control. There is a part of me that feels very in the way and out of control. Then there is the part of me that is very quiet and acquiescent. I'm in conflict about these two aspects of myself."

"My stomach just hangs there." *means* "There are a number of issues in my life right now that I need to address, but I feel stuck and everything just hangs in the balance."

"My stomach has terrible stretch marks since the birth of my daughter." *means* "Being stretched is a main theme in my life. I have great conflict about taking care of my daughter and, at the same time, pursuing my own career."

Midriff

"My midriff is unsmooth and ripply." *means* "I'm going through a midlife crisis. I'm over fifty and I have to deal with what's next."

"My middle section is horrible, it's just too much." *means* "I feel caught in the middle. My daughter is a lesbian and she and her partner are having a baby. I feel fine about this, but I am so worried about how my community will receive them. Will I end up having to defend them? I'm in the middle."

Breasts

"My breasts are too big. They don't fit in anything comfortably." *means* "I don't want to be too big and not fit in. I worry about being too much for everybody."

"My breasts are pendulous—they hang." *means* "I feel like I hang onto other people. I feel too dependent."

"My breasts are saggy and flabby. They're soft and not firm." *means* "I feel like I'm not firm a lot of the time, that I'm wishy-washy."

"My breasts are heavy and enormous, in a thick, full way, dense." *means* "I feel impenetrable and solid. I don't let people get close."

"My breasts are too small and undeveloped—I hate them." *means* "I often feel undeveloped. In some ways, I remain very childish."

"My breasts stick out too much and attract too much attention." *means* "I feel like I attract too much attention and never really fit in anywhere—not at work and not at home."

"My breasts are too jiggly." *means* "I'm not solid enough right now to do what I think I need to do."

Thighs

"I've got real thunder thighs." *means* "I make too much noise."

"My thighs are lumpy and bumpy." *means* "I feel that I'm very uneven—friendly one day, unfriendly the next, happy one day, unhappy the next."

"My thighs are out of shape." *means* "I never force myself to do things."

"My thighs are ripply." *means* "I'm very indecisive."

"My thighs bulge." *means* "I feel like I'm always sticking out."

"I have elephant legs." *means* "I feel big, clumsy, and awkward."

"My thighs are gross and disgusting." *means* "I feel like I'm overwhelming, too assertive and aggressive."

"My thighs are flabby." *means* "I feel disgusted by my sexual needs—they're always hanging around."

"My thighs wobble." *means* "If only I weren't so shaky and insecure—wobbly. I feel like I should be firm and decisive. I don't believe in myself. I need to firm up."

"I have the fattest, ugliest thighs in the world." *means* "It's like saying, 'You're the worst.' When my mother was angry—and she was angry a lot—that's what she'd say: 'You're the worst.' "

"My thighs are blubbery, loose, and watery like a whale." *means* "This reminds me of tears. I'm living with a man who is dying and I'm at loose ends."

Upper Arms

"My arms are floppy, weak, and vulnerable." *means* "Like my mother, I don't stand up for myself."

"There's flab hanging off my arms." *means* "Flab for me equals ambivalence, going back and forth, never being decisive."

"The backs of my arms are thick." *means* "I'm too tough—I don't let myself feel things."

"They're so flabby." *means* "I associate flabby upper arms with my grandmother. Now I have flab, too. I feel undesirable because I'm older. To me, getting older means being invisible and less sexual."

"My arms are hanging, loose, and bumpy." *means* "I'm in the midst of a very ugly divorce that will leave me hanging loose."

Buttocks

"I have a big rear end." *means* "I feel like I take up too much space."

"There's just too much back there." *means* "I realize, as I say it, that I've been very depressed about getting older."

"My behind is disgustingly large and obtrusive." *means* "I do things to the extreme. I take over conversations."

"I have a grotesque behind." *means* "I grew up in a home where I felt threatened by my father sexually. When I say grotesque, I mean *dirty*. That's how I felt as a child—dirty."

"My behind is ripply." *means* "To me, ripply is like loose, as in not being a good girl, feeling too sexy."

"I have a big ass." *means* "I feel like I make an ass of myself. I grew up in a family where girls were teased and the butt of many jokes."

"My ass sags. It's tired and abused." *means* "I hear myself referring to how drained I feel from caring for my family and working full time. I also remember that my father used to hit me on my rear end a lot."

"It's too big, too fat." *means* "I've got so much to do that I can never get caught up. I'm just not up to the job, it's too big for me."

Face

"My face is jowly. I wish my jaw were firmer." *means* "I'd like to be more definitive."

"My chin is so weak and ugly." *means* "I feel weak. I want to appear and feel stronger."

"I hate my double chin." *means* "I'm in such conflict about wanting to be the best at what I do and feeling I should be more modest and less competitive. I want to be seen and yet I don't. I lead a double life. On the outside I'm very showy, but on the inside I'm more insecure."

"My face is imperfect, nonsymmetrical, repellent, unworthy, freakish." *means* "I've always felt this way about my face because of my cleft palate. But, now I realize that I'm really talking about parts of myself that I can't confront. I end up dumping all of those feelings on my face because it's a convenient target."

Hips

"My hips are too big, out of proportion, and grotesque." *means* "I'm talking about my needs. In my family, my needs seem too big."

"My hips are as wide as a shelf." *means* "My kids are grown, one is getting married, and I'm fifty years old. Since I haven't moved forward in anything, I feel like *I'm* on a shelf."

General

"I have big hips, a huge rear end, and a small bust—nothing goes together well." *means* "I often feel like I'm never going to get my act together."

"I'm horsey looking." *means* "I'm like a workhorse, always letting people dump things on me."

"I look at myself and I say, 'Disgusting.' " *means* "I was molested as a child by my uncle. I think that hating my body has to do with taking the rap and feeling like I was the disgusting one. It's easier to hate my body than to feel the rage I feel towards him."

Moving Beyond Bad Body Thoughts

Decoding your bad body thoughts allows you to identify your real concerns. What do you do after you figure out what problems you have been covering up with fat talk and bad body thoughts? It is easiest to begin answering this question by focusing on what you should *not* do. For example, you should not replace the yelling and punishment of bad body thoughts with yelling of another variety.

"I decoded my bad body thoughts," said Laura, who used to yell at herself for having a protruding stomach. "I figured out that they were really about my wish for more attention—but then I just picked right up where I left off and began yelling at myself for wanting more attention. I made the leap to figuring out what my problem was, but then I used it as another reason to treat myself badly."

If you are going to banish bad body thoughts, you must also

banish the harsh criticism they convey. You have to call upon the caretaker within yourself and, together, try a little tenderness. After all, what is the crime for which you are meting out such stern punishment? Does Laura's secret wish for attention merit the kind of contempt she has heaped upon herself for so many years? Would she treat her own children so harshly if they expressed the same wish?

Often, women yell at themselves simply because they do not know what else to do. They yell because they are frustrated, just as many parents resort to yelling constantly at their kids because they lack other parenting skills. Women who continue to yell at themselves, despite the fact that it consistently proves to be ineffective, need to develop different self-parenting skills.

Consider Laura's situation. She is grappling with a tough and complicated issue. Basically, she feels that she is loud and bossy. This self-image conflicts with how she as a woman believes she "should" act. Generations of women have struggled with this "should be" image. In order to emerge from the struggle intact, we need to question everything we have ever been told about who we are "supposed" to be.

Self-flagellation and self-contempt are counterproductive to this effort. Remember, you have been attacking yourself with angry bad body thoughts for many, many years. Your yelling has only led to depression and more entrenched resistance. The more Laura has attempted to flatten herself/her stomach, for example, the more she has protruded. Instead, she must approach the frustrating task of unraveling and examining her "shoulds" with patience, courage, tenderness, and intelligence.

Consider the case of Lois, a woman in Wisconsin. When Lois did the body-part exercise, she found herself thinking about what a "blob" she was. When Lois decoded the word *blob,* she realized that she often feels wishy-washy and indecisive.

"If someone asks me where I'd like to go for dinner," Lois explained, "I'll always say, 'Wherever you like. You choose.' Or if someone says, 'Let's go shopping today instead of going to the museum as we'd planned,' I'll always say, 'Fine,' without even thinking about it."

Lois is angry at herself for always accommodating other people's wishes and needs. She knows that she has always kept her real desires hidden, but she has never been able to do anything about it. She remembers that as a child, she was often chastised for wanting too much. "Who do you think you are?" her parents would ask when she expressed a wish of her own. Eventually, Lois learned to stop asking for what she wanted, and eventually she lost sight of her own desires as well. When Lois says that she'll go wherever, eat whatever, and do whatever, she is not exaggerating. She buried her preferences so long ago, and so deeply, that she no longer recognizes them herself.

The time has come for Lois to treat herself kindly as she attempts to unearth those preferences. They are her buried treasures, and their excavation will require a good deal of patience and energy.

Lois also must begin to challenge her belief that being wishy-washy is bad. Although she certainly would like to learn more about her own likes and dislikes and feel freer to express them, she needs to explore the contempt with which she regards her current inclination to blend in and accommodate others. As Lois learns to be gentle with herself, she will come to know more of what she wants and eventually will be able to risk voicing her desires. She will have to be patient. It will take time for her to trust that people welcome her input and, as that happens, she will also begin to see that those who react the way her family did no longer hold sway.

The nurturing caretaker you are trying to develop within yourself not only accepts you unconditionally but also challenges the values you have always accepted without question. Just as she asks, "Who says that a perfect stomach is flat?" she also asks, "Who says that being decisive is better than being flexible?" "Who says that being assertive is better than being accommodating?" We all have qualities we wish to change, but what do these qualities have to do with our basic human worth? Our internal caretaker's position is unequivocal: "I love you the way you are. If you are disturbed by qualities that cause you pain, I will certainly try to help you change. But I accept you *as is*, right now."

As you unravel the issues beneath your bad body thoughts, it is important to understand that you have kept these thoughts and feelings hidden for good reasons. You were ashamed of them; you were frightened to reveal them. You, like all of us, have internalized cultural judgments that were transmitted to you by your family. Until you can question cultural standards rather than conform to them, and until you can give up these judgments in favor of sympathetic understanding, you will need to hide your real thoughts and desires behind bad body thoughts.

When you read women's responses to the body-part exercise, for example, doesn't it become apparent that much of what we are yelling at ourselves for reflects the misogynistic stance of our culture? When we protest that we are "too big," it is because we are trying to squeeze ourselves into the small space we are allotted. When we assert that we "look monstrous," we are agreeing that our desires make us unappealing.

Once we recognize why we are hiding our feelings, wishes, and aspirations, we must question the standards we have accepted without challenge. Do *you* believe a woman should be seen and not heard? Do *you* believe that women want too much? Do *you* want too much? Remember that each bad body thought you intercept and uncloak is a step forward for you individually and for all women as well.

As we have said, the ambivalence so many of us feel about our female bodies and our female selves comes from living in a culture in which women are treated badly. Unfortunately, the extreme loathing many women feel toward their bodies first took root in families where we felt unwanted or were actively abused. As you can see from the body-part exercise, many of us felt rejected in myriad ways. When children are badly treated, they assume, quite simply, that they are bad.

Marianne, a participant in a San Francisco workshop, recognized the implications of her bad body thoughts and shared her insight with us. "I realize that I go further than simply saying, 'I'm fat.' I actually tell myself, with all the hatred I can muster, that I *deserve* to be fat. I'm just beginning to question what I really do deserve. And I am beginning to see that I certainly didn't deserve the treatment I received as a child. I see now that, for years, I've been repeating to myself what I heard coming at me from my parents. It wasn't just about my being fat; it was about everything. I believed that I deserved their contempt. Bad body thoughts became my main weapon against myself. I'll tell you truthfully, I'm scared about the rage that's buried in my bad body thoughts. Where will it go? I can't imagine not having that self-abuse as my constant companion."

Marianne, like each of us, was born deserving unconditional love and acceptance. But, whether we got what we needed as children or not, the time has come to supply it to ourselves. If, like Marianne, you feel frightened of the feelings buried beneath your bad body thoughts, you may want to seek professional help as you go about curing your Bad Body Fever.

Going the Distance

One evening in our New York workshop, we were having a discussion about bad body thoughts when Janice spoke up. "As I'm listening," she said, "I realize that I hardly ever have bad body thoughts anymore. I really can't think of the last time I felt fat. It seems like a miracle."

Janice's transformation is not a miracle at all. She has been using our approach for a long time and she has worked very hard at becoming aware of her bad body thoughts, setting them aside, and trying to understand why she has them and what they really express.

What impressed all of us in the group, however, was how extraordinarily gentle Janice had become with herself. She also was quick to catch the slightest hint of self-criticism or impatience when another group member spoke. Janice is proof that the more we are able to entertain a wide range of thoughts and feelings without passing judgment, the less need we have to disguise our feelings with bad body thoughts.

Janice has developed a reliable internal caretaker who speaks very gently and can look at all thoughts and feelings sympathetically. This caretaker guards her against the harshness and criticalness that are the basic ingredients of every bad body thought. There are few models in the world for such caretaking, but when we meet a woman like Janice, we see that it is possible, with practice, to let go of bad body thoughts and address the issues they disguise.

As an aid on your journey, we recommend a book by Marcia Hutchinson called *Transforming Body Image.* Marcia has developed a series of exercises designed to help you befriend your body. Here is one exercise we find particularly helpful. You will need a pen or pencil and some paper. As you did in the body-part exercise, pick a part of your body that you dislike and write down how you feel about it and what you usually say about it.

Having done that, put your pen or pencil in your nondominant hand and respond as if you were now your beleaguered body part. In other words, speak as your stomach, your breasts, or your legs and address what has been said to you. How do you feel being told that you are too fat, or that you are disgusting, or that you are flabby? Now is your chance to speak up. What would you like to say? What do you need? How do you want to be treated?

After your body part has had its say, return your pen to your dominant hand and respond. The goal is to generate a dialogue with this part of your body until you have resolved as much as you possibly can between you.

We have used Marcia's exercise at some of our workshops and would like to share a few of the dialogues with you. These dialogues become more poignant if you imagine the body-part responses as if they were written in a childlike, uncertain hand.

Mary: My stomach is disgusting. I hate it. I think it's grotesque.

Mary's stomach: I am a baby place. I gave you the children you thought you would never have. I deserve respect.

Mary: Believe it or not, I've never thought of that before. I've always hated you so much.

Mary's stomach: But not when the babies were in me. Then we were friends.

Mary: You're right. I enjoyed you then. I'm truly sorry. I'll try to remember.

Mary's stomach: I hope so. It hurts me to have you look at me with disgust.

Mary: I don't think I'll forget this.

Mary's stomach: It's okay. I love you.

Mary: I love you, too.

Pam: My butt—I hate how big it is. It makes me feel gigantic. When it hurts from sitting, I feel annoyed. It ruins the line of all my clothes.

Pam's butt: Please take better care of me. I help you every day to walk and move in this world. Move me more. I hurt if you sit so much. I need to move. You ignore me. What's so wrong with me?

Pam: I like the way you speak up for yourself, but to tell the truth, I'm frightened by your power and presence. You are very large. It's hard for me to accept and respect you, but I do promise to move you more.

Pam's butt: Your promise is not real. You really don't like to move me.

Pam: No, I don't, but my promise is real. I can only remind you that you frighten and embarrass me. I have to learn that we are one and the same. I want to work this out.

Pam's butt: I need movement. I want to dance.

Lucy: I ridicule my whole body and feel shame about it. I can't accept that the changes in it are "age appropriate."

Lucy's body: I'm doing just what I'm supposed to do and you tell me I'm bad. I don't know what you expect of me. I'm never right. Please let me be. I feel so alone and unwanted.

Lucy: I didn't realize what I was doing and I'm sorry to have hurt you. Tell me what I can do to be supportive.

Lucy's body: Don't nag. Don't criticize. Keep your mouth shut unless you can be supportive.

Lucy: I'm not always aware of what I'm saying, but I'll try. Please let me know if I slip.

Lucy's body: I'd like to feel we are on the same side. Right now I feel like we are adversaries. Let's keep talking.

Marilyn: My waist. I hate that it's so thick.

Marilyn's waist: I hurt. I don't deserve your hate. I need to be petted and caressed, not beaten down. I need to be set free and not always covered up because you're ashamed of me.

Marilyn: What specifically do you need?

Marilyn's waist: Looser waistbands. Larger belts. Don't hide me. Show me off.

Think about it this way. If you, as an adult, lived with someone who was as abusive to you as you are to your body, you would have the option of moving out. Your body has no such choice. Day after day it suffers your remarks, your grimaces, and your endless attacks on its size and shape.

Stopping your bad body thoughts by noticing them, setting them aside, and creating an atmosphere in which all of your thoughts and feelings can exist free of disguise is the first step in curing Bad Body Fever. *Befriending your body* is the next.

Chapter

4

BEFRIENDING YOUR BODY

CURING BAD BODY FEVER REQUIRES THAT YOU CHALLENGE CULTURAL attitudes about women's bodies in general and yours in particular. As we discussed in the previous chapter, you must first make the decision to stop attacking yourself with bad body thoughts. However, you also must take action by seeking out experiences that will enable you to develop a genuinely positive feeling about your body. We emphasize the word *genuine* to differentiate our approach from the "think positive" approaches that tell you to say good things about your body even if you don't really feel them. We know that when you hate your body, you do not hate it any less just because you tell yourself that you are beautiful. We also do not think it is a good idea for you to look in the mirror and try to find one or two things about your body that you like, as some other approaches suggest. Doing that implies that certain parts of you are attractive and others are not. All standards of beauty are time limited and arbitrary, determined, as they are, by qualities a particular culture values. You have simply learned the beauty rules of your culture. Indeed, you have learned them too well.

We urge you repeatedly—but gently—to challenge the external authority that taught you to look at yourself with disgust. *Who says that one body is more attractive than another?* is the question you must always have in mind. Your genuine positive feelings will emerge in the course of challenging old beliefs and treating yourself differently.

Positive feelings about your body? For many women, the idea of actually befriending their bodies seems impossible. Our experience has shown us that it *is* possible to develop a new way of seeing yourself and a new way of feeling. In order to create this unprecedented perspective, however, you must first be willing to make the effort to see yourself differently than you ever have before. And, as you make this bold and courageous effort, you must be willing to respond to any bad body thoughts you experience with a resounding "Who says . . . ?"

This is how it works.

Seeing Yourself Differently

In the Mirror

Bad body thoughts are often triggered when you glimpse your own reflection in a mirror or shop window. The mirror work we suggested in our first book was designed to help you recapture the power of your own reflection. Rather than avoiding the mirror, we urged you to use it: to abandon the punishing lens of cultural bias and criticism and to learn to see yourself in a bold, fresh, and nonjudgmental way.

In the years since we wrote *Overcoming Overeating,* we have seen just how difficult it is for women to look at their own reflections without judgment. What do you say when you see your reflection if you don't say, "Yuck?" We suggest that when you look at yourself in the mirror you say something like this:

> "This is my body. What I see is the reflection of my genetic heritage, my aging, my history of dieting, and my history with food."

If you are a compulsive eater, your reflection is one of a person who has needed to turn to food for comfort. In the past, you have regarded this need as a shameful transgression and you have berated yourself for it. Now, however, it is time to evaluate your need as nothing more or less than what it is: a piece of your history reflected in the mirror. Your need to use food for comfort is nothing to yell about and nothing to cringe from; it is simply one of several factors that contributes to the way you look.

As you continue to look at your reflection in a nonjudgmental way, we suggest that you say the following:

> "I may never look very different from the way I look right now. I am going to try to inhabit my body, dress myself, and enjoy my body as much as I can. It is my home. I will not continue to speak to myself about my body in the unkind ways I have learned. I am going to come to terms with myself at this size."

As your gaze becomes more focused on specific parts of your body, it is time to begin questioning the external authority you have internalized. Don't be shy. Look closely and ask in a loud, strong voice, "*Who says that my thighs are not beautiful? Just who says?*"

Allow some time for the challenge to penetrate. Think about it while you continue to look at yourself. Who says that your thighs are not beautiful? The answer is, *everyone.* There is no question that the collective "we" does assert with certainty that there *is* such a thing as the "perfect" thigh. Barbie has it, but you don't. Barbie also has a perfect butt and perfect breasts. But the truth is that Barbie is plastic and you are not. Barbie does not have a genetic heritage, but you do. She does not age, but you do. And she does not eat—from either physiological hunger or psychological hunger—but you do.

Take a deep breath when you look at yourself. You need to see yourself without judgments so that you can grow into your body right out to your edges. One way to begin growing is to look at your body in light of the context in which you grew up.

The Context of Your Family

Take some time to look at family photographs. Look at your parents, grandparents, your aunts and uncles, your great-grandparents if possible. If you look at photographs from both sides of your family that include previous generations, it is likely that you will begin to see some patterns. Somewhere in your ancestry are people with bodies shaped very much like your own.

"Looking through family albums was extremely useful for

me," said Helaine, a workshop participant. "It enabled me to finally acknowledge that I come from a long line of women who were shaped very much like I am now. We're a lot rounder than today's ideal, but I love the connection I feel with the women in my family photographs. I love the fact that I'm part of a *we.*"

Clarissa Pinkola Estés tells a related story in a wonderful chapter on the body in her book *Women Who Run With the Wolves.* Inculcated with the belief as a child that her body size indicated a lack of self-control, she finally journeyed to Mexico as an adult to find some of her ancestral people. The women of the tribe—"strong, flirtatious, and commanding in their size"—were concerned that Estés was not fat enough. They explained that "women are *La Tierra,* made round like the earth herself, for the earth holds so much."

A Genuinely Positive Perspective

We have stressed how important it is for women to relinquish their judgmental perspective and look at themselves in a neutral way. But Irene, a participant in a New York workshop, challenged us on the issue of neutrality. "I don't think it's enough to just accept your body," she said. "In order to see myself differently, I had to reach a point where I could look at a woman who is as large as I am and genuinely think that she looked terrific."

When we first began our work with women with eating problems, we stressed the importance of living as if you would never lose weight and we urged women to embrace their largeness in a bold, positive way. As Irene spoke, we realized that over the years, we had subtly softened our position. We had settled for neutrality because the women we worked with so strongly resisted the idea of ever really liking their bodies.

Irene reminded us that it is important to move beyond neutrality. Ultimately, you cannot cure your Bad Body Fever until you have genuinely positive feelings about your body. Perhaps listening to the experiences of women who have reached this turning point of genuinely befriending their bodies will prove to you that it *is* possible.

Maria: Hugging Others—Embracing Herself

Maria, a woman in Colorado, found the impetus to develop a new perspective on her body by actually hugging other large women. "I was at a weekend conference related to my work," she explained, "and I made some good connections with the other women there. We were all saying good-bye and hugging one another. One of the women was about my size and when I hugged her, I was struck by how good she felt *because* she was so soft and big. I laughed out loud and actually told her how much I liked hugging her and why. I'm sure it wasn't the first time I'd hugged another large woman, but in the past I was too upset about my own size to enjoy hugging anyone, let alone someone large. I think I anesthetized myself whenever hugging was going on. This time, the hug was really special."

Joanna: Talking to Her Arms

During this discussion, Joanna described a technique that worked for her. "I've always hated my upper arms," she said with some embarrassment. "They're soft and wobbly. A few months ago, I spontaneously started stroking them while I looked at myself in the mirror. Then, as crazy as this sounds, I actually began to talk to them. I spent time every day looking in the mirror and getting acquainted with my upper arms in a new way. It's unbelievable to me, but I actually like them now. I think that the way they wobble is endearing, and I love the soft, squishy way they feel. Now I'm ready to begin making friends with my hips. Touching myself in addition to looking at myself has been very helpful."

Vivian: Looking Beyond Her Size

"For a long time," said Vivian, who wrote to us from Cleveland, "I tried to see myself accurately whenever I looked in the mirror. I thought the point of mirror work was to come to terms with exactly how large I really am. Now, however, I understand mirror work differently. When I look in the mirror now, I don't really focus on size because size, as an issue, is not what's important to me. If I'm larger today or smaller today, either is okay.

What matters is that I recognize myself in the mirror and that I regard myself with acceptance simply because of who I am. I greet myself in the mirror, and that's very pleasurable."

Patricia: Working with Photographs

While you are in the process of becoming comfortable with looking at yourself in the mirror, it may be helpful to begin looking at yourself in photographs. Patricia Schwarz, a photographer from Berkeley whom we met at the 1992 AHELP conference (Association for the Health Enrichment of Large People), has very strong feelings about size acceptance. Patricia, a large woman herself, specializes in photographing large women, and her photographs are extraordinarily beautiful. We have no doubt that if the mixed-size audience who watched her slide show that evening had been asked how they felt about large bodies, they would have responded en masse, "Magnificent!" Flesh, mass, form, and power all add up to magnificence from Schwarz's perspective—a perspective that is undeniably contagious.

Schwarz encourages other large women to enhance their size acceptance by collecting representations of fat things: objects, photos, and museum postcards. Beyond that, however, she urges them to take hold of a camera and begin to see the world of their bodies differently.

We have often asked members of our groups to photograph each other with an instant camera. Patricia suggests that when you take photographs of each other, you allow the model to be the director and determine where she wants the focus to go. As the model, you might want a picture of a part of your body that you have a particularly difficult time accepting; or you may want to see yourself "just being" in front of the camera; or you might want a real portrait. You decide.

This kind of photographic work is best done in groups of three or four. If you are more comfortable doing it alone, however, you can use a tripod and timer. The most important point is to look at the photos closely and talk to yourself or to others about what you see. What do you like? What do you hate? Let it all out, then look again. This time, however, let your inner caretaker respond to the photograph as well. Her perspective is gentle, tender, and loving, and it is a perspective you need to hear.

The Taboo Against Looking at Yourself

One of the reasons so many women have a difficult time doing mirror work—and perhaps one of the reasons we are so susceptible to bad body thoughts when we see our own reflections—involves a cultural taboo against taking pleasure in being seen by ourselves or by other people. The idea of disrobing and standing in front of a mirror studying one's own reflection is downright embarrassing for many of us.

What is this embarrassment really about? A woman named Kim gave us a clue. "I keep trying to work in front of the mirror," she said, "and I'm fine as long as I keep my clothes on. But as soon as I get undressed, I feel disgust. I know that I'm supposed to step away from the mirror as soon as I get judgmental, but I get judgmental the minute I take my clothes off!"

Kim tried thinking out loud in an effort to explore what she thought was so terrible about her naked reflection in the mirror. Much to her surprise, she began talking about her five-year-old niece, who parades about the house—dressed and undressed—showing off her body to anyone who's there. "I think it's great that she's so free," said Kim, "but even at her age I would have been mortified walking around like that."

For Kim, and for most of us, the taboo against looking at ourselves and being seen by others has to do with what we have learned are forbidden pleasures, the innocent sexual pleasures children take in displaying and looking at their own bodies, and the more mature sexual pleasures we experience as adults. Kim is not disgusted by her body per se when she looks in the mirror. She is disgusted by her strong desire to display her body and to be seen by others. Rather than experience that desire, she obscures her view and punishes herself with harsh bad body thoughts.

In this process of befriending our bodies, how do we overcome our sense of shame? How do we bring ourselves full circle to the point where we can indulge our natural, early impulse to look at ourselves and take pleasure in what we see? Watch the delight of a young child who stands before the mirror just before she climbs into the bathtub. She wiggles. She sings. She makes all kinds of faces. How can we reclaim that delight? Perhaps by dancing, wiggling, singing, and making faces now!

As we said earlier, it is important to challenge your bad body thoughts with a bold, "Who says . . . ?" Beyond that, however, the best techniques we have found for overcoming the shame that initially accompanies mirror work have come from the women in our workshops.

"Who says that youth is more attractive than age?"

"I started doing yoga recently," said Celia, a woman from California. "One morning I was running late, so I did it without any clothes on in my room. I have a full-length mirror. At first I was stunned by what I saw reflected in the mirror. Then I became simply fascinated. I've done very little exercise in the past and I'm finding that my body does all sorts of things I didn't know about—like when I stand on my head, everything, *absolutely everything,* hangs! I'm fifty-six-years-old, but I guess I really didn't know what that meant until I saw myself in the mirror upside down! Oddly enough, rather than get depressed about it, I found myself fascinated. I'm a sculptor and I was enthralled by the shape and form of my own body. Somehow, my interest took precedence over any judgments. So now I always do my yoga naked."

Celia used her own words and her own actions, but they added up to precisely the kind of challenge we are advocating. *Who says that a youthful body is the most attractive? Just who made up that rule?*

"Who says that fat is bad?"

Ann, from Montana, made a commitment to dealing with her bad body thoughts by apologizing to herself for them, challenging them, and letting them go. After a few months she began to notice that she was feeling better about herself than she had in years. "The good feelings were like a high," she said, "but the one thing that consistently brought me crashing down was catching a glimpse of myself in the mirror. As good as I felt about myself, whenever I saw myself in the mirror, I'd be shocked by my size."

Ann's story makes it clear that feeling fat and feeling thin, with their concomitant bad and good feelings, have little to do with actual body size. Her experience is not unusual. Many women who have been challenging their bad body thoughts and feeling much better about themselves lose their new perspective the moment they unexpectedly glimpse themselves in the mirror. Suddenly they see themselves through the "outside" eyes of a fat phobic/woman phobic culture that obliterates their newer, clearer vision. When this happens to you, it is important to remind yourself that your negative judgment is actually a bad body thought and must be handled accordingly. Apologize, challenge, let it go, and try to learn from the experience. What were you really criticizing? The fact that you had allowed yourself to feel so good?

Ultimately, Ann dealt with the issue by looking at her reflection more and more frequently and giving herself the opportunity to associate her good feelings with what she saw. *Who says that fat is bad and thin is good? Just who devised that ridiculous rule?*

"Who says that thin is sexy?"

Claire, from Virginia, took courage in hand and decided to make some really bold moves to help herself with her mirror work. "I figured that as long as I was going to break the taboo and really look at and enjoy my body, I might as well do it in style," she said. "I searched through flea markets and antique stores until I found a big, old mirror still gilded on the frame. I set it up in my bedroom. Next, I dug up some wonderful old fringed scarves and fabulous fabric remnants I've collected over the years. Then I undressed and lay down in front of the mirror as if I were an artist's model, hundreds of years ago, posing for a portrait. I draped myself with different scarves and fabric and thought of Titian and Degas. I'd never seen myself that way before and it was absolutely thrilling. I felt so womanly and sexy and powerful. From now on, whenever I feel shaky about myself, I plan to get out the scarves and repeat the experience. It works wonders!"

In other words, *who says that feeling big and powerful isn't sexy? Just who thought that one up?*

"Who says flesh is ugly?"

At another workshop, Lorraine told us that she had recently started belly dancing classes as part of her struggle to accept her body. One night she went to a club where some women from her class were going to perform. First, she watched the professionals, all of whom were thin. She wondered, anxiously, what would happen when her friends began to perform. They each weighed more than 200 pounds. She was sure they were in for an awful humiliation.

Her friends' performance was astonishing. They had such a sense of themselves and communicated such delight in their bodies that the audience was enchanted. "I was bowled over by their grace, their costumes, and their radiance," she said. "I never would have dreamed such a thing possible."

Now, when this woman practices her belly dancing in the mirror, her delight is even greater than it was before. *Who says that a flat stomach is the ideal? They certainly haven't seen my belly dance!*

A Word of Caution

As you proceed with your mirror work, it is important to remain respectful of your personal history. For example, Susan, in Chicago, told her group that it had taken her a very long time to be able to look at herself without clothes on. "I was molested when I was a kid," she said, "and seeing my naked reflection made me feel very vulnerable and very guilty." If you have a history of sexual abuse, you need to go very slowly in this work and do everything you can to make yourself feel safe. The key here, as we have said before, is to call upon your internal caretaker to guide you. She knows what pace is best for you and she knows that pushing harder never works.

Obstacles to Maintaining Good Feelings About Your Body

For many women the ability to feel good about their bodies is ephemeral. "There's no question but that I'm really feeling a lot better about my body," said Bea. "I can spend time in front of the mirror and really enjoy my body as it is. I even dance around a little and can almost enjoy feeling substantial. But at some point in the day, I invariably head outside, and that's when it all begins to unravel. I start comparing myself to other women and lose the good feelings I had in the privacy of my home. I'm at a point now where I can stop my bad body thoughts when I notice them, but I can't recapture the feelings of pleasure that I had about my body before I left the house."

Many women report similar experiences. Their mirror work buoys their self-perspective while they are at home, but their old problems return as soon as they leave their houses. The moment they step outside into the world, they become vulnerable to the tremendous external pressure to denigrate their bodies and, before long, they find themselves yearning for a culturally idealized shape.

Even if you can only feel good about your body in the safety of your home, it is important to appreciate how significant your accomplishment is. It means that you have carved out some territory for yourself. Eventually, the work you are doing in the privacy of your home will sustain you outside as well. Stretching your territory is easier, however, if you remain mindful of the fact that befriending your body is a truly courageous act.

The Pressure to Compete

As you continue to explore this process of befriending your body, it is important to notice how you feel about the women and men around you. Most of us were raised to regard other women as competitors for male attention. We were trained early on to believe that the woman with the "best" body would "win" the best man. Is it any wonder that we are uncomfortable when we step out of our homes into an arena in which we are *supposed* to compare our bodies to the bodies of our so-called competitors?

Are we really in competition with other women in the ways we have been taught? Are physical attributes really the basis of meaningful romantic relationships? Anyone who looks closely at couples as they walk down a street can see that skinny men walk hand in hand with fat women, tall women arm in arm with short men. On screen, Hollywood may couple people on the basis of their looks, but off screen, most handsome men do not marry Sophia Loren look-alikes (who, by the way, married a short, fat, bald man named Carlo Ponti—not Cary Grant!).

There are, of course, people who believe that their own status and worthiness are enhanced if their lovers measure up to the culture's coveted body type of the moment. These people are certainly not good prospects for becoming accepting, loving companions. The reality, however, is that most men and women are drawn to each other for reasons that go far beyond body type. The same is true for gay and lesbian couples. "Chemistry" between people has more to do with the unconscious links we draw between people in the present and people who were important to us as children than it does with busts and biceps. As long as mothers and fathers continue to come in a variety of shapes and sizes, mates will, too.

Suzanne, a participant in a New York workshop, had a terrible time at a party she and her boyfriend attended because she couldn't help but compare her body, unfavorably, to the bodies of the other women there. "I was convinced," she said, "that he would be attracted to this friend of mine he'd never met before, because she has a gorgeous—by that I mean thin—body."

When Suzanne expressed her concern to her boyfriend later that night, he laughed. "What's so funny?" Suzanne asked, confused by his laughter. "Well," he said, "I can't believe you think that just because your friend has a great body, I'd lose all control and leave you. Is that all you think I care about? There's more to me than that . . . and there's more to you than that, too. And I certainly hope your friend has more going for her than her great body."

Everybody in the room nodded as Suzanne spoke. It was clear that we could relate to what she was saying. We could all picture ourselves in the situation—falling back into thinking that thin is good—and being certain that the perfect body mesmerizes every man. Why do we all share so simplistic a notion of how men think? What does this notion tell us about ourselves? What does it tell us about men? Clearly, our view of men as mindless creatures entirely controlled by the size and shape of the female body is both a belittling put-down of men and a strong statement about the power of the female body.

That evening we talked about how as women, we are not striving to be thin for the sake of thinness. We are striving to be thin so that we can be powerful, irresistible. If we are going to pour a lifetime's energy into perfecting our bodies, at least, in the end, we hope to be rewarded.

Body Power

Longstanding cultural myths have their roots in our earliest needs and experiences. In order to understand the hold of these myths—that people form relationships entirely on the basis of a woman's body shape and that women really can become powerful just by changing the shape of their bodies—we need to look back in time.

From the perspective of a small child, a mother's body has all kinds of magical capacities and attributes. Mother, after all, has the body from which babies emerge; she has the body that nurtures those babies; and she has the body that attracts Father's attention as well. Beyond all of this, however, is the fact that, as very young children, our mothers' bodies are also central to our lives. We want our mothers; we yearn for them; we hold onto their skirts and bury our faces in their thighs; we run to them for comfort, safety, and pleasure. This early perception of a body that is so much more powerful than our own provides the foundation for the fantasy of the power of the female body.

When we talked about the power of our mothers' bodies in a workshop one night, it was clear that we had struck a familiar chord. "That feels right to me," said Marilyn. "I've often thought about why I'm so focused on other women's bodies. I've assumed all along it was because I was worried that men would be drawn away from me to the bodies that I think are better than my own. But now it occurs to me that *I'm* actually the one who's doing all the looking at these other women. No one's forcing me to look, but I feel drawn to them. It *must* have to do with my early feelings about wanting my mother as well as wanting to be able to compete with her."

Pauline joined in. "Long after my daughter stopped nursing, she just couldn't get enough of my body," she said. "She was always cuddling, touching, hugging, kissing. She went through phases where, like a jealous lover, she didn't want to share me with anyone, and she also went through a stage when she told me quite sincerely that she was going to marry her daddy and I'd have to find another house. My body was everything to her. She wanted to devour me, to be just like me, to get rid of me, and then to come back to me for comfort."

"The next time I find myself focused on how great I think another woman's body is," said Louise, "I'm going to try to own up to the fact that I'm looking at her wistfully and admiringly rather than just jealously. Maybe if I allow myself to admire her, she won't seem like some powerful, threatening mommy who's going to take all the men away. Who knows? Maybe we could both be beautiful and powerful. What a radical idea!"

When we see other women's bodies as threats, we weaken ourselves. As the saying goes, "Divide and conquer." As long as women continue to focus their energies on worrying about each other's bodies, we weaken ourselves individually and collectively. If, instead, we could look at other women's bodies and appreciate and enjoy what we see, we would be strengthening ourselves. We would be asserting that women's bodies are lovely—ours and our mothers' included. And we would free ourselves to use our power to move ahead in the world.

Woman to Woman

Of course, allowing ourselves to look at another woman's body and enjoy it brings us into a head-on confrontation with the strong taboo against having sexual responses to members of our own sex. We learned, early on, that women's bodies were for men. Our mothers' bodies were for our fathers' pleasures. But the truth is, if we cannot allow ourselves to take any pleasure in other women's bodies, we will never be able to take pleasure in our own.

Donna Pittman, a psychotherapist whom we mentioned earlier, joined us at the week-long Overcoming Overeating workshop we conduct each year at Lake Austin Spa Resort in Texas and helped us learn to enjoy looking at each other's bodies. She led a series of exercises for the group using movement and guided fantasy. Toward the end of the day, she told us that she wanted to help us feel comfortable wearing our bathing suits now that summer was upon us. Although she acknowledged that it might be difficult, Donna asked us to pair up in our swimsuits and take turns looking at each other. For two long minutes our partners walked around and around, looking us up and down, before changing places. Once each woman had had a chance to look at someone else and be looked at herself, it was time to talk about all our experiences.

Some women felt devastated by being looked at; others, much to their surprise, found it more difficult to look than to be looked at. By the end of the discussion, we had all made a very exciting discovery: A body is a body is a body. In other words, we are all the same and we are all different—we are all composed of a variety of interesting shapes.

By the end of the week, this same group of women, all of

whom had come to feel much more comfortable in their bodies, decided to hold a workshop in the indoor pool. Because we had the resort to ourselves that week, we could make bathing suits optional. Some of us decided to liberate ourselves from our bathing suits, but, more importantly, we all decided to liberate ourselves from old, worn-out ideas—like the idea that we are not supposed to look at each other; like the idea that someone must look better, and someone must look worse; like the idea that fat is ugly. Remarkably, liberation turned out to be a lot easier than anyone would have expected.

By the end of the week, everyone in this close circle of women was overwhelmed by their newfound perspective. They said they would never forget how remarkable each and every body looked, with bathing suits or without them. We actually reached a point where it was difficult for any of us to imagine how the ideal of thinness had ever taken hold.

Who says that protruding bones look better than cushiony flesh? Who says that angular looks better than round? Just who came up with that crazy idea?

We left the Spa experience enthralled by our own female bodies and by the bodies of our friends as well. Our eyes were clear as we headed back out into the world. Our new goal was to dress the bodies that we had befriended in a way that would decorate rather than conceal them.

Chapter

5

MOVING INTO YOUR BODY

ONCE YOU BEGIN SEEING YOURSELF DIFFERENTLY, YOU WILL WANT TO dress yourself differently as well. Most women recall that, back in their dieting days, they always went shopping for clothing when they had reached their goal weight. Shopping for clothing for their thin body was a celebration, a reward for having achieved a goal.

We like the idea of buying wonderful clothing to celebrate the achievement of a goal. The problem is that you have been celebrating the wrong accomplishment. Rather than buy clothing to celebrate your thinness, we suggest that *you buy a wardrobe for yourself to celebrate your size acceptance.*

DRESSING TO SIZE

Dressing for who you are, rather than for who others think you should be, is a tangible manifestation of the psychological work you have been doing. Each article of clothing that you buy to celebrate size acceptance is a reminder that you value yourself and that you deserve to be treated tenderly and lovingly. And each article of clothing that you bought to celebrate weight loss is like a bad body thought waiting in the wings. By getting rid of clothing that is too small, you are ridding yourself of bad body thoughts as well.

Still, many women have a hard time clearing out their closets and dressing themselves for the here and now. They look at their size eight clothes and feel a stab of longing; then they look at themselves in the mirror and feel simply overwhelmed. Does this sound familiar to you? How can you overcome your resistance to curing this aspect of Bad Body Fever? Once again, the answers we offer come from our interactions with the women in our workshops.

Call upon Your Internal Caretaker

Whenever you encounter difficulty with the symptoms of Bad Body Fever, it is important to remember that you have an internal caretaker who is eager to help you get beyond the rough spots. She is there to encourage you. She understands why you feel nostalgic about your size eights, but she is quite clear that you are every bit as acceptable and deserving now as you were when that clothing fit you. She is sorry for the pain you have felt in response to your body all these years, but she is excited about helping you create an image that will delight you right now. In fact, when you bemoan having *outgrown* something, she is there to remind you that *growth* is not a bad word. She has all sorts of original ideas, like taking a favorite item of clothing that no longer fits you and having a seamstress reproduce it in your present size.

Beyond offering this kind of support, your internal caretaker also always remembers that your bad body thoughts are never about your body. She knows that you do not want to dress nicely when you are feeling lousy about yourself. But she will help you shift the focus from your body to whatever is really bothering you, and she will help you get beyond your problem the way a good mother helps a child sort things out. She may sing a bit, coo a bit, talk things through with you, and help you negotiate a plan for the future.

Practice Dressing in the Privacy of Your Home

When you first began doing your mirror work, you were most comfortable in the privacy of your own home. After a while, hopefully you became more comfortable with the idea of moving beyond the mirror into the outside world. This same process of stretching your "safe" territory holds true with regard to dressing. The world we all live in is still terribly judgmental, and these harsh judgments of a sexist, antifat world can be intimidating. The best way to deal with this intimidation is to take things slowly. Your first step can take place entirely "in your head": We urge you to stop thinking about clothing as a form of camouflage and to begin thinking about what kinds of clothes you would really like to wear.

During our first workshop at Lake Austin Spa, everyone seemed to buy biking shorts in the hottest colors available. Most of the women recognized that it would be some time before they were comfortable wearing their shorts in the outside world, but they were thoroughly able to enjoy wearing them at the workshop. And the more comfortable they felt among their peers, the better prepared they felt to face the stares of strangers.

Be Sensitive to Your Personal History

As you attempt to dress yourself in the kind of clothes you really like, it is important to be sensitive to your personal history. Naomi, one of our New York workshop participants, made the point that she was literally unable to distinguish between clothing that she liked and clothing that made her look thinner.

"I'm sixty years old," she said. "For forty-five of those years, I've shopped for clothes that made me look thinner. And before that, my mother shopped for my clothing with the same goal in mind. When I look in the mirror and try to decide whether or not I like something, I'm sure that I'm still making my selection on that basis. If I put on pants, for example, and I see the bulge of my thighs, I won't buy those pants."

Many of us share Naomi's experience. We can't expect to look at a bulge that we have spent a lifetime trying to cover up and suddenly decide to show it off. Remember, feeling fat is a manifestation of the more general feeling that you are not okay the way you are. Millions of us have spent our lives poisoned by this feeling of inadequacy, and as we struggle to overcome it, we must be gentle with ourselves.

Create a Strong Support Network

One way to overcome external pressures as you attempt to dress yourself for the here and now is by creating a strong support network. Have a "Come As You Are, Not As You Should Be" party. Don't be shy about using your support network as a reality check when you step into the outside world and confront the many people who will be urging you to cover up. You need each other.

"The first time I went clothes shopping after a workshop," said a woman named Midge, "I had a hard time with a saleswoman. She kept urging me to try the clothes she thought were 'slimming.' Finally, I mustered the courage to tell her that I wasn't interested in disguising my shape. I expected her to just let it drop, but she went right on. 'What's the harm?' she asked. 'Don't you want to look as good as you can?' "

If the "well-meaning" advice of salespeople is more than you want to cope with, you might do well to shop with a supportive friend or begin your new shopping adventure by mail. One woman at a recent workshop mentioned that she had discovered all kinds of terrific catalogs in *Radiance* magazine. Another pointed out that many mainstream catalogs now have large-size sections. "Eventually I'll be ready to try things on at my local stores," she said, "but for the time being, I'm most comfortable in the privacy of my home. If I like things, I keep them; if I don't, I send them back . . . without having to explain anything to anyone." Freda Rosenberg, a body image consultant in Philadelphia, has put together *Freda's Secrets*, a guide to catalogs that sell large-size clothing.

Whether you shop in stores or by mail, it is important to make the distinction between dressing so that you feel attractive and dressing so that you feel acceptable to others. Millions of women spend untold hours and millions of dollars attempting to dress themselves in a manner that garners acceptance. Such widespread effort suggests that there is something sadly amiss in their basic feeling about themselves. When you feel yourself slipping into the rut of dressing to please others, we suggest the following exercise.

"Imagine If . . ." Exercise

Imagine that your body type somehow becomes the cultural ideal. Every magazine you open has models in it who are built exactly like you—rather than 20 percent thinner than the average woman, as is currently the case. How would you do things differently in your life? How would you dress? What would you eat? How would you feel when you looked in the mirror?

"I couldn't believe it," said one woman. "Just by saying 'imagine if . . .' I suddenly felt comfortable and accepted for who I was. For the first time in my life, I didn't feel like there was anything I had to *change*. What relief!"

Another woman in a California workshop was quick to say, "I would let go and love myself." As soon as she uttered these words, she felt overwhelmed by sadness. "I guess I never realized how withholding I am toward myself," she said. "I never realized that I could feel a lot better about myself simply by declaring that I'm my own ideal. I'm so used to measuring myself by other people's standards."

"I was disturbed by the exercise," said another participant. "I went from a caterpillar to a butterfly too fast. What would I do with myself if I weren't thinking about how I could change my body?"

"Freedom," said one woman emphatically. "All I could think about was no longer having to be so aware of how I looked. I could move naturally."

"I'd wear better clothes," someone else said.

"It's amazing to realize that the world doesn't have to change in order for me to feel okay. A change just has to occur in my own head."

"When I tried this exercise, I focused entirely on the fact that I could go to a store and pick out whatever I wanted—clothing would no longer serve as camouflage."

"I would take greater risks in what I wore," said a woman who had always worn big tent dresses in an effort to hide her body. "I'd wear brighter colors and stand out."

"I felt happy for a moment," said another woman, "but then I felt very angry about all the judgments I still live with."

"I saw myself very clearly in a red-sequined dress," someone said triumphantly, "and do you know what? I have a fancy party coming up and I'm going to find that dress for myself. I've been working with this approach for long enough now to feel that I can finally live in my own body!"

Several of the women who did this exercise were surprised to discover that they felt uncomfortable suddenly becoming the cultural norm. "I was concerned about being top dog," one participant said. "I'm used to envying women who I think have great bodies, and I don't want to be in a position where others envy me."

"I realized that I'd have a hard time adjusting to all that attention," said someone else. "I always say that I want my body to be more like the ideal, but I see now that even if it were in vogue to be large, I still wouldn't be comfortable revealing my body."

"Not me," a woman from the crowd shouted in a loud, clear voice. "I did this exercise and felt *ecstatic.* I felt like crowing. My time had finally come!"

Why Bother Imagining?

The value of an exercise like the one we have just described is that it forces you to think about the beliefs and values that influence the wardrobe you select. When you actually stop and think about what you would choose to wear if you weren't concerned with making yourself look slimmer, you are forced to confront two issues: first, how big a factor "looking slimmer" is in your choice of clothing and, second, what kinds of clothes you really yearn to wear. What kinds of colors do you like? What kinds of fabric do you feel best in? Do you really like loose-fitting clothing? Do you prefer the feel of fabric clinging to your body? How do you feel about vintage clothing? Do you like a sophisticated look? Casual? These kinds of questions are fun to think about, and you deserve that pleasure. They get bypassed, however, when your entire focus goes to whether or not something makes you look slim or fat.

"I always thought about how I looked in clothes rather than how I felt," said Ginger in San Francisco. "Now my first consideration is how an item of clothing feels—the fit and the fabric. In the past I would look in the mirror to see whether or not I 'looked good.' 'Looking good' was my only criterion, and I knew that 'looking good' was really a code for looking slim. Now I look in the mirror to find out if *I* like the way I look. Let me tell you," she added, "there's a world of difference between those two things!"

Making a Commitment

Even with lots of support and all of the techniques we have just discussed, learning to dress yourself for the here and now may be very difficult. It is important, when you encounter difficulty, to remind yourself that the struggle to develop an independent stance about your size is a difficult one and that it requires an ongoing commitment.

Sara, who attended our New York workshop, is a case in point. "I did everything you suggested," she said, "and for a while I was doing fine. I bought a lot of clothing and spent a lot of money. Doing that made a huge difference in how I felt. But now that clothing is too tight and I'm in a panic. I know that you say we should never put on the brakes, so I keep up my supplies of food. But how much bigger do I have to get? The last size I bought was so large, I can't imagine going higher. And I simply can't spend any more money on clothing."

Some old-timers in the group smiled knowingly when Sara finished talking. Their smiles did not reflect insensitivity but, rather, a sense of recognition. They remembered saying similar things at some point in the past, and they knew that we would respond to Sara in the same way we had responded to them.

Accepting yourself unconditionally means precisely what it says—*without conditions.* We were sympathetic to Sara's sense of panic, but we did point out that her panic reflects the fact that somewhere, deep down, she believes that there is a size at which she will not be acceptable, even to herself. That belief is at the root of her Bad Body Fever and must be met with a challenge and, ultimately, with acceptance.

Who says that any particular size is the largest that is acceptable? Just who sets such limits?

Moving Yourself Differently

People often ask us about the role of exercise in curing Bad Body Fever and compulsive eating. Since we stress the importance of caring for your body by seeing yourself differently, and dressing yourself differently, it would make sense to assume that exercise would also have a place in that care.

We are very much in favor of movement and exercise. We know, however, that many women think about exercise in tandem with diets—as a means toward weight loss. In order to make movement or exercise a permanent part of your life, you must disassociate it from the issue of losing weight. Then you must challenge your ideas about what your body can and cannot do.

Exercise—A Means to an End

Exercising to lose weight has the same built-in problems as dieting. We buy health club memberships, exercise machines, running shoes, and work-out videos in the same compulsive way we enroll in the latest diet program. More often than not, the gym membership lapses before we've had a chance to get our money's worth. The exercise bike collects dust in a corner of the bedroom. After a few days of rain, we never manage to get back to jogging. And the exercise videos cannot compete with the movies we rent for pure entertainment.

We engage in exercise that aims at weight loss as punishment for not looking like the models in the fashion magazines; we then rebel against that punishment because we also yearn to be accepted *as we are.* There is an alternative kind of exercise, however. We can exercise for strength, for endurance, and for the pure pleasure of moving our bodies in the ways they were intended to be moved. You can learn to ask yourself when, what kind, and how much exercise/movement your body needs. Unfortunately, years of cultural conditioning have complicated our ability to ask and answer these questions. Just as we allowed many cultural "shoulds" to stand in the way of our natural appetites, we have also restricted ourselves from moving in ways that would make us feel good.

"When I was young, I used to take modern dance classes," recalled Jessie in one workshop. "I remember being in perpetual motion even when I wasn't in class. I remember that dancing and moving my body gave me a sense of power and well-being. I wish I had the guts to take a class today, but at my size I just can't get myself to do it. I think everyone would laugh at me. I'm sure I'd be the largest woman in the class."

Jessie needs to challenge her assumptions with a firm "Who says?" Who says that only thin women have a right to delight in moving their bodies? Who says that you cannot enjoy moving your body at any size? Why can't you take a swim class or a belly-dancing class if you'd like? Just who says that slim hips move better? Who says that thin legs kick higher?

Ilene, a woman in a California workshop, challenged the status quo precisely as we had suggested. "I decided that your position on exercise is correct," she said. "Why shouldn't I enjoy my body and move it the way I want? So I started to play tennis again after twenty years of not playing. At first it was hard going, but I persevered. After a few months of playing regularly, I complained to my instructor that I was frustrated because I missed so many balls. I was sure it had to do with the fact that I was fat and couldn't run fast enough to reach them. I've always blamed my shortcomings on my weight, and I was ready to do it again. Luckily, my instructor had a different perspective. He said that I simply did not have the skill or the physical stamina to reach those balls and that it would take much more time and practice before I did. He was right—and months later I was doing much better."

Exercise and movement should be *pleasurable.* No matter how you choose to move, it should be for the purpose of experiencing and enjoying your body, regardless of your shape. We are all entitled to this kind of pleasure. Think back to your childhood. Can you remember a time when it was fun to wiggle, squirm, run, jump, hop, and skip? It is important to recapture that early pleasure. If you cannot remember such a time, it is important to explore your history and figure out what interfered.

Pat Lyons, coauthor with Debbie Burgard of *Great Shape*, suggests an exercise to facilitate this exploration. It involves constructing an activity continuum. At the upper-left corner of a blank page of paper, write "Sally Sofa"; in the upper-right corner, write "Mary Marathoner." Sally represents total inactivity, Mary represents exercise, exercise, and more exercise, and the space in between represents all the gradations. Down the left-hand side of the page, make a list of ages—6, 10, 14, 18, 21, 25, 30, and so on. Now plot your activity level by putting an asterisk where you would place yourself at various ages along this continuum. At the age of six, were you closer to Mary, to Sally, or somewhere in the middle? Continue through the years, thinking about each age. What made it possible or not possible to move your body? What did you enjoy doing? What was no fun? Where would you like to be today on this continuum? If you are not there, what is getting in your way?

Many of our workshop participants were amazed to discover how active they had once been and how much that activity meant to them. Everyone who had become sedentary wished they were still active. Is that true for you? If so, how can you make that wish come true? Begin by focusing on the pleasure you once felt when you moved and think about recapturing that pleasure today.

Measuring Your Progress

In *Overcoming Overeating* we urged readers to throw away their scales. Scales, we said, are part of the old system. We rely on them as external evaluators to measure our success and acceptability. Such evaluators have no place in a world of size acceptance. Our new evaluators are internal; we can learn to turn to ourselves to determine how we look.

Not surprisingly, many people have a difficult time parting with their scales. "It's like saying good-bye to a longtime companion," one woman said. "For years my scale greeted me every morning when I woke up and again every night before I went to sleep. I've always told myself that the scale is impartial. It's not easy for me suddenly to see how truly biased its information is!"

Checking in to see whether you have gained or lost weight does not measure your progress as you battle Bad Body Fever. The progress you need to measure now is much more complicated than it was when you simply wanted to lose weight. Now you need to consider whether or not you are living by your own rules. Are you allowing yourself to enjoy your body at your current size? Are you dressing to please yourself? Are you finding new ways to talk to yourself? Your bathroom scale cannot measure any of these things—only *you* can.

The fact that scales no longer have an "official" role to play in your life does not mean that you will not be tempted to check one out from time to time. Some people weigh themselves secretly. "I just wanted to see if I was accurate about what's happening to my weight," is the typical explanation. Or, "I was visiting a friend and there it was in the bathroom. I just couldn't resist." Or, "I told the nurse that I didn't want to know my weight, but when she left the room, I couldn't keep myself from looking."

We understand that it is odd to live in a weight-obsessed world without occasionally stepping on a scale. It is important to remember, however, that we never really used these scales to tell us how much we *weighed.* We used them to tell us if we were *good* or *bad.* "I can't believe I ever said this," said one woman. "But, I clearly remember saying, after I weighed in at a Weight Watcher's meeting, 'I was a *bad girl* yesterday. I ate too much for dinner and I gained a pound.' "

Without a scale to measure how good or bad we've been, many of us feel adrift. Connie, a participant in a New York workshop, is a case in point. Connie had been making great progress in combating her Bad Body Fever. She was dressing to please herself, eating when, what, and as much as she was hungry for, and feeling happier and more secure than she ever had before. Then one evening she decided to step on the scale. "I was horrified," she told the group. "I weighed more than I had ever weighed before."

Why had Connie stepped on the scale? Why, when she had been feeling so good about herself, did she do something to put her good feelings in jeopardy? What could have possessed her?

When we asked Connie to think about what had happened just prior to her stepping on the scale, she thought of several things. First, her four-year-old niece had said, "Aunt Connie, you have a fat stomach." Connie explained, "I had no trouble telling her that people come in all different shapes, that some are fat and some are thin. But the fact was, her comment really hurt."

In addition, Connie told us that her husband had been giving her a hard time about feeding herself on demand. "He really doesn't like having all the food in the house, and he and the rest of the family keep pointing out that it doesn't look like this approach to my eating is doing anything for me," Connie said. "Somehow, with all the pressure, I just had to get on the scale. As soon as I did, I felt horrible and thought about quitting our group and going on a diet."

Connie's story is an excellent illustration of the convergence of external pressure and internal resistance. In fact, she was barraged by external pressure to do something about her weight. But, as she eventually acknowledged, the external pressure would not have sent her to the scale unless she, herself, had continued to harbor doubts about how she was doing with this new approach. Connie's family felt that she was on the wrong track because she was not losing weight. Evidently, at the moment she jumped on the scale, she must have agreed with them. At that moment, she bought into the idea that weight loss should be her goal and her sole criterion for success.

As the group discussed Connie's situation, she came to a realization. "The fact that my family was so unsupportive just when I was beginning to really feel good about myself was very disturbing to me," Connie said. "But I realize now that not only have I been eating differently, I've been acting differently as well. I've been a lot less passive than I usually am about all kinds of things. I suspect that their real problem has more to do with the fact that I'm not as compliant as I once was than it does with my weight. Jumping on the scale was a way to become my old compliant self again."

How might Connie respond differently to the pressure her family exerts? We suggested that, the next time her family comments on her weight, she say something like, "I understand that you believe that my weight is an indication of my progress. I used to believe that as well, but I no longer use my weight as a measurement. Now, I'm after very different things."

Can You *Really* Change the Way You Feel About Your Body?

Throughout these chapters we have talked about ways to change the way you feel about your body. We have consistently stressed the fact that making this change is very difficult. After all, for most of our lives we have been "mainstream" in our thinking about size and weight. Developing an independent stance—and then holding on to it in the face of daily challenges—requires a great deal of ongoing effort. We are swimming upstream, and the current against which we are pressing is very strong.

We understand that there will be times when you feel exhausted by your struggle. Indeed, we expect that there will be times when it seems entirely impossible for you to hold your own against this current. The fact is, however, that there are women who have developed a deep fondness for their bodies—whatever their size. The women who do this most successfully are those who take on the job of becoming their own best caretakers most seriously. They go the distance, break all the rules, and insist on granting themselves unconditional self-acceptance. They no longer seek the love and validation they crave from those around them. Instead, they look in the mirror, wiggle, move around, and take delight in what they see. Although such women are unusual, their number is increasing.

For many of us, size acceptance requires daily acts of faith. As we rise from our beds in the morning, our fat today/thin today evaluations feel as familiar as our nightgowns. Our new, independent perspective on our bodies has faded during the night. Hopefully, before we reach the bathroom, we remember who we are in the present and say something loving to the reflection in the mirror that awaits our greeting. We take extra care in selecting an outfit for the day. And if, during the day, we feel vulnerable to the external pressures for weight loss, we realize that something is being triggered *within* that requires investigation.

Carole, a participant in our New York workshop, put it well when she said, "I used to think that someday, I'd be totally free of fat feelings and bad body thoughts, but now I see it differently. The external pressure that fuels my body hatred is enormous. Sometimes it really is easier for me to be upset with my body than to be upset with my life. But the struggle is most manageable if I take it one small step at a time."

Carole told the group about one such small step, which she had taken a few days earlier. "I got my hair cut the other day and when I walked past the mirror in the entrance hall of my house, I didn't like what I saw," she said. "In the past, I would have stared at the mirror with disgust and made some comment about how fat I looked. This time, though, I looked in the mirror and said to myself, 'Oh, I never like the look of newly cut hair. I like the way my hair looks when it's had a chance to grow a bit.' For me," Carole concluded, "that represented a real step forward."

Other members of the group responded to Carole's story by recounting their own small steps. "I tried on something I'd bought last year," said Arlene. "It was too tight. But before I had a chance to dump on myself, I remembered that when I bought it, I had asked if they had it in the next size, but they didn't. I put it in the give-away bag without another thought."

"I took a giant step forward," said Estelle, "by allowing myself to have a professional massage. I'd always wanted to have a massage but felt too uncomfortable about allowing someone to see and touch my body so intimately. I asked a friend to check out a particular masseuse on the issue of large-size bodies, and it turned out that she is a real advocate of size acceptance. She put me in charge and told me to tell her if anything felt uncomfortable. She wanted me to feel safe—and I really did. It was so liberating to allow myself to be touched like that. In fact, the only down side was that the experience made me aware of how harshly I had treated myself in the past, when I didn't believe that my large body deserved to be treated well."

All of the women in this group had taken steps forward. Are they fever free? No. But for the most part, they are in remission and are determined to treat themselves kindly and responsibly whenever the symptoms of Bad Body Fever reappear.

Part Two

Reclaiming Your Appetite

Chapter

6

DIETING: AN ESCAPE FROM FREEDOM

AS A RESULT OF BAD BODY FEVER, MANY OF YOU HAVE SPENT YOUR lives trapped in a painful paradox. You are always trying to make yourselves smaller by dieting, yet you rebel against your own best efforts to *be* smaller by binging. To us, your binges are a sign that a fight for freedom is alive and well within you. Unfortunately, you have not been able to create a climate in which your fight succeeds. Each time you binge your way free of one diet, you simply find another to take its place.

When we wrote *Overcoming Overeating,* we went public with an approach to eater's problems that was based on our twenty years of experience working with compulsive eaters. Central to this approach is the idea that women can stop worrying about their weight and abandon diets once and for all.

Our readers were people who had signed up for Atkins, Jenny Craig, Weight Watchers, Optifast, Pritikin—you name it—and had then binged their way out of all of them. Their binging was an attempt, either conscious or unconscious, to free themselves from unnecessary and punitive food restrictions. Binging, however, does not free people; it is simply a reaction to the restrictions of diets. In terms of eating, freedom means abandoning diets and learning to live comfortably in a world of food. We knew that our suggestion to go for complete freedom from diets would be controversial and difficult for many women to hear.

Our View of Dieting

It was clear to us before we wrote our first book that diets simply do not work. Our own experience with dieting was the same as the experiences of the thousands of chronic dieters all over the country who attend our workshops. Everyone loses weight on a diet—and everyone gains it back. Indeed, the fact that ninety-five percent of all dieters regain their weight, plus some, is the foundation on which a $37 billion diet industry is built. The ultimate irony is that, if diets worked, there would be no diet industry.

Before we urged people to abandon dieting, however, we took a good look at what it is about diets that ensures their failure. Why, we asked, does dieting inevitably lead to binging?

Every diet is premised on two beliefs: that you are not okay the way you are and that food is an enemy from which you need protection. We will look at these two premises more closely later. For now, it is enough to understand that every time we begin a diet, we are seeking acceptability and protection—but in the end, we get neither.

Our View of Binging

In a culture that avidly supports dieting, it is easy to see why most women regard their inability to keep weight off as a personal failure. "If only I'd had more willpower," the standard lament goes, "I wouldn't have binged my way out of this diet."

We view the failure of diets from a very different perspective. Indeed, we see binging as a sign of healthy rebellion against the two beliefs on which all diets are based. We recognize that each time a woman binges, she is rebelling against the notion that there is something inherently wrong with her. Binging is also a rebellion against the restraints of diets, all of which declare certain foods off-limits, thus creating an exaggerated yearning for the forbidden foods. Indeed, dieting is the main cause of compulsive eating.

Rather than chastise the women in our workshops for their lack of willpower, we congratulate them on having the courage it takes to rebel against the totally senseless and demeaning rules of diets and we introduce them to our plan to cure compulsive eating. The truth is that for anyone with an eating problem, food itself is never the real problem. The real problem is their need to use food as a tranquilizer rather than as a fuel.

Dumping Diets

In recent years, much of the medical establishment has acknowledged the failure of diets to produce lasting weight loss. In March of 1992, the National Institutes of Health made an official declaration that diets do not work, thereby legitimizing a suspicion most diet-weary women already held. The medical world, however, has not yet offered an alternative to diets. From our perspective the alternative is self-evident: If diets don't work, get rid of them!

Our approach is designed to undo the damage caused by dieting. We teach compulsive eaters to trust themselves around food, to learn about their own appetites, and to recognize that there is nothing inherently wrong with them.

Chronic dieters spend most of their lives berating themselves for how much they eat and for having bodies that do not meet an idealized cultural standard. Their chastisements mimic our harshest cultural attitudes about eating and weight, and the more they denigrate themselves, the more they turn to food for comfort. Although there is no way to change this kind of behavior overnight, we urge our readers to ease the pain of self-inflicted condemnation, first by developing an awareness of it and, then, by gradually eliminating it.

All dieters categorize food as being either fattening or nonfattening. This dichotomized view of food further aggravates eating problems by creating cravings that, when indulged, lead back to bad body thoughts . . . that lead back to dieting . . . that lead back to binging.

Our solution is to "legalize" and "equalize" all food—in other words, to do away with the notion that certain foods are forbidden. All foods should be abundantly available and regarded as equal. The goal is to learn to think about food as a way to satisfy physiological or stomach hunger, just as we all did at the beginning of our lives, and to eat whatever we are hungry for, whenever we are hungry.

If you are a compulsive eater, when you feel in trouble emotionally, you experience what we call psychological hunger, or mouth hunger, and you turn to food as a means of calming yourself. Under the dual pressures of dieting and your own anxiety, you have lost your basic hunger/food connection; you use food as a tranquilizer instead of as a fuel. Each time you use food in this way, you are actually using it as a symbol of the comfort that came from early nurturance and caretaking. The only way to break the cycle of turning to food for psychological hunger is to learn to feed yourself "on demand," just as mothers of infants today are encouraged to do by their pediatricians.

Demand feeding functions in the same way for you as an adult as it did for you as an infant. Each time an infant is fed when she is hungry, changed when she is wet, and comforted when she is upset, she learns that there is a world outside herself that cares about her feelings and meets her needs. This kind of attentiveness is the hallmark of good caretaking—and good caretaking is what you need in order to free yourself from dieting and compulsive eating.

Demand feeding reestablishes the basic hunger/food connection that was destroyed during your years of compulsive eating and dieting. Each time you feed yourself when you are hungry, you demonstrate that you are able to care for yourself in an attuned way. The more reliable you are as a self-feeder, the more emotionally secure you will feel and the less likely you will be to turn to food for reasons other than hunger. You will have less anxiety in general, and you will feel better equipped to name your problems and deal with them directly. Imagine never thinking about food except when you are hungry. Imagine *thinking* about your problems, rather than *eating* about them.

The Initial Reaction to Not Dieting

In *Overcoming Overeating*, we looked at how compulsive eaters—people who have spent most of their lives either dieting or binging—could actually end the diet/binge cycle. In the years since we wrote the book, we have observed a consistent pattern in the process of diet dumping. Most compulsive eaters initially respond to our suggestion to replace dieting with demand feeding with suspicion and mistrust. "This is going to be a disaster," one woman said. "If I swear off dieting forever, I'll keep eating until I burst." "If I don't yell at myself about being fat," said another, "I'll keep getting fatter and fatter."

However, once people face the fact that dieting itself has been making them fatter, they are willing to hear us out. They are pleased to hear us say that their inability to stay on diets is actually a sign of their mental health. They are so pleased, in fact, that after some understandable hesitation, they start to experiment with not dieting—and they feel elated.

"It's really true," one woman said. "During those first few weeks I thought I'd never stop eating doughnuts. But I did stop! My home is filled with cookies, cake, ice cream, and all sorts of stuff, but I don't feel driven to eat." "I'm eating less and losing some weight," another member of the group chimed in. "I can't believe the freedom I feel. I'll never go on a diet again."

Backsliding

The chains that bind women to diets and bad body thoughts, however, are not so easily broken. Women who have spent years or decades absorbed by bad body thoughts have a hard time letting go of the habit of dumping on themselves. And women who have spent a lifetime checking in with the scale have a hard time sticking to their resolve to abandon diets once and for all.

The initial exhilaration most people feel when they get off the diet/binge cycle is soon tempered by the realization that living without diets is not easy.

"When I'm dieting, I'm thinking about food all the time," one woman said, "but at least I'm also losing lots of weight. Now I'm very conscious of how I use food, but I'm worried that I'm gaining weight."

"In the beginning," said another, "I thought it would be a snap to eat whatever I wanted whenever I was hungry. But I soon found out that I don't really know when I'm hungry, and I also don't know what it is that I really crave. I'm so used to craving the things I'm not supposed to have that, once the restrictions are lifted, it's hard to figure things out."

"It's much easier for me to think about how full or empty my plate is than it is for me to think about how full or empty my stomach is," commented one woman at a workshop.

After the initial exhilaration of our nondiet approach wears off, many people cope with their new uncertainty in an interesting way—they subtly turn the Overcoming Overeating principles into a diet. They yearn for a set of rules to tell them what and what not to eat, a set of rules that will free them from the burden of looking within themselves. After turning our approach into a system of do's and don'ts, they ultimately rebel against those rules in the same way they have rebelled against diets.

"I had a good week," a woman named Alice reported. "I ate out of control only three times." Alice does not realize that her self-evaluation is as judgmental as it was in her dieting days. She does not hear the aching need for approval in her voice, nor does she realize that she is still trying to be someone's "good girl."

This rebellion against our nondiet approach happens gradually, typically beginning with judgmental remarks like the one Alice made. Then, the demand feeding approach suddenly begins to feel like too much work. "I just don't have the time to keep buying food for myself," one woman said. "It's too much effort to keep figuring out when I'm hungry and what and how much I want to eat," said another. All of these feelings culminate in a yearning for the old salad days when a sheet of paper answered all questions about what to eat for breakfast, lunch, and dinner.

It is not surprising that people backslide and attempt to turn this radical approach into a diet. Women who are clearly willing to rebel against diets by binging, are not necessarily ready to give up those diets in order to explore the possibilities of life without them. As with any compulsive behavior, people do whatever they can to get back to safe, familiar ground.

Why We Backslide

Why is it so hard to let go of dieting and develop an independent point of view about eating and weight? In order to answer that question, we need to look at the place of diets in our culture. The fact that anyone is able to say "I'm not dieting anymore" is a miracle when we consider the incalculable pressure in our culture to monitor food intake. The increasingly alarming statistics on anorexia, bulimia, and chronic dieting attest to that pressure. The message for women, in particular, is that our bodies are not right and that, in order to make them right, we must eat as little as possible. This message is prominently conveyed in the windows of shops all over this country, broadcast over the airwaves, and plastered on the pages of magazines and newspapers. Even when those very same publications report the latest findings on the ineffectiveness of dieting, they continue to promote dieting.

The week of June 30, 1991, the *New York Times* cited two independent studies that discredited the effectiveness of dieting. One study reported that when people who are not at risk for heart disease limit their fat intake, they increase their life span by only three months. The other study reported that "yo-yo dieting" not only impeded weight loss but created dangers as well. Women between the ages of thirty and forty who repeatedly lost and gained the same ten pounds actually shortened their life expectancy.

Later that week the *New York Times* columnist Jane Brody featured a quiz by Dr. Kelly Brownell, the author of the second study, that continued to promote dieting. The quiz was titled "How to Determine Your Readiness to Diet," and the point of the column was that dieters, not diets, are the problem. If dieters were just ready to diet, diets would work!

The Social Conventions Underlying Dieting

Dieting has become a social convention and, unfortunately, social conventions are harder to change than laws. Civil rights laws of the sixties, for example, guaranteed equal job opportunities to all people, but two decades later our attitudes toward minorities continue to influence the reality of those opportunities in both powerful and subtle ways, regardless of the laws.

Social conventions, like those that have accumulated around dieting, are not written down and, often, are not even spoken directly. For example, most people assume that all large people eat too much and should be on diets. And most people believe that we should all watch our weight. Ideals like these become part of our inner fabric and are very difficult to identify, let alone alter, even in light of overwhelming evidence that shows them to be destructive.

We understand their feelings when women using our approach say, in one way or another, "I don't want to be different from everyone else," or "I hate the way people look at me when I'm hungry and take something out of my food bag, the way you suggest." We also understand that these judgmental looks you receive have more to do with what kind of food you are carrying around than with the fact that you're carrying it. "When I brought my carrot sticks and water-packed tuna to work, everyone understood that I was dieting and they left me alone," commented one woman in a Chicago workshop. "They even congratulated me on my willpower. Now I have a jar of M&M's on my desk and you should hear the comments."

Whatever efforts women make to get smaller, however strange or extreme, fall within the bounds of normal and receive approval or even praise. When those efforts are abandoned, perhaps even announced—"I'm never going on another diet"—the woman suddenly finds herself in quite a different category. She becomes a rebel, and even if she herself admires rebels, she may not feel comfortable being one. For all of us, the fear of being ostracized and isolated is very powerful.

Fear, however, is not the only obstacle we encounter as we attempt to rid ourselves of the tyranny of diets. Eventually, we each must face the fact that, on a deep, inner level, we agree with the social program implicit in diets, and we will continue to backslide until we question some of our assumptions.

The Roots of Our Participation

As we saw in our examination of Bad Body Fever, in order for external pressure to have an effect on us, it must strike an inner chord. When Erich Fromm explored the psychological basis for the rise of fascism in his book *Escape from Freedom,* published in 1941, he stated that "ideas can become powerful forces, but only to the extent to which they are answers to specific human needs prominent in a given social character." The idea of dieting is just such a social force that answers the need women feel to transform themselves.

Naomi Wolf contends that, as women become more powerful in our culture, they encounter more and more pressure to make themselves smaller—to make themselves "less." Consider an ad for Dynatrim that read, "In 14 days be *less* of a person." Why would a woman agree to become "less of a person"? Why do women succumb to the pressure to shape their bodies rather than the world?

Modern culture rests upon many implicit divisions and polarizations among people: rich/poor, educated/uneducated, white/black, young/old, male/female. Everyone's internalization of the values inherent in these divisions leads to a sense of inferiority in the less powerful groups. We believe that this culturally induced sense of inferiority among women makes us feel less capable, in need of instruction, and desperate to become someone other than who we are. These feelings of inadequacy leave us vulnerable to the self-destructive suggestion to remake our bodies by dieting. It is amazing and very sad that millions of women still believe that they should have less, be less, and, most important, never be themselves.

The Search for Structure

Diets tell us how to live one aspect of our lives that often has far-reaching ramifications. Diets provide us with a structure that makes us feel secure. "Whenever I go on a diet, I feel this wave of relief that suddenly I'm back in control," said a woman at a Montana workshop. Sadly, the illusion of control we feel when we go on diets has nothing to do with self-control.

In a workshop one evening, we were discussing everyone's fear of living without diets and found ourselves talking in a more general way about our fear of living without structure. One of the participants remembered the endless discussions she had had during college when the traditional system of grading was switched to a system of pass/fail. "People thought nobody would bother to study without the lure of an A. Was there a natural urge to learn, or were people going to just party all day long?"

Another woman remembered how everyone at her college had felt when the administration abandoned curfews and rules about members of the opposite sex visiting each other's dormitories. "People worried about whether there would be wild orgies," she said. "It just seemed that if you let go of structure and rules, chaos would fill the gap. Now, coed dorms are the norm." In whatever context, the prospect of freedom is frightening.

Erich Fromm explains this fear as "the dialectic character of growing freedom." In order to develop, we must break the bonds that limit us; yet those same bonds have made us feel secure. As we become freer and more able to express our individuality, we also experience the insecurity of being more alone in the world. We all look for ways to solve this problem of aloneness. Dieting masquerades as one solution to the existential problems presented by freedom.

Consider the developing child. Both literally and figuratively, the more she grows and the more capable she is of doing things for herself, the less able she is to be held the way she was when she was an infant. She no longer fits into her mother's arms in the same way she once did. Yet she yearns for that "fit" at the same time she yearns for her independence.

The Search for Safety

A diet—like curfews and grades and our mother's arms—offers safety in the form of rules and regulations for eating that, if faithfully followed, promise weight loss. In this culture, along with weight loss comes the promise of a new, utterly satisfying life. Diets, like mommies, are expected to make it all better.

For those of you who have spent your lives dieting and binging, this issue of external versus internal authority may be critical. As soon as you begin a diet, you no longer need to make decisions about each mouthful. The diet makes those decisions for you. Your life is simpler. You do what you are supposed to do, sit back, and wait for the weight to come off and your life to change. And while you are dieting, you feel virtuous because you are living up to cultural guidelines. In short, you feel like a "good girl."

Without the diet, you feel wild, unfocused, and without known boundaries. With the diet, you feel secure and in control. Without the diet, you feel the disapproving gaze of those around you. With the diet, you have their admiration. For people who have been dieting (at their parent's insistence) since childhood, watching what they eat makes them feel like themselves. Without the diet, they feel a loss of identity. Unfortunately, the very comfort that comes from living within the confines of a diet is also its liability.

Once you get your weight down to where you think you want it, you congratulate yourself and feel very good . . . for the moment. Soon, however, it becomes clear that the diet, like an overprotective parent who makes all the child's decisions and restricts her developing independence, did nothing to help you solve your eating problem. Your obsession with the diet simply puts the problem on hold. Like the prisoner whose problems were not solved by being incarcerated, you leave your diet no different than you were when you began it. And like the ex-con who continues to break laws because nothing has changed in his life, you continue to eat compulsively whenever you are diet-free.

Despite the fact that dieting is thought of as a sign of accepting self-responsibility, it is really a way of placing responsibility for yourself in someone else's hands, however invisible the owner of those hands may be. Diets are addictive because they create the illusion of a safe structure that can contain your eating impulses—just as your mother's arms once set the boundaries of your world. As long as you rely on diets to feel safe, however, real freedom and growth will continue to elude you—just as growth eludes the child who clings to her mother and cannot risk the uncertainty of separation.

It is hard for most compulsive eaters to believe that they have the internal mechanisms necessary to guide them through a world of unrestricted food. It helps to remember that we were all born with perfectly adequate signals for hunger and satiation. As infants, we did not need anyone to tell us when we were hungry or when we were full. The sooner you rediscover that inner knowledge, the sooner you will be able to move ahead.

Backlash

Every revolutionary change in consciousness elicits an opposite reaction. That is the nature of change whether on a personal or a worldwide scale. (We commonly express this phenomenon in the adage "Two steps forward, one step back.") The women's movement, so strong during the 1970s, experienced a conservative backlash in the 1980s. As Susan Faludi documents in her book *Backlash*, political, economic, and personal barriers against women reemerged during the last decade with a vengeance.

The 1990s have seen a feminist resurgence that bodes well for a remobilization against dieting and body hatred. Backlash, however, is an ongoing phenomenon. Not only do the usual advocates of family values ridicule feminist demands, but others who purport to speak in the voice of the "new feminism" imply that our war has already been won—we should enjoy our power and stop raising the issue of our victimization.

This backlash has its parallels on the antidieting front as well. For a brief period of time, our antidieting movement was big news. We made such a splash that, overnight, the word *diet* disappeared from the diet industry's literature. Instead we began hearing about "lifestyle changes" and the "nondiet."

Some of those nondiets were quite transparent. After all, a weight watcher is a weight watcher is a weight watcher. Others, however, were more deceptive. In *Stop the Insanity*, for example, Susan Powter traded in the insanity of traditional diets for the "sanity" of low fat/high exercise regimes. In other words, she talked the talk but walked a dieter's walk.

There is always a harsh reaction to progressive struggles. However, as people come within reach of the kind of freedom they seek, they invariably discover that, beyond the external backlash that confronts them, they have internal hurdles to confront as well. As products of our culture, we have internalized its rules. In order to free ourselves from a cultural injunction like dieting, we must overcome both external and internal resistances.

Living in this culture, each of you has learned many things that are not only incorrect but also dangerous. For example, you have learned that your female body is not perfectly lovely the way it is. As we have said, in order to clear your vision of such negative judgments, you must question every idea you have ever had about your body and your weight. In particular, you must recognize that *just because everyone says that fat is bad and dieting is healthy, that does not make it so.*

How do you say that dieting is ridiculous—and mean it—when you believe deeply that it is essential? How do you summon up the courage to free yourself from the structure of a diet when you are terrified of losing control? How do you stand alone against a tidal wave of propaganda that is fueled by the diet industry?

The Struggle Against Dieting

It is clear that we need a strong antidieting movement. We need slogans.

"Dieting is dangerous for your health."

"Become more of a person."

"Eat Dessert First."

"One size *does not* fit all."

There are some people in Texas who are already wearing T-shirts that read "I Used to Diet But I'm Okay Now."

As part of creating that movement, we urge you to form your own groups. Joining forces with others goes a long way toward solving your problem. Each Overcoming Overeating group should be dedicated to creating a safe, supportive environment that fosters self-esteem and encourages the kind of inner exploration that ultimately will cure compulsive eating. The more your new ideas are nurtured, the more they will germinate and grow, replacing your old ways of thinking.

A front-page headline in the *New York Times* on April 12, 1992, read, "A Growing Movement Fights Diets Instead of Fat." "Based on their own experience," the article went on to say, "emboldened by well-publicized findings suggesting that 'yo-yo' dieting may be detrimental and bolstered by recent Government inquiries into the false advertising claims of some diet companies, a growing number of women are joining in an antidiet movement. They are forming support groups and ceasing to diet with a resolve similar to that of secretaries who 20 years ago stopped getting coffee for their bosses. Others have smashed their bathroom scales with the abandon that some women in the 1960s burned their bras." The next time you consider weighing in for a new diet, bolster your resolve by recalling a banner a group of antidieters carried during a demonstration in Dayton, Ohio: "Scales Are for Fish, Not for Women."

Joining forces with others is essential to solving your problem, but as we have said, the external pressure to diet is only one part of the struggle. The feelings that you have about yourself that have led to a lifetime of dieting are embedded in your psyche. Deep inside, you really do believe that you deserve to have less and be less. Re-creating yourself as a person who *should* have, rather than a person who *should not* have, is terribly difficult, even with the support of a group. Learning to trust the "rebel within" who binged her way out of diets takes time, as does learning to replace the rebellious act of binging with a strong, independent approach to eating.

Feeding yourself on demand is a fundamental aspect of self-care that will eventually have a profound impact on how you feel about yourself. Because this independent approach to eating runs counter to cultural guidelines, your internal caretaker has an important supporting role to play in the process of your becoming a nondieter.

Good caretakers have three essential qualities: They trust themselves, they have the courage to be different, and they have lots of patience coupled with resolve. As we go on, we will explore these qualities in depth, but for now it is enough to touch on each one briefly.

Learning to Trust Yourself

Before you can cure your compulsive eating, you need to take your actions very seriously; you need to believe that the impulse that led you to binge out of every diet you ever went on was a good impulse, worthy of exploration. An attuned caretaker would say, "You really do know best. You were telling yourself something important each time you binged out of a diet and it's about time you began to listen. If you keep going off diets, it's because they don't agree with you. If anyone says, 'Here, have some of this diet soup,' you should answer them, 'No thanks, I'm allergic.' "

Finding the Courage to Be Different

In order to cure compulsive eating, you must develop the courage to stand alone, to be different from most of the people around you. Separating yourself from your group in this way can be intimidating and even frightening. That's why "being there for yourself," trite as the phrase sounds, is so essential.

Think of it this way. You're scared to take this step and you long for support. There is more to you than your fear, however. There is the part of you that has taken care of others when they were scared and there is the part of you that has felt scared and been taken care of by others. You may believe that the caretaking you received as a child was flawed. Nevertheless, as an adult you have given and received all kinds of caretaking. It is now within your power to pick and choose among models.

You can create an attuned and understanding you who will be there to respond to the frightened you, and you can play both of these roles simultaneously. The frightened you may tremble under the gaze of disapproving onlookers, but the caretaker you can place the disapproval in its rightful perspective. "It's your body and your life," this voice will remind you. "You really cannot afford to be swayed by those whose disapproval has already caused you so much suffering. If you stick with your point of view, they may, over time, become more accepting. And if they don't, eventually you won't care as much because your own approval will matter much more."

Developing Patience and Resolve

Your compulsive eating problem has developed slowly, over many years, and curing it will take time. We hope that, in the course of reading this book, you will become convinced that your resistance to freeing yourself from body hatred and from diets is completely understandable and merits your patient respect. Resistance and backsliding do slow you down and can be very frustrating, but they also provide security.

The helpful and loving caretaker you are trying to develop understands that growth occurs in fits and starts. She remains excited about what you learned to do yesterday even when you revert to your old way of handling things today. She is eager for you to develop a new relationship to food and to your body, but she is not in a hurry—she does not want you to feel overwhelmed. Because she understands how frightened you are about doing something as radical as living without body hatred and dieting, she is willing to examine each and every "yes, but." This new caretaker of yours is confident that with determination and patience, the two of you together will make progress. Each time you feel overwhelmed and hopeless, she will say, "Don't worry, *we'll* figure it out." The *we* is crucial—you are not as alone as you thought!

How can this caretaker be so sure that, together, you will solve your eating and body image problems? She is certain because she knows she will do whatever it takes to free you—she does not want you to suffer anymore. She is the voice within you who is enraged at how much of your life's time and energy has been drained by this obsession with eating and weight. She is patient, loving, gentle, and kind. She is also determined. Although the two of you do not yet have all the answers, she has confidence that, together, you will learn all you need to know. In the meantime, she has some words of wisdom for you:

"You are not incurable. Compulsive eating is not a disease from which you will be forever recovering.

"There are many reasons why you became addicted to diets and to food, but you will be able to solve your eating problem even before you understand all of the emotional issues that led you to food.

"You will probably regain the weight you lost on your last diet, but not because of demand feeding. You have always regained the weight lost on diets; that's the binge phase of the dieting cycle. It is possible that by feeding yourself on demand, your weight will stabilize sooner.

"You are engaged in a process. You are going to be tempted to throw in the towel and sign up for another diet, but you will eventually feel more comfortable living without restrictions.

"You *can* eat your way out of an eating problem!"

Chapter

7

BACK TO THE BEGINNING: KNOWING WHEN TO EAT

A FIVE-YEAR-OLD WALKS INTO THE KITCHEN AND SAYS, "I'M HUNGRY." In the most matter-of-fact voice her mother answers, "Eat something." The connection between when we feel hungry and when we eat is a simple one. Or is it? Sometimes, instead of saying simply, "Eat something," a parent might say, "What! You can't be hungry. You just ate dinner." Or, "Don't eat anything now. Dinner will be ready in a half hour. You can eat then."

Hunger is a biological drive that is satisfied by food. That drive is first evident at birth when a newborn begins to suckle. No one ever urged a newborn to put off satisfying her hunger until breakfast . . . or lunch . . . or dinner. But somehow, over the course of childhood, the hunger/food connection in many of us is consistently and purposefully obscured.

The beliefs we hold about when we should eat originate in our homes and are reinforced by our culture. We learn that there are appropriate places and times for food and, more often than not, those times have nothing to do with what is going on inside our stomachs. We also learn that there is an appropriate shape for our bodies that may very well have nothing to do with our genetic destiny. So, we eat when we are supposed to, and in accordance with diets that promise to mold us into an acceptable shape.

By the time we reach adulthood, many of us have forgotten what we came into the world knowing: to eat when we are hungry, to not eat when we are not hungry. Indeed, many of us have actually forgotten what stomach hunger feels like because food has acquired a meaning that has nothing to do with satisfying stomach hunger. Curing compulsive eating requires "regressing" to the point where your hunger/food connection is as clear and strong as it was the day you were born. Getting to that point involves a two-pronged process of *action* and *understanding*. Traditionally, the only action compulsive eaters have been urged to take is to diet, and the only understanding they have been encouraged to reach is an understanding of the "problems" that led them to misuse food. However, the action and understanding that we propose are very different.

We promote an understanding of how compulsive eating works—how you learned to use food for comfort. Somewhere along the line, your hunger/food connection was short-circuited. This damage probably occurred either as a result of dieting, which quarantines many foods as off-limits, or as a result of using food to offer yourself solace when you were anxious. In either case, a pattern was established whereby food became a source of comfort rather than a source of nourishment. And hunger was lost.

Eventually you will need to learn a lot about the particular problems that send you in search of food, but first you must find the break in the circuitry and repair it. How can you do this? Surprisingly enough, by *eating*.

The action part of our approach involves doing just that. The only way to repair your short-circuit is to eat each time you feel a glimmer of stomach hunger. We urge compulsive eaters to abandon all external rituals and schedules and begin focusing on their individual biological cues. It is only by focusing inward that you can begin to rediscover stomach hunger and the genuine gratification—both physiological and psychological—that comes from heeding its call.

The idea that people should eat when they are hungry, and not eat when they are not, seems very simple. Implementing this simple idea, however, proves to be quite difficult. After all, we are encouraging you to eat often when you have spent a lifetime trying not to eat. You have learned to believe that food is your problem and that the solution is to stay away from it. This belief is at the heart of all diets. We know, however, that your problem is not the food itself, but what you use food for. Do you eat when you are hungry? Or do you eat when you are having feelings that are difficult for you to handle?

When you reach for food as an antidote to an unwanted emotion, you are really reaching out for caretaking. You feel a need to be soothed and calmed, you turn to yourself for comfort, but you are unable to provide it. Diets do not address the core fact that you are not sufficiently able to comfort yourself.

When we are anxious, simply understanding the source of the anxiety is often not enough to bring relief. We need an internal soothing presence to help us modulate the anxiety. Developing this internal caretaker is a big task, for it requires unconditional acceptance of ourselves, however we look and feel, whether we see ourselves as fat, thin, hungry, scared, lonely, or needy. Becoming an attuned self-caretaker begins with detecting stomach hunger and responding by feeding yourself on demand.

We said earlier that the hunger/food connection, as it is established in infancy, is basic to developing an internal sense of security and trust. As an adult, learning to feed yourself when you are hungry serves precisely the same function, because each time you feed yourself when you are hungry, you are demonstrating to yourself that you can meet your own needs. This nurturing response, repeated many times each day, ultimately makes you feel more grounded and secure.

No matter how many times we explain to compulsive eaters that the cure for compulsive eating involves eating when they are hungry, they continue to have a difficult time understanding how prescribing the "symptom"—eating—could possibly be curative. We finally recognized this inability to grasp the concept as an expression of natural, human resistance to change.

Resistance is neither good nor bad; it is simply the expression of a natural inclination to cling to what is familiar. Your reluctance to do things differently deserves your respect and consideration. After all, by resisting something new, you are asserting your unassailable right to remain just the way you are.

Resistance to making eating on demand a priority expresses itself in many ways. You might hear yourself protesting:

> "It's a nuisance to have to stop and feed myself in the way you suggest—many times a day."
>
> "It's antisocial to eat when I feel like it and not wait for others."
>
> "It's embarrassing to suddenly take out food when no one else is eating. It makes me feel too needy."

Let's take a look at what lies behind each of these expressions of resistance.

It's a Nuisance

Why is it a nuisance to feed yourself whenever you are hungry? If you accept the premise that feeding yourself every time you are hungry is a basic requirement for developing an internal caretaker, then it follows that your unwillingness to feed yourself many times each day reflects an unwillingness to take on this job. Before you can make any progress in overcoming your patterns of overeating, you need to identify the source of your unwillingness.

One reason you may not want the job of caretaker is that you are still angry about never having been appropriately cared for by others. You still wish that someone else would notice your suffering and make up for the deficit. Even though you know that your wish will never come true—that what's past is past—you continue to hold onto the fantasy. Taking good care of yourself implies an acceptance of the painful reality of your past deprivation.

Another reason you might regard feeding yourself many times each day as a nuisance is that you feel emotionally drained. The years you have managed to get by without a proper caretaker have tired you and left you without the necessary energy and resources for the job. You neglect yourself the way you felt neglected as a child. In essence, you become the mother who says, "How can you be hungry again when I just fed you?"

How do you move beyond your anger and feel the energy to start taking proper care of yourself? Unfortunately, most compulsive eaters are not ready to assume the role of self-caretakers until they are completely fed up with dieting. "After gaining all the weight back from my second round of liquid diets, I realized that diets would never solve my problem," said a woman who wrote to us from Ohio. "The idea of ever starting another diet is just unacceptable."

Only when you have hit bottom on the diet route are you willing to face the hard work involved in learning to care for yourself. Even then, you still have to fight the fantasy that someone, or some diet, will come along and make everything all better.

This process of becoming a self-nurturer is a slow one that involves moving from one experience of stomach hunger to the next. With each feeding, you feel more cared for and more secure. It quickly becomes evident that feeding yourself when you are hungry makes you feel much better than depriving yourself ever did. These good feelings multiply, making it possible to imagine a time when you will no longer turn to food unless you are physiologically hungry.

It's Antisocial

Eating when you are hungry means breaking with the tradition of eating three meals a day. The scheduling of meals three times a day evolved from the needs of the workplace rather than the needs of the body. Eating has been determined by a time clock rather than by our own biological clocks. You need to rediscover your own individual "eating clock"—and that means giving up meals in favor of eating experiences each time you are hungry.

The resistance we encounter when we suggest giving up meals is extraordinary. It's as if we are suggesting that people must do something as un-American as giving up their families. The intensity of this response is significant and we take it seriously.

When the women who attend our workshops talk about the problems they encounter dropping three square meals a day in favor of eating whenever they are hungry, it becomes clear that eating on demand stirs up fears of independence. Learning to find your pattern of hunger is about learning to find yourself, separate and apart from anyone else. Your hunger is like your signature: It is unique.

This fear of independence is expressed on two levels: in your external world ("What will family or coworkers think?") and in your internal world ("I'm uncomfortable eating on my own" and "When I see others eating, I want to eat, too").

The External World

"My family doesn't like my eating this way."

"My husband wants us all to eat together," said Barbara soon after she had begun her efforts to eat on demand. "He feels that we have such little time together that the least we can do is to sit down to a meal each night. I've told him I'm willing to see to it that dinner is on the table, but if I'm hungry earlier, I'm going to eat then. I've begun to do that. I sit with him while he eats and usually sip a cup of tea, but I can see that it still bothers him. And it's just as much of a problem with my kids. I feel like a hypocrite telling them not to snack before dinner now that I know that they'd be a lot happier eating when they're hungry."

Some variation of Barbara's story is an often-repeated theme.

"My husband has always done the cooking," Theresa said. "He really enjoys it. It's a letdown for him now that I don't get hungry in time to eat the dinners he fixes."

"I'm trying to follow my hunger," said Maggie. "As a result, when I went out to eat with my friend the other night, I wasn't hungry. I'd eaten a couple of hours before. The whole time we sat together, my friend kept urging me to eat. It was clear that she felt uncomfortable eating while I was just having coffee, and her discomfort was very hard for me to ignore."

Eating when you are hungry challenges social conventions. The convention of mealtime involves the expectation that everyone will be hungry for the same thing at the same time and, if they are not, they will accommodate each other by eating even if they are not hungry or do not want the food that is being served.

When you reject conventional eating patterns, it means that you no longer use food as a bridge to connect to others. You will eat with them if you are hungry and you will sit with them if you are not.

Sometimes, the people around you—who have not gone through a process of re-thinking conventional eating—will experience your choice as a personal rejection. If that is the case, it helps to remind yourself that their feelings of rejection do not mean that you are rejecting them. The only thing you are doing is *not eating when you are not hungry*. The more comfortable you are with this position, the easier it becomes to deal with their discomfort. A tip: We have discovered that the world gives you considerably more difficulty if you have doubts about what you are doing. The more confident you are about your choices, the fewer problems you will have with the world.

When we talk about the social problems around demand feeding, it is helpful to look at the power we have attributed to food as a connector. Food is symbolic of love. Breaking bread together is supposed to connote caring and closeness. In our experience, compulsive eaters are more likely to use food to disconnect from their immediate surroundings than to connect. When, for example, we suggest that people stop eating when they are full, they often report feeling anxious. "What will I do if I'm not eating?" Jill asked. "Just sit there and talk?" Jill feels more comfortable when she can use food as a buffer between herself and others; she feels more exposed when the food is not there.

Barbara, the woman whose husband felt strongly about eating together at dinner, talked about her experience a few weeks later when her husband was away on business for several days.

"It was great," she said. "I cooked when I felt like it and always had stuff to heat or eat in the refrigerator. I told the kids that while Dad was away, we would take a vacation from regular meals. We'd just eat what we wanted when we were hungry, and I'd be available to help anyone prepare something they couldn't find.

"I lined up babysitters for a few evenings," Barbara continued, "and made dates with friends. Not having a regular dinnertime was so liberating that, in the beginning, I felt exhilarated. But a funny thing happened. I found myself feeling guilty about going out so much and having such a great time. I realized that I hadn't put my four-year-old to bed for three nights in a row, and I started to feel like a bad mother."

Barbara went on to say that the feelings she had about not being with her child at bedtime started to seem familiar. "I felt the same way about not being with her at bedtime as I feel about not eating dinner with the family every night. I realized that I always set up shoulds for myself. I try to live by standards that I've never really thought about and that have nothing to do with what's going on inside me. Who's counting how many nights I put my child to bed? I think I *should* be there for most bedtimes, when the reality is that she and I have a very close relationship and spend lots of time together apart from bedtimes. Who says that putting a child to bed is the essence of mothering? Who says that having dinner together every night promotes closeness?"

The week had given Barbara a clearer perspective on how best to mesh her needs with the needs of her family. When her husband returned from his business trip, she felt better able to talk to him. "He has agreed to try something different around dinners," Barbara reported. "He's not completely happy about it, but that's okay with me. I'm convinced that the family will end up spending more time together in the long run."

"I can demand feed myself at home, but not at work."

One of the first objections people raise when we recommend demand feeding involves the workplace. "I couldn't possibly bring food into my office. My coworkers just wouldn't understand," said one woman when we talked about the importance of eating whenever hungry. "How can I eat in the classroom when the kids are not allowed to?" asked another.

The specific obstacles to demand feeding that these people raise are less significant than the speed with which they raise them. We are consistently struck by the passion with which compulsive eaters attempt to maintain the status quo. It is more difficult to eat on your own schedule in some jobs than it is in others, but it has been our experience that when people are ready to listen to their own hunger, they generally find ways to make their workplace more flexible.

Cynthia, a woman who first felt that it would be impossible to feed herself on demand while she was at work, told us how she overcame her resistance. "I never thought I could do what you prescribe on a teacher's schedule," she explained. "After all, I'm always with the kids. But once I stopped thinking about all the reasons why I couldn't eat on demand, I began to find ways that I could. I realized that it's not a problem for me to step outside my door for a minute or two. I do it when I need to use the bathroom or confer with another teacher, so why not do the same thing to feed myself? Now, I bring delicious food with me to work and take bites when I need to."

Think about the environment in which you work. If you were absolutely committed to responding to your hunger every time you felt it, how many times each day could you make room for it? Could you stop for a minute at your desk each time you felt hungry? Could you divide up your breaks differently? Would you have to speak to a supervisor about making some changes, or could you do some experimenting on your own? What would you do if you had a medical problem that required having something to eat every few hours? The reality is that you do have a serious problem that requires your attention.

The Internal World

"My husband doesn't mind not eating together.* I *mind."

"My husband doesn't seem to care if I just sit with him while he's eating," said Monica, "but I don't like it. It just doesn't feel comfortable to me." We encouraged Monica to explore further. "In part," she said, "I feel like I should be providing a real meal every night, but I think it's more than that. It sounds crazy, but I don't feel I'm really with him if I'm just sitting there not sharing the food. It's not as cozy. It just doesn't feel right to me."

Other people in Monica's group nodded in agreement. But some of the old-timers smiled. Connie said, "I can remember feeling that way, but now I'm so glad when we don't have plans for dinner. At this point, I have enough experience eating on demand that I can take the edge off my hunger by eating just a little bit and still be hungry for a planned meal. But it's always a real pleasure to have a number of days in a row when I can eat entirely on my own schedule."

"When I started doing this, I thought I'd miss the nightly dinner routine, but I think my partner and I both feel a lot freer without it," said Lisa. "We still spend the evening together when we're both home, but our time together isn't centered on food. If we're hungry for the same thing at the same time, great. If not, we each take what we want when we want it."

"When I first moved in with my boyfriend," said Wilma, "we had a romantic dinner every night, but then reality set in and it became difficult for both of us. We don't really like the same kind of food and we aren't always hungry at the same time. We sat down and talked about what we most valued about our romantic dinners and decided that it was the quiet time together, talking in an unrushed, open-ended way. We substituted a nightly walk for dinner and managed to hold onto what we valued without sacrificing our individual appetites."

Allowing yourself to get hungry on your schedule helps to define you. Eating because someone else is hungry or because it's time to eat blurs your boundaries and obscures your definition. Sometimes, however, the feeling of having a blurred boundary is confused with the feeling of closeness. Such is the case with Monica who likes the blur she feels when she and her husband eat the same thing at the same time.

We certainly appreciate that sharing a meal with someone you love can be pleasurable. There is a big difference, however, between *eating a meal as a joint experience and eating meals you are not hungry for as a joining experience.*

Many people are not as honest as Monica about this issue. Rather than own up to their own role in eating for the sake of others, they continue to say, "I can't eat when I'm hungry: *they* won't let me." More often than not, however, "*They* won't let me" is a projection of their own reluctance rather than an accurate assessment of their dinner companions' feelings.

Discomfort at being separate, alone, or different is usually at the heart of your reluctance to discovering your own eating schedule. The sense of "being in your own skin" that comes with carefully heeding your hunger signals takes some getting used to. But, once you make the leap inward, you begin to feel a new kind of comfort that more than makes up for the fantasy you are relinquishing.

"If I see others eating, I want to eat, too."

"I can resolve to just sit at the table and have something to drink if I'm not hungry," said Beverly, "but I always end up eating if I'm out with someone. I may just ask for a bite or a few french fries, but I can't stop thinking about the food. The other night when I wasn't hungry, my roommate said, 'Listen, you always say that you don't want anything and then you keep picking at *my* food. This time, why don't you just fix yourself a plate and then leave it if you don't want it.' "

For Beverly, it is the compelling pull of food itself that makes it hard to eat only in response to hunger. The food beckons to her for two possible reasons.

Many foods are off-limits for the chronic dieter, which makes them automatically alluring. Early on in this nondieting process, before food loses its glow, you may find it hard to simply sit while others are eating. It takes time to "legalize" food and believe that it will always be there for you. But once food loses its forbidden quality, it also loses its allure. You know you can have whatever you want when you want it.

What does it mean when you have successfully legalized your food but are still unable to stay away from your friend's plate? It must mean that you are having feelings that you are compelled to deflect with food. In other words, you are feeling driven to eat from mouth hunger. The food on the plate is incidental; you simply want to eat to avoid the feeling.

As it turned out, Beverly had not done a complete job of legalizing. She was telling herself that she could eat whatever she wanted, but she was still afraid to bring a lot of the food she wanted into the house and put it on a shelf labeled "Bev." She picked at the food on the table because she did not really believe that she would no longer deprive herself.

It Makes Me Feel Too Needy

Although the social aspect of eating is a major hurdle for people who are trying to find stomach hunger, it is not the only problem. When you say, "I'm hungry," you are saying that you have a need to eat. Acknowledging needs can be very difficult for women, many of whom believe that, if they acknowledge any needs at all, they will be overwhelmed by a lifetime of accumulated, unexpressed ones.

In a patriarchal culture it should come as no surprise that women have greater difficulty expressing their needs than do men. For centuries, when food was scarce, men and boys were fed first and women ate the leftovers. Girls grow up, even today, learning to sense what it is that men want from them, and attempting to curtail their own wishes accordingly. Women in our culture have been taught to subjugate their needs to the needs of others. Girls sit around a tray of cookies, no one taking the last one even though they all want it. Boys sit around a plate of cookies, eager to get all they can. "It never occurs to me to eat the last piece of meat on a tray," said one woman at a workshop. "I always urge my husband or son to take it, even if I'm still feeling hungry and they're not."

Our attempts to suppress our needs are never really successful. Once a need exists, it presses for some kind of satisfaction. Even as we see to it that the needs of others are being met, we are wishing that others would do the same for us. When they don't, we feel disappointed or angry. A three-step cycle is set in motion: I want; I feel unentitled to have; I attempt to get or steal something for myself, but I do it in such a way that I punish myself at the same time.

Let's say you want something—love, sex, attention, power, admiration, comfort. You feel guilty about your desire and try to renounce it. But you still want what you want. Instead of going after what you really want—the love, sex, attention, power, or comfort—you go after something else that feels forbidden. For example, you eat a brownie. Afterwards, you feel disgusted with yourself and, as punishment, you scream at yourself for having eaten something forbidden. You then take it a step further and renounce your needs by putting yourself on a diet.

This same scenario plays itself out in many ways in women's lives. If we don't eat compulsively when we deny our needs, we may shop compulsively, or pursue sex in the same compulsive way. We tell ourselves that we have conquered our wishes when really we have done nothing more than disguise them. In the end, we always feel guilty for having sought satisfaction.

Beyond feeling guilty about wanting to have their needs met, many women feel frightened about opening up this Pandora's box. They do not believe that they can simply feed their hunger and then move onto something else. "I worry about what will happen if I really let myself feel hunger," one woman said. "If I allow myself to have food on demand, I'm afraid I'll never stop demanding. I'll be hungry all the time."

For some, this feeling is the end result of years of attempting to control or deny needs. Compulsive eaters often fear that they will be insatiable precisely because they have not allowed themselves to be properly nurtured. They are convinced that without all kinds of external rules and regulations, like diets and very specific mealtimes, they will run amok. The fear is that giving up mealtimes leads to chaos; the reality is that letting go of external constraints puts us back in touch with our internal needs. Babies know when they have had enough to eat—and so do adults who make the effort to find out. Food on demand may feel out of synch when you *think* about it, but it leads to inner calm and strength when you *do* it.

It Embarrasses Me

The reason that eating can be a source of embarrassment is because it is embedded in our earliest infantile experiences. Eating is connected to the way we were welcomed into the world and to our early experiences with sensuality, sexuality, and aggression. No one is more aware of these connections between eating and sexuality, sensuality, and aggression than the compulsive eater. She uses food to comfort herself precisely because it represents these early gratifications. Even when she eats in response to stomach hunger, the shame she feels about these infantile associations may carry over.

The roots of shame in relation to food are complex. It is helpful to consider them from a few perspectives.

Unrequited Love

All babies come into the world feeling themselves to be the center of a universe that exists to meet their needs. Shame is what we feel when we discover that this is not the case. An infant whose mother ignores her cry for attention feels this shame very early on. All of us, however, feel it eventually. "Shame," writes Helen Block Lewis in her book *Shame and Guilt in Neurosis,* "is a universal reaction to unrequited love."

Responding to your hunger means welcoming yourself many times a day. Do you deserve such a welcome? Are you worth the fuss? If your sense of entitlement fluctuates—and whose does not—you may at times feel reluctant to feed yourself as well as we are suggesting.

Early Sexual Association

As infants, we simply go after food. We suck, we bite, we grab, we make messes. Sometimes, when we are around babies we get in touch with that early part of us that recalls taking the world in through our mouths and spitting some of it back out.

We hear ourselves saying things like "You're so delicious," or "I could just eat you up." It is no accident that we use these oral images to express our love for babies. These words reflect a recollection of a time when we, too, experienced the world through our mouths, when pleasure in eating was our infantile version of sexuality.

Even when we are not near infants, we never completely forget or renounce the aggressive, biting component of that early eating experience or the bliss of our early sucking. Just as devouring was part of our primitive way of loving, we continue to play sexually at devouring and being devoured as adults. Glimmers of the early link between eating and sexuality persist throughout our lives. Therefore, when we say we are embarrassed to eat in public or to be caught eating at all, we may be making that link unconsciously. Eating always has the dual potential of offering gratification and causing shame.

Failing to Meet Expectations

A failure to meet social and developmental standards leads to shame. Once a child is toilet trained, an "accident" evokes shame. A six-year-old would be mortified if a friend discovered that she used a bottle to go to sleep. As both children and adults, we experience shame when we fail to live up to an ideal that was set for us and that we have accepted as our own. Compulsive eaters have a history of feeling ashamed by their need to use food for comfort. They feel embarrassed that they cannot cope with whatever is bothering them in a different way. And even when they begin to use food to satisfy stomach hunger, their lifetime habit of feeling embarrassed about eating lingers.

Shame and Eating

Although we can examine different sources of shame, the *feeling* of shame is the same, regardless of the source. Linda told us, "The other day I hopped into a cab to go crosstown because I was late for a meeting. I felt hungry. I had food with me, but I was too embarrassed to take it out and eat it. What would the cab driver think?" The reality is that the cab driver probably would not even notice. Occasionally, a driver might notice and, particularly if he owns the cab, might say, "Hey, lady. This isn't a restaurant. I don't want a mess in my cab." In that case, his voice is very much like the voice of a mother who complains about picking up crumbs all over the house and restricts eating to the kitchen. The request is not unreasonable. He is not commenting on your hunger so much as he is safeguarding his property. If you did not feel ashamed of being caught in the act, you might not have any difficulty reassuring the cab driver that you would be careful. Your shame, however, would make his comment far more searing than it was intended to be.

Lori reported, "I wanted to eat something during a meeting yesterday, but I just couldn't bring myself to do it. It was only 10:30 in the morning. What would people think about a woman my size eating at that time of day? They'd think I couldn't control myself until lunch." Lori is struggling with two issues. The first is her size: It is very difficult for large women to eat in public even at mealtimes. The second is being "mature" enough to delay gratification. When you take out a sandwich at a meeting and begin to eat because you're hungry, it *looks like* you have no control; it *looks like* you are eating compulsively. The reality is that, by eating when you are hungry, you are *asserting* your control.

The shame you feel in these situations is a hangover from your days as a compulsive eater and an indication that you are still buying into the myth that eating should be restricted to mealtimes. This shame makes you vulnerable to the way others perceive you and also interferes with the good feelings that arise from demand feeding.

One woman in a workshop reported an insight into her husband's criticism that raised the question of who was more mature, a person who eats when hungry or a person who feels intimidated by the so-called grown-up rules:

> My husband is very irritated by my efforts to eat whenever I'm hungry. He keeps asking me why I can't wait until we get home. After all, it's only a matter of a few minutes. Sometimes he gets sarcastic and asks what I think will happen if I wait a few minutes, as though I really believe I'll die if I don't eat. That kind of comment rattles me. Last time he said it, however, I tried to think about it, and I actually managed to gain some perspective. In fact, I'm starting to see that it's really *his* problem. I had this image of all these good little boys feeling proud of themselves for

> being able to exercise control—or what they think of as discipline. My husband is still worried about being good, about doing what he thinks he should do when he should do it.

Another woman raised the issue of sexuality in a way that struck a chord among the other participants: "If I eat in my office at some time other than the regular lunchtime, I feel that I'm breaking a taboo. When I eat in public, I'm so self-conscious. It feels somehow that eating ought to be private, unless you're doing it with other people."

If we listen to this woman's language carefully, the level of shame makes it clear that she is talking more about sex than about food. As other people in the group began to think about it, they admitted to similar feelings. "This sounds crazy," Ella said, "but when other people watch me eat—particularly when I'm eating at an irregular time—I feel like they're watching me open up a private part of myself."

Everyone laughed, but there was clearly a nervous edge to the laughter. They all related to the eating/sexuality connection as a source of shame. We noticed, however, that the shame was most intense for women who had been considered fat as children.

"When I'm eating in the office and someone walks in," said Ella, one such woman, "I feel incredibly humiliated. It's as though I've been caught doing something naughty."

"Yes," said Jeanne, another woman whose history of dieting goes back to childhood. "Me, too. It doesn't even matter that I'm hungry. Even if I'm having cottage cheese, I'm embarrassed."

These women had been scrutinized very closely as children. They had been forbidden to eat other than at mealtimes. "When someone comes in and sees me eating at my desk," said Jeanne, "it's exactly like having my mother walk into the room. You'd think I was doing, goodness knows what! When I was a kid, eating between meals was as forbidden as touching myself. And, here we are, talking about it in the same way, talking about a fear of getting caught. What can we do about those feelings?"

This discussion highlights the fact that people with a childhood history of dieting have even more trouble than most when it comes to eating freely. They want desperately not to be noticed when they eat, and eating in a place as public as their office runs counter to that wish.

Although we cannot erase a painful history, it is helpful for such women to try to maintain an awareness of the fact that they are reacting as if they were still children and their colleagues were their mothers. Today, as adults, they can do things they could not have done as children. For example, if a colleague sees you eating and says something like, "Having an early lunch?" you can answer, "Yes, I'm hungry now." If the colleague says nothing, but looks at you in a disapproving way—the way your mother once did—you can remind yourself that you are an adult and that eating is not a sin.

Your mother may have put many foods off-limit and may not have accepted your body size, but it is important for you to be aware when you dump those same negative judgments on yourself. As an adult, you now make your own rules. One woman actually developed a comforting litany, which she recites to herself whenever she feels uncomfortable: "What my parents did was harmful to me, but I am now in charge of reversing that damage. I am going to eat whenever I'm hungry and in front of whomever happens to be around." This woman knew that she would feel uncomfortable for a while, but she also knew that the only real way out of the problem was to eat often, each time her hunger said, "Feed me."

Turning the Nondiet into a Diet

When faced with your resistance to reestablishing your hunger/food connection, you may feel antisocial, infantile, isolated, and ashamed. In response to these difficult feelings, you may attempt to turn the Overcoming Overeating approach into yet another diet in order to make yourself more comfortable. We have seen this happen many times. Of course, no one does this deliberately, but the thirst for rules and the force of habit are very strong. "Oh, I get it," the veteran dieter says when we talk about demand feeding. "The cure for compulsive eating is to eat only from stomach hunger."

Although many compulsive eaters are more comfortable following rules than trying to tune into their own hunger, the attempt to turn stomach hunger into a rule inevitably backfires.

Compulsive eaters are defined by their need to use food for emotional reasons rather than to satisfy stomach hunger. As a compulsive eater, until you build a solid foundation of eating from stomach hunger, you will continue to experience mouth hunger.

As this new system of self-care develops gradually, you will feel secure and well grounded enough to begin to consider "sitting with" your feelings rather than eating your way through them. There is no way to rush this process. A compulsive eater cannot simply *will* away mouth hunger. Nudge yourself gently in the direction of stomach hunger, but if you need to eat from mouth hunger, then do so without scolding yourself.

Becoming a Caretaker Rather Than a Rule-Giver

Our ears perk up suspiciously whenever someone says: "I know I *should* be waiting until I'm hungry," or "I know I *should* be carrying food with me," or "I know I *should* at least ask myself if I can wait until I'm hungry." The *should* tells us that the person is living by rules in a punitive mind-set rather than with desire in a loving perspective. Sometimes a person actually says, "I know I *shouldn't* be thinking about *shoulds*, but . . ."

We understand that all people have difficulty bucking the shoulds and the should nots of childhood. It can be comforting to have an internal parent creating structure by telling you what to do, even if you respond to that voice with rebellion. It is our hope, however, that you will learn how to transform the voice in your head from that of a rule-giver to that of a caretaker. You have already experienced enough shoulds to last a lifetime. They may give you the comfort of structure, but they do not give you the joy of being *you.*

The caretaker we have in mind is more eager to soothe you than keep you in line. She looks forward to your getting hungry many times each day and does not worry about mouth hunger. She knows that mouth hunger will eventually fade away. In the meantime, she responds to mouth hunger with compassion. "Right now you are feeling anxious and food is the only thing you find calming. Eventually, we will find better ways to deal with your feelings, but, for now, I will get you exactly what you want to eat. I'm sure that you will experience stomach hunger again soon."

This internal caretaker is wise and has no need to resort to the old shoulds. Instead she asks, "Are you hungry now?" "What would you like?" She understands that good feeding will lessen your anxiety. She encourages you to respect your hunger signals whenever they appear, and she helps you get beyond the social barriers, the feeling of neediness, the embarrassment, the fear of insatiability, and the resistance to caring for yourself in a loving way. She urges you to eat whenever you are hungry, and she reassures you that she will be right there with you to handle your doubts and fears. Best of all, *she remembers when eating was fun!*

Chapter

8

LEGALIZING FOOD

OUR NONDIETING SOLUTION TO THE PROBLEM OF COMPULSIVE EATING has received a great deal of media attention. Invariably, however, the part of our program reporters are most eager to question is the idea of legalizing food. We say that before you can feed yourself on demand—that is, give yourself the food you are hungry for, in the quantity you desire, whenever you are hungry for it—it is necessary to make all foods equal in a psychological sense. In other words, regardless of their nutritional values, carrots and ice cream must have equal standing in your mind.

Legalizing food is the step you must take to put into action your commitment to never diet again. Legalizing is a means to an end. In order to cure your eating problem, you must first demonstrate to yourself that you will never deprive yourself of any food. You cannot do that as long as you evaluate foods as being good or bad in terms of their fat and caloric contents. Indeed, the very first lesson of the Old Testament, the story of Adam and Eve, is that nothing adds more to the allure of food than labeling it "forbidden."

Although the intent of most food categorizing is to help people lose weight, the reality is that the intent backfires. It is true that foods do have different nutritional and caloric values, but the polarization of food as either "fattening" or "nonfattening" has turned millions of us into food junkies. When we lift the bans we have put on food by making all food items legal, the allure quickly disappears. We can then shift our attention away from the labels and back to our hunger.

It is significant that our concept of legalizing has become the focus of so much attention and anxiety, both from the media and from our workshop participants.

"When you talk about the need to see all foods as equal, are you actually saying that compulsive eaters should think about a piece of pecan pie in the same way they think about a stalk of celery?" one incredulous interviewer asked.

"That's crazy," said a woman in a Chicago workshop. "Are you actually saying that we should eat whatever we want? I know myself. I'll eat cake until I burst!"

The panic with which people respond to this idea of legalizing all foods reflects the extent to which they are actually terrified—of *food.* People with eating problems believe that food is their enemy. We know however, that their real problem is how they have learned to use food. As we said earlier, compulsive eaters use food as a tranquilizer rather than as a fuel. You can solve that problem by reconnecting food with physiological hunger—by feeding yourself on demand—but you can't feed yourself on demand until you have made peace with food.

Legalizing food involves, first, bringing all of your formerly forbidden foods into your home in very large quantities. For example, if you love ice cream and it has been off-limits, figure out how much you could possibly eat in one day and then buy three times that amount. Surround yourself with large quantities of the foods you crave so that what you eat will not be determined by the amount in your cupboard.

Beyond that, you need to make a commitment to replenish your supply as soon as it starts to dwindle. And, most important, you have to swear off yelling at yourself when you eat the foods you bring home. Think about it this way: Your goal is to legalize both food and eating.

Everyone trembles at the idea of stocking their homes in the way we have just described. *Everyone* is terrified of losing control—of the gorging they believe will follow legalizing all food. They discover, however, that when they surround themselves with the foods they love *and* stop yelling at themselves for eating it, their cravings begin to diminish almost immediately.

"I expected to feel frantic," said a woman at a Houston workshop, "but by the end of the first week of being surrounded by so much food, I could hardly believe the sense of calm I felt."

We all feel good when we are surrounded by the things we love. Our shelves are lined with books that excite us intellectually. We hang paintings and photographs on our walls to please our eyes. We play music that delights our ears. Yet when it comes to food, everything is different. If you love chocolate, you buy celery.

The indisputable fact is, we relax when we are in an environment that pleases us. As a compulsive eater you need to think of food as part of your environment. The sooner you begin to create a pleasing food environment for yourself, the sooner you will be able to relax around food.

Many people feel concerned that buying more food than they can possibly eat is a terrible waste. We explain that they are buying food for two reasons and both are equally important. Some of the food is for eating, but the surplus is there to symbolize caretaking, support, and permission to eat. Think about your surplus food the way you might think about your favorite wallpaper. If you feel pleased and comforted just looking at all your supplies, the food has served its function just as well as when you eat it.

Most compulsive eaters have a hard time imagining the impact of legalizing food until they have actually done it. Consider this excerpt from a letter we received from Kelsey McMillan after she attended an Overcoming Overeating workshop in Houston, Texas:

> I woke up this morning and asked myself, "Well are you going to do it? Have you got the guts to change your life forever and be what you want to be?" "Get out of my way," I answered. "I've got a shopping list to make." At first, my mind was blank—except for the thought of a sausage and pepperoni pizza. But I gave myself a pep talk. I said, "I know that you're afraid. But listen, you're not perfect and you won't be failing if you overlook something right now. Just work with what you can think of now." So I relaxed.
>
> The first things to hit the list, after the known quantities were: pizza, corn chips, and queso. Now, I can't tell you how hard it was to talk myself into this delicacy. Not because it was so terrifying, but because it had to be the right queso—which is my

own recipe. But dammit, my queso is a time-consuming pain in the ass to make! So I crossed it off.

Next came strawberry shortcake. I added strawberries, cake shells, and whipped cream to the list. "Wait a minute," I thought. "Maybe there's some new product in the freezer section to simulate this and I won't have to make it. Yes, that would save trouble and it would be ready at all times. 'Now just a goddamn minute,' I heard my inner child say. 'You are worth the trouble! You make queso for other people all the time. If they're worth it, so are you! And strawberry shortcake? It's not that much trouble. Make ten or twenty of them and keep them in the refrigerator. You want it. DO IT!' "

The rest of the list consisted of convenience foods and snacks, which, in the recent past, I have rebuked myself so mercilessly for eating.

I shower and wash my hair. I can hardly wait. I put on a bright Hawaiian shirt (I guess that's redundant, huh?) and shorts. I style my hair. I put on jewelry. Hey, I'm really getting dressed for this, aren't I? I must feel it's a special occasion.

I deliberately select a store I know is practically deserted at this time of day. I want no judgmental glances. And I want to proceed at a slow pace to help myself stay calm. I walk through the automatic doors and grab a basket. Suddenly, I hear the theme from *Jaws.* I pause by the specials' bin to catch my breath.

"You're okay," I breathe.

"We can do this," says my inner child.

I strut purposefully over to the strawberries at the end of the produce section and select a quart. I turn to look at the bagels, as if facing a firing squad.

"It's not too late," I warn. "Strawberries are safe. Just break and run to the checkout stand."

Then I hear myself say with renewed courage, "Do it." I carefully inspect the bagels to make sure I get exactly what I want and grab three packages. Then I grab two packages of Italian breadsticks. Confidently I stroll to the bread aisle. There, at the end of the aisle is a large display of tuna fish with a banner encouraging me to eat light. I look at the display, then walk away with a toss of my head, saying, "Go to hell, tuna fish."

Around the corner is the peanut butter. I select the biggest jar of Peter Pan creamy on the shelf. Then it's on to the chips. I pick up two large bags of potato chips, two large bags of corn chips, and three bags of Cheetos. Whew! I look around to see if anyone is watching. Wait, who cares? I start to giggle.

I begin searching the rows of sweets. "Can I help you find something?" asks the girl stocking the shelves.

"Chocolate-covered raisins," I answer.

"Thanks, but I'm going to need more," I say timidly, as she points them out and hands me one.

"How many more?" she asks.

I swallow. "Four."

"You want four in all, or four more?"

"Four more," I answer, thrusting out my chest and chin. (And I dare you to say anything about it, I think to myself.)

I move on to the meat counter and take the platoon-size package of hamburger meat. Then I'm in dairy products. Am I sure I want to get the stuff for queso? Of course. I struggle to overcome my panic just to remember what I need. Okay, all done. I'm grinning to myself. Time to check out.

The woman finishes scanning my booty and the total comes to $104. I'm relieved. Without realizing it, I had told myself that if the total didn't exceed $100, then I must not really be serious about this.

"Looks like you're having a party," observed the checker.

"I sure am."

Kelsey McMillan meant business when she swore off diets. She struggled over the legalizing process, but she emerged a winner. Not everyone is so successful. Many of you, like Kelsey, get off to a good start when you attempt to legalize food. You stock your house with large quantities of your favorite foods and feel great relief as you shed the restraints that limited your life for so long. You see clearly that the more "legal" a food is, the less driven you feel to eat it. But, after a while, you begin to notice yourself slipping into old patterns.

You start feeling irritated with yourself that you are hungry for ice cream. You start wanting to have less food around. You wonder why you're not eating cottage cheese. You find yourself wandering in the diet section of the supermarket and thinking about the caloric content of the food you are eating.

All of these feelings signal your reluctance to completely abandon your old dieting mentality. If, based on your own experience, it feels good to surround yourself with the foods you love, why do you slip back into the old, familiar patterns of restriction? What is behind your resistance to legalizing food?

Forbidden Food—Forbidden Feelings

Compulsive eaters who have been using the Overcoming Overeating approach for a long time often notice that when they are in trouble—when they reach for food out of mouth hunger rather than stomach hunger—the food they reach for is always one that had once been forbidden.

"A few months ago I lost my job," said Sandra, who legalized food nearly a decade ago. "Since then I've had an insatiable hunger for ice cream. And it's not just the ice cream I want. It's the toppings, too. The other night I made myself a bowl with hot fudge sauce, walnuts, and whipped cream."

Sandra knows better than to dump on herself for what she eats. "I spent too many years of my life hating myself for the foods I ate, and I won't ever fall into that trap again," she explains. "But I do find it curious that I never feel a craving for lettuce when I'm going through a hard time and I'm in search of comfort. Maybe it's just a matter of old habits dying hard."

The "old habit" to which Sandra refers is the ritual of compulsive eating. Compulsive eaters need forbidden foods in order for the ritual to serve its implicit purpose. For example, your best friend calls to say that she has just gotten a promotion and part of you is thrilled for her. At the same time, you experience other, conflicting feelings—perhaps envy or even the first bubblings of competitive rage. These feelings make you uncomfortable. Rather than allow yourself to experience the feelings that you consider bad, you reach out for a "bad" food. And when you finish eating the bad food, you tell yourself that *you* are bad for having eaten it. *It is easier to feel bad because you have eaten a forbidden food than it is to feel bad because you are envious of a good friend.*

When compulsive eaters legalize food and take away its charge, they can no longer use "bad" food to disguise what they really think is bad about themselves. *It can be difficult to keep food legal if you have many feelings that you consider illegal.*

Consider the situation of a woman named Martha. A few months after Martha legalized food, she went to a Christmas party at her husband's law firm. "I thought I'd have no trouble with the food, because I had fully legalized it months ago," Martha explained. "I have everything I want around me all the time, but, boy, was I ever surprised. I couldn't keep away from the hors d'oeuvres. I ate every canapé in sight. And I felt drawn to the dessert table all evening. That night, when I came home, I was disgusted with myself. I didn't know why I was so out of control."

We asked Martha to review the evening in her mind, to try to remember exactly what happened just before she headed for the food. After some thought, Martha recalled making eye contact with a recently hired attorney. "He was very handsome," Martha said, "and he reminded me of an old boyfriend from years ago."

At some point during the evening, this new attorney caught Martha staring at him and she looked away in embarrassment. In that split second, Martha had had some fleeting, forbidden fantasy of something happening between this man and herself. Martha, who sees herself as a happily married woman, found her attraction to this man very frightening. Even the idea of having an affair—an idea she would *not* act upon—was too scary for her to allow into consciousness. So, instead, she ate. She ate the forbidden fruits rather than face the forbidden wish, and she ended up feeling disgusted with herself about the food rather than about her sexual feelings.

Eventually, Martha learned that she could harbor wishes, fantasies, and feelings without ever acting on them. Once you learn that lesson, you will be able to sit with these once forbidden feelings and thoughts rather than run to food for comfort and cover.

For many, however, taking the charge away from food constitutes a loss.

"I can see that I fight against the idea that all foods are legal," said Irene in a Texas workshop. "Sometimes I just need to be naughty, and food has always been the way I've done that. I'll be sitting at home with a full fridge and start thinking about doughnuts or something else that isn't in my house at that moment. I'll get in the car and head for the local convenience store, just like I did in my old diet/binge days. At those moments, my need to create something forbidden is very strong. Sometimes, the next day, I'll be able to figure out what I was running from when I jumped in the car, but the chase is very compelling."

Nancy, in that same workshop, could relate to Irene's predicament. "I have all this food in the house that I'd have given my right arm for in the past. Now there's no thrill and I have nothing yet to replace it. It's a real loss!"

The Signals of Backsliding

As you advance in the process of feeding yourself on demand, it is always important to be aware of whether you really do regard all foods as equal, or whether you are allowing yourself to backslide. Remember that as much as you want to be rid of your compulsive eating, you have come to rely on forbidden foods to cover a variety of forbidden feelings. It is tempting to keep certain foods "special" for times when you need some way to handle your anxiety or guilt. Backsliding can be subtle, camouflaged by a number of different disguises. The more familiar you are with these disguises, the more effectively you will learn to deal with them.

Diminishing Supplies

Always having large quantities of the foods you love at hand is critical to the process of legalizing. As a rule, everyone starts this process by doing just that—stocking up. There is no question that the biggest surprise for people in the early stages of legalizing food is that, contrary to popular belief, the more food you have at hand, the less you eat. Scarcity produces anxiety; surplus makes people feel more secure.

Roberta, who read our first book and later attended a workshop, reported, "I could hardly believe that when I surrounded myself with M&M's I began to eat less of them. Just having them around was a relief. They didn't call out to me in the way that they always had. In fact, I just forgot about them."

After a while, however, Roberta's experience with legalizing took a typical turn. "About two months after I made the decision to legalize," said Roberta, "I was in a showroom doing business and I found myself face to face with a big glass bowl of M&M's. It didn't take long for me to realize that those M&M's had become the focus of my attention. Should I have one? Should I not have one? I could hardly concentrate on my work. Finally, I took a few, but as soon as I popped them into my mouth, I realized that a few wouldn't do. I left the showroom with a handful in my pocket and I thought about M&M's all day.

I also overate all day. The next morning I got up and bought a package of M&M's, which I proceeded to inhale. What went wrong?"

When we asked Roberta why she hadn't gone right from the showroom to a supermarket to buy ten large bags of M&M's, she shrugged her shoulders, as if to say, "I don't know." And when we asked why, the next morning, she had limited herself to one bag of M&M's, she shrugged again. Roberta had legalized her favorite candy months before and knew they were no longer off-limits. Unfortunately, knowing is not always enough.

As soon as Roberta allowed her supply of M&M's to diminish, she reempowered them. She had probably felt some discomfort in the showroom that had nothing to do with food. Rather than experience that discomfort, however, she focused on the M&M's, which had been a forbidden food. She ended up feeling bad about eating the M&M's instead of feeling the discomfort that sent her to them. If Roberta had left the showroom and bought ten large bags of M&M's as soon as she noticed that they had become charged for her again, she would have neutralized their power to distract her from whatever it was that had bothered her.

When food is simply tasty and available rather than special but forbidden, it is no longer an effective tranquilizer. In other words, the victory of ending your compulsivity around food requires a significant loss—the loss of food as a tranquilizer. With surplus on your shelves, food recedes and your feelings emerge.

Bettina, a woman in New York, told us how she had reinforced her commitment to legalizing. "Last Friday I had a strong urge for chocolate," she said. "Because I wasn't hungry, I knew that the urge was a signal to stock up. So I went to the supermarket and bought about twenty candy bars. Over the course of the next few days, I noticed that every time I went to the cupboard to get a candy bar, I felt like I was sneaking. Something didn't feel right. I figured I needed to make a bigger commitment to myself.

"That night," Bettina continued, "I went to one of those gigantic discount stores with a $50 bill in my pocket and the determination to spend it all on candy. I always think about children around the world starving when I do something that smacks of any self-indulgence, so I felt a bit guilty. But then I realized that I wouldn't feel guilty at all if I were going to spend

$50 on lettuce and raw vegetables. My guilt had more to do with the kind of food I was buying than with buying food per se."

When Bettina got to the checkout counter, the woman at the register asked her if she was going to have a party. "I just nodded a big yes," Bettina said. "When I got home, I spread my mountain of candy out all over the table and took a good look at it.

"That was three days ago," Bettina concluded. "I've eaten three pieces of candy since then. When I go to work in my studio, I pack up the candy and bring it with me; and when I come back home, I unpack it. It's a lot of work to carry it around and I hate doing it, but I also recognize that it's what I need to do. Lately," Bettina added, "I've been craving nectarines and salad. It's really different not to have food on my mind at all."

The people in Bettina's group had lots of different reactions to her story. Mostly, they were impressed by her ability to go the distance. "You really were able to give to yourself in an unconditional way," one woman said. "I always put limits on what I'm willing to do for myself," said another. "I'll buy myself *just so much* clothing, and *just so much* food. But you really lifted the limits. It's pretty dramatic to see what happens when you do."

Bettina's story is an excellent example of what happens when you get beyond talk and are ready to take care of yourself. She recognized that she needed $50 worth of candy to convince herself that she was lifting the limits and the judgments. She became a nurturing caretaker for herself by saying, in effect, "If you need me to buy this candy, I will. And if you need me to bring the candy to work, I'll do that, too. You can rely on me to give you what you need. As long as I'm around, you have nothing to worry about . . . and I'm not going anywhere!" No one had any doubts that Bettina's commitment to legalizing was a big first step in her becoming an attuned self-caretaker.

How do you know when to go out and buy more of something? Just as it is not good for your car if you wait until the fuel gauge is on empty to refill, so it is not good for you to wait until your pantry is empty. As soon as your supplies drop halfway, go out and buy more. The minute a food begins to feel charged, it means that your supply needs to be replenished.

Do not be fooled by the initial high you feel when you first legalize food. Although you may no longer be craving your formerly forbidden foods, you still need to be sure they remain in your life. Remember that legalizing food means becoming comfortable with it, not eliminating it. Maintaining the comfortable environment you created when you first legalize food is an ongoing process that requires vigilance.

Look-But-Don't-Touch Food

Some of you supply yourselves with abundant food but simultaneously make a very secret decision—secret, sometimes, even from yourself—that you will not eat it. You bring the food into your kitchen, just as you were told to do, but deep down you decide to do your best not to touch your food supply. Although we urge you to enhance your environment by bringing food into your home, the legalizing process will not work if you turn your home into a look-but-don't-touch food museum. When a compulsive eater stocks food with the expectation that she will not eat it, she is keeping that food forbidden.

Sometimes this same scenario plays itself out with a twist. Jane, from Montana, noticed that even though she was maintaining her food supply, she was questioning herself each time she ate. "I suddenly realized that I was putting myself through a third degree before I put anything in my mouth," Jane said. " 'Do you really want this?' 'Do you really need this?' Technically, I wasn't yelling at myself," Jane concluded, "but I realized that I was experiencing my interrogation in the same way I used to experience my yelling." The more you question yourself in this punitive way, the more forbidden the food remains and the more driven you will be to eat it.

Another common twist on the stock-up-but-don't-eat approach to legalizing involves what we call fence-sitting. "Okay," one typical fence-sitter said, "I'll go out and buy the food, but I'm terrified that I'm going to eat my way through my supply in record time and be fatter than ever." This fence-sitter is convinced that legalizing will exaggerate her lack of control, so she never bothers to restock her supply when it is half gone. She puts on weight and blames it on legalizing rather than on the fact that *she never really legalized food.* She would keep food around only if she did not eat too much of it. This is fence-sitting, not a commitment to abandon diets forever.

Keeping Your Distance from Food

Some compulsive eaters sabotage the legalizing process by rationalizing their empty refrigerators. "I don't see what the trouble is," said Genie. "I live in New York City where I have every food at my fingertips. I've even got an all-night deli on my corner. All I need to do is give myself permission to eat what I want when I want it. Once I've done that, anytime I want something, I'll just run out and get it."

We have heard all kinds of reasons for people not bringing food into their homes. Some people, like Genie, assure us that they will run out and get whatever they want whenever they want it. Others tell us that the food will spoil. Others say they do not have room in their homes for the food they want. And still others say that if they keep food in their homes, other people will get to it before they do.

The reasons people cite for not bringing large quantities of food into their homes are less important than the fact that if food is not within reach when you want it, the legalizing process simply will not work. As long as you attempt to create a distance between yourself and the food you are hungry for, you will end up overeating.

If you do not have food in the house and do not feel like running out to a deli, you will overeat on whatever is available in an effort to find some kind of satisfaction for your craving. And, if you do take the trouble to go out for the food you want, the way Genie assures us she will, you are likely to eat more than you really want while you can get your hands on it.

The Right to Choose

Another subtle way compulsive eaters backslide after they have legalized food is to limit their supplies to only those foods that were formerly forbidden. "When I went shopping after I made the decision to legalize," said Nan, from San Diego, "all I bought was junk. My house was filled with cookies, ice cream, and candy. I even filled a large bowl with gumdrops."

It makes sense that, given permission, people with a history of dieting go for what has always been off-limits. Nan probably filled a jar with gumdrops because they had been forbidden to her as a child. But if you limit your pantry to formerly forbidden foods and eat nothing else, you will eventually gain weight and pin the blame for your weight gain on the legalizing process.

When you legalize food, it is important to get beyond the foods that have always been forbidden and really figure out what it is you want. You have to break down all food barriers and even legalize nonfattening foods so that they can be eaten without your feeling punished or deprived. Remember that by trying a variety of foods, you will find what is truly appetizing to you, whether it is high or low in calories. There are times when a crisp stalk of celery is exactly what your stomach wants. If the only foods at hand are candy and cake, you will not have an opportunity to learn about all of your different kinds of hunger.

But What about My Health?

One of the most common paths away from legalizing is an understandable concern about issues of health and nutrition. We have always urged people with certain health problems to be cautious. But often, when a compulsive eater purports to eliminate food from her diet for health reasons, her real motivation is fear. You feel safer not having certain foods available because they are the foods that you typically binge on when you lift your self-imposed restraints.

The basic question to ask yourself is whether you are eliminating certain foods out of fear or as a result of a spiritual or philosophical belief system, such as adherence to religious dietary restrictions or macrobiotic or vegetarian limitations. Here is the litmus test: Ask yourself if you feel compelled to overeat foods you have eliminated whenever you have access to them. If you do not, then you are clearly comfortable with the parameters you have drawn around food. If, on the other hand, you feel drawn to the very foods you have forbidden yourself, you are probably afraid of the power they hold over you. As long as you remain engaged in your power struggle with them, you will continue to rebel and binge.

Consider the case of Felicia, who wrote to us after reading *Overcoming Overeating.* "I've decided to remove sugar from my diet. I feel addicted to sweets. The minute I eat something with sugar, I want more. It's better to avoid it entirely." Felicia's observation seems reasonable. But is it?

Every chronic dieter feels addicted to sweets and wants to remove them from view—and every chronic dieter has an exaggerated yearning for sweets once they are removed from view. Felicia overloads on sweets whenever she is at a social function where they are being served. She binges on these foods because they are forbidden, not because she is addicted. Whenever you eliminate foods because of fear, you will feel like a junkie in withdrawal, and you will binge on those foods whenever the opportunity arises.

At a Houston workshop Karin asked, "What about allergies or diabetes or high cholesterol? Are you suggesting that people with these problems ignore them?"

Of course not. Clearly, some people need to modify their eating when they have a diagnosed medical condition that has been proven to respond to specific dietary restrictions. This kind of modification is a respectful response to your body's internal needs. Your body is telling you it cannot process certain foods. Listening to your body is very different from imposing external judgments that declare certain foods bad or forbidden.

Interestingly, some dietitians have found that legalizing food may improve those conditions in which certain foods are traditionally avoided. Dana Armstrong, a dietitian who works with Alan King, M.D., an endocrinologist, in Salinas, California, reports that some diabetics who have legalized food and learned to feed themselves on demand have improved blood sugar control. Those of you with a medical condition requiring professional attention should always consult a physician or dietitian. Remember, though, that legalizing food always makes you feel more relaxed and, ultimately, less driven to eat any particular food. *Freedom reduces cravings.*

We all want to live long, healthy, and productive lives. If we knew which foods would ensure this positive outcome, we would be the first to urge everyone to eat them exclusively. The reality is, however, that no one has come up with the definitive word on nutrition. A look at nutritional advice over the last three decades leaves us more confused than enlightened. During one decade we were eliminating carbohydrates; during the next, we were watching our cholesterol and extolling the value of carbohydrates. What we know for sure is that when compulsive eaters deny themselves certain foods for health reasons, they crave precisely these foods. Conversely, when they legalize all foods, they have fewer cravings and can figure out what their bodies need—from the inside out.

Just Came Off a Diet

"I lost a lot of weight recently," a workshop participant we will call Donna told us, "and now I want to use your approach because it makes so much sense. But I also want to maintain this weight loss. I'm afraid I won't be able to with your approach."

Donna has reason to be concerned, but not about legalizing. Ninety-eight percent of people who diet regain their weight, plus some. Anyone who has just come off a diet, with all the concomitant taboos and yelling, is bound to binge. You may think that you are binging because you have legalized food, but your binging is really a reaction to the deprivation of the diet. In this situation, weight gain is virtually inevitable, but it's because of the diet, not legalizing food. In fact, legalizing food reduces your impulse to binge.

Once you have completely legalized foods—once you genuinely regard all foods as being equal in a psychological sense—you will gain a new respect for your appetite and begin to understand what a remarkable instrument your internal hunger barometer is. You can trust your body to know the difference between a protein, a fat, a carbohydrate, and a sugar, and you can trust it, as well, to let you know just what it needs and when it needs it.

Welcome to the Food House Fantasy

We have developed a fantasy that we use to help workshop participants find out how they are doing with the legalizing process and what work they have yet to do. You can participate in this fantasy by reading what follows or by reading it into a tape recorder and then playing it back for yourself. But first, as we do in our workshops, we suggest that you find a comfortable position, close your eyes, take deep breaths, and allow yourself to focus on the regular, easy rhythm of your breathing. When you are relaxed enough to enter the realm of fantasy, you can begin.

Imagine yourself alone in a beautiful meadow filled with wildflowers and the sound of birds singing. The sun warms your skin, and you are struck by the beauty of all that surrounds you. You see a path leading from the meadow into a wooded area and you decide to follow it. The woods are damp, plush, and green, redolent of pine. The path narrows, but you continue to follow it. Up ahead, in a clearing lit by streaks of sunlight, you see a house. As you approach, you notice a sign over the front door. On the sign is your name and the words FOOD HOUSE.

You open the front door and walk in. Inside you find a house filled with all the foods you have ever wanted. You feel the accumulation of years of tension leave your body as you realize that you have found a treasure. Look around. Take your time. You have as long as you need.

When you decide to leave, remember that you can return whenever you want. You know where this house is. You know how to find it. Now, go to the meadow and rest for a while. Then open your eyes.

What was your fantasy house like? How did it feel when you stepped inside? What happened? The participants in our workshops have reported a wide range of experiences.

"The sign over my door looked like the Baskin Robbins sign, but with my name instead," said one woman. "It was like an ice cream parlor inside with world-class chocolate ice cream all over. I just basked in the ice cream. I felt absolutely no fear, and that surprised me. All I felt was pleasure. I was totally relaxed. I didn't even want to eat that much of the ice cream. I just liked being there. I hated to leave, but when I remembered that I could always come back, I felt better. I guess I'm going to stock up on my favorite ice creams, in huge quantities."

"I didn't expect what I saw in my fantasy," said a woman named Paula. "I love chocolate, sweets, and all kinds of food, but what I saw in my house was lobster with butter. There's almost nothing I love more than lobster, but I never buy it for myself because it's so expensive. But while I was in my fantasy house, I began to think. Sometimes when I get a real craving for lobster, I go out and eat something less expensive, but end up feeling unsatisfied. So I eat more . . . and more. Then, when I'm still not satisfied, I try eating something else. I might eat several times within a half hour and still not feel satisfied. By the time I'm finished eating, I realize that I've spent lots of money and gotten virtually no satisfaction. If I'd bought the lobster in the first place, I would have eaten less, spent less, and felt much better."

"I was shocked by what my house looked like," said a woman at a New York workshop. "I walked into a beautifully decorated country kitchen. The cabinets were honey oak with see-through glass doors. The dishes were French faience, neatly stacked and displayed. Condiments, rice, and pasta were also displayed in glass jars. The table was elegantly set with candles, cloth napkins, a tablecloth, and flowers. I sat down and felt terrific. My kitchen at home is a mess. I live in a tiny New York City apartment. My kitchen is unappetizing. I have no adequate working space, the paint on my cabinets is peeling, and my pots and pans are all scratched and dented and missing handles. It's not a very pleasant place in which to work or eat. I guess one thing is clear from this fantasy," this woman concluded. "I'd better fix up my kitchen in addition to legalizing my food."

"In my fantasy, I was the head chef in a four-star restaurant," one woman explained with satisfaction. "I went from chef to chef to see that everything was prepared perfectly. From time to time, I'd taste something, but the funny thing was, I wasn't really interested in eating. I felt best just looking at all the food. Strangely enough, now that I think of it, the foods I've been eating since I legalized are not the foods I saw in my fantasy house—they're not the gourmet foods I usually prepare for my friends. The foods I've been craving lately are all the things my parents prepared especially for me when I was a child, like my father's fried-egg sandwich and my mother's Kraft cheese and macaroni. I wonder if what I really want is to be served and cared for the way I've cared for others all these years."

Not everyone has such an easy time allowing themselves entry into their fantasy food house. One woman reported that she got to the front door of her house and found it locked. "I was relieved," she said. "The whole idea terrifies me." Another participant managed to get into her house but found it empty. "I couldn't visualize anything," she said. And still another woman said that she went into her house, saw all of her favorite binge foods, and ran out into the woods, screaming.

These people share an absolute terror of food. For them, the experience of being surrounded by the foods they most desire is akin to the experience of a soldier, abandoned by his troop, finding himself surrounded by the enemy. These people have not yet learned that food is not their enemy and that their relationship with food need not be a battle.

If your fear is too great when you begin to legalize food, we suggest that you start by bringing in one favorite food at a time in a large quantity. As you build confidence in your ability to be in control of food rather than have food control you, you can add to your pantry. The sooner you reach a point of lifting all food bans, however, the sooner you will overcome your problems with food. It is also helpful to remind yourself that legalizing is just a means toward an end. The larger goal is demand feeding.

Consider the case of a New York artist named Sue. Sue drove her station wagon upstate to the Entenmann's factory, where she bought every type of cake, doughnut, cookie, and pastry that they make. She put down the rear seats in her station wagon and loaded up. She came home, opened up her dining room table, set out a beautiful tablecloth, and sculpted a monument to forbidden foods from all of her purchases.

When Sue's husband came home from work, he walked into the dining room and couldn't believe his eyes.

"What the hell is going on?" he said.

"I've decided never to be frightened of food again," Sue answered. "I also am never going to deprive myself of any food. I've had it with diets. This sculpture represents the first day of the rest of my diet-free life."

Chapter 9

Knowing What to Eat

ONCE YOU HAVE LEGALIZED FOOD AND BEGUN TO EAT IN ACCORDANCE with your stomach's schedule rather than in accordance with a cultural clock, it is time for you to begin to think about what you want to eat. Finding out what your body craves at any given moment of hunger is another important piece of the puzzle that will reveal precisely who you are as an eater.

Finding the perfect match between your hunger and what you want to eat can be very difficult for compulsive eaters because you have spent most of your life dieting, binging, and generally disregarding your internal cues about hunger and satiety. In order to find out what you want each time you are hungry, you need to ask yourself, "What exactly is my body craving?" You then need to test a variety of foods in your imagination to identify if you want something warm or cold, salty or sweet, spicy or bland, heavy or light, fatty or lean. In order to do this, you need to go beyond your taste buds and imagine what the food will feel like when it arrives in your stomach. As a compulsive eater, you tend to approach the "what" of demand feeding in very much the same way you approach legalizing: You leap forward—and then you resist.

The Roots of Resistance to Eating What You Want

When compulsive eaters attempt to think about making a perfect hunger/food match, they notice that their efforts raise all kinds of emotional issues which, on the surface, have nothing to do with food. Asking yourself what you want to eat turns out to be a loving question that requires you to declare something about your preferences and desires. You may find yourself responding reluctantly to such offers of love, feeling inhibited about stating your desires. Why?

"I feel undeserving."

"When I began to spend time thinking about what I wanted to eat," said Brenda, "I was struck by the fact that I never ask myself that question about *anything*. A lot of the time, I feel like it just doesn't matter what I eat."

Like Brenda, many compulsive eaters assume that their wishes and desires do not deserve attention, an assumption that often has its roots in childhood. Brenda, for example, recalls feeling overlooked as a child. "I come from a very large family," she told us, "and I don't ever remember being asked how I felt about anything. Clothing would appear in my drawers because it was on sale or because someone else outgrew it. The one time I recall saying that I didn't like something, my mother made me feel terribly guilty for being 'selfish' and inconsiderate." Brenda learned as a child that it was better to submerge her wishes rather than risk feeling guilty and humiliated. That early lesson resounds today when she tries to think about what she would like to eat when she's hungry.

"I've always assumed that women should give, not receive."

Alice, responding to Brenda, said that she also has a hard time thinking about her needs, but for a different reason. "My mother really nurtured me," Alice explained, "but she never took care of herself and her own needs. She always fussed over the kids and my father and I got a strong message that, as an adult, a woman is supposed to neglect herself and tend to others."

Women often feel unentitled. A boy who reaches out for what he wants is regarded as healthy and aggressive. A girl who does the same is often chastised for not being ladylike. The NBC program "Dateline" (December 29, 1992) focused on the difference between the way boys and girls are treated in the classroom. A progressive sixth-grade teacher agreed to be filmed in her classroom to see if she demonstrated any gender bias in her teaching. She was shocked to discover that she called on boys more often than girls, even when the girls had been waving their hands for a long time. This teacher, who was totally unaware of her bias, saw how often she looked past a girl to call on a boy who did not even have his hand raised. She also encouraged boys to elaborate on their answers more frequently than she did girls.

The girls in this class and in most classes learn more in school than history, science, math, and English. They learn that their thoughts, feelings, and development are not as important as those of their male counterparts. Some of them grow up to apply that lesson to food and eating, believing that they are not entitled to pay attention to their own eating needs.

"I'm uncomfortable exposing my needs."

Many women at our workshops talk about feeling too exposed when they attempt to match their food with their appetites. "When I take the time to stop and really think about what food will match my hunger," said Jenny at a Houston workshop, "I almost feel like I'm naked in public. It's such a strange reaction, but it's what I feel."

The truth is that Jenny's reaction isn't really all that strange. Some of us feel generally uncomfortable with our desires. As we have said, hunger is a primitive desire that evokes early feelings of connection, love, aggression, neediness, intimacy, and sensual pleasure. Pinpointing and satisfying a specific hunger as an adult may very well trigger these early, more infantile responses. When that happens, it is likely that you will feel the same sense of embarrassment as Jenny did.

"I'm reluctant to make choices."

As compulsive eaters attempt to decide just what food will match their hunger, many of them discover that they have a hard time making decisions in general. "I buy all kinds of food and go through them all in my head whenever I'm hungry," said Sue, "but I usually end up feeling so frustrated. I just can't zero in on one thing."

Upon further exploration, it turned out that Sue was in the throes of deciding about a career change and, possibly, a relocation. These decisions were paralyzing her. Rather than make a decision about what she wanted to do, Sue was inclined to put everything on hold. "At least that way," she said, "I can keep my options open."

Despite Sue's wish, refusing to make decisions does not always mean that our options remain open. While making a choice does open up one door and close another, if we wait too long before making a move, sometimes all the doors rust shut.

The issue behind Sue's fear of losing any option is an understandable wish to "have it all." Throughout our lives, however, making one choice means abandoning some other possibility. Having it all remains an illusion, a fantasy. Learning to feed yourself exactly what your body craves, whenever you are hungry, and stopping as soon as you have had enough brings the issue of limits to the foreground of your consciousness. You are hungry at certain times and not others; you are hungry for a limited amount of food each time you eat; and, each time you are hungry, you are hungry for one particular type of food and not some other. You may *feel* insatiable, but your appetite is actually quite limited.

If you think about this issue of food choices from a more long-range perspective, you have endless opportunities rather than repeated limitations. For example, if you choose rice pudding at three o'clock in the afternoon, it is likely that you will crave something else the next time you are hungry. Each eating experience offers the opportunity to make a new choice, and you have a lifetime of eating experiences ahead of you. Those experiences will be much more satisfying if you learn to respect your wishes.

"I don't like standing out."

Compulsive eaters often long to blend in, to disappear in the crowd. Defining your food needs at a particular moment underscores the fact that we are all individuals with individual likes and dislikes. "What if I want a hamburger in the morning," asked a woman who often ate out, "or some scrambled eggs and bacon in the evening? It embarrasses me. I'd much rather choose something else and fit in than heed my appetite and stand out."

It may feel strange at first to see that your food choices do not mesh with the world around you. You must keep in mind, however, that you have been eating "appropriately" for years—and it has not been good for you.

The Signs of Resistance

The resistance compulsive eaters experience when they first attempt to eat precisely what they are hungry for expresses itself in many indirect ways. It is important to recognize these subtle signs of resistance so that you can deal with the underlying issues and experience the pleasure that comes from eating exactly what you want when you are hungry.

Money

Compulsive eaters very often express their resistance to demand feeding—and particularly to making a perfect match between their hunger and what they eat—by focusing on the cost of the food. Money, to be sure, is a very real issue for many people, but there are ways to cope with limited financial resources without sabotaging your demand feeding.

"In the past," said a Chicago workshop participant named Roberta, "I had trouble spending the money necessary to stock up on all the foods I wanted. It was my way of holding onto the feeling that I was a marginal kind of person, not worthy of that kind of indulgence. Now, however, I no longer feel that way. I really want to treat myself well, to provide myself with the things I want, but the fact is that I'm unemployed. I *really* don't have the money now to go out and buy a huge supply of food. I'm worried about paying my electric bill, let alone filling my refrigerator."

Because Roberta was committed to caring for herself, however, she found a way to do it. "I can no longer afford the prepared foods that I used to depend on," she said, "so I've figured out a way to improvise. When I think about an expensive prepared food that I want, I remind myself that the up side of unemployment is that now I have the time to cook things for myself. Most of the dishes I love are much less expensive if I make them from scratch. So I'm cooking up big batches of the things that I like and I'm keeping a running wish list of the things that I can't afford, so that as soon as I start making money again, I will buy them for myself."

Roberta has also discovered that an occasional splurge can be economical in the long run. "If I really want good Belgian chocolate and I buy the cheap stuff, I end up eating lots and lots of it in an effort to find some satisfaction," she explained. "It ends up costing as much as if I'd just gone out and gotten myself one perfect square of what I wanted."

It is important to remember that the more accurate a match you make between your hunger and the foods you eat, the less you will eat. If you go for the Belgian chocolate, or the expensive cheese, or the lobster as soon as you want it, you may very well end up saving yourself time and money. Beyond that, you will spare yourself the stuffed, unpleasant feeling of having eaten a great deal of something you really did not want.

"The most important thing I've learned," Roberta concluded, "is that there is a big difference between saying I can't make the match because I can't afford the food I want and saying I can't have what I want because it is forbidden. Acknowledging that I just don't have the money right now is a restriction, but it's not a judgment about what I should or should not eat. I know that I deserve to have whatever I want, and when I can provide myself with those things, I will."

Dana, a woman in a Denver workshop, pointed out, "I spend a lot of money just buying the food required to maintain my weight, and God knows, I've spent a fortune on diets over the years. It couldn't possibly cost me more if I were to stock up the way you suggest and really buy the things I want. But still, I resist doing that. My resistance to spending the money to stock my kitchen with the foods I crave must really have more to do with my resistance to making a commitment to providing for myself."

Dana's observation is a good one. If you are having trouble spending money on food, check to be sure that you are not feeling resistant about giving yourself what you need. Remind yourself that you are worth the investment.

Dwindling Supplies

When people tell us that they have trouble making a good match between what they are hungry for and what they eat, we often discover some form of underlying neglect. They don't necessarily say that they cannot spend the money, as Roberta did, but they shop as though they cannot spend the money and then later, when they peruse their pantry shelves in search of the right food to match their hunger, they don't see what they desire.

Just as stocking the house was essential to the legalizing process, making a good match between what you want to eat and what you actually eat requires providing yourself with an ample selection. Quantity and quality offer you the opportunity to think about what your stomach wants rather than what you have on hand.

"Just this week," said Ruth from New York, "I saw what happens when I don't maintain my supplies. Invariably, I start eating things that don't match my hunger and I end up eating much more because I'm never satisfied. It happens again and again. I see the value of stocking up and being generous with myself, but then I get lazy, or neglectful, or stingy. It's rough taking on this job of being a good caretaker as a forever proposition, but I'm beginning to realize that I have a choice. *Am I going to provide for myself comfortably, or am I going to spend my life looking for comfort in food?*"

"I have a related problem," said Judy, a participant in the same workshop. "I come from a large family. There was very little time for individual attention and fuss. My mother was stretched to the limit and we each had to do a lot of our own providing. I resent having to keep the house stocked. It's like I run out of steam and feel overburdened the way my mother did. I see that it's great having the food around, but I guess I really want someone else to provide it. I've actually thought about hiring someone to do a couple of hours of shopping for me each week. I guess if I were really serious about providing for myself, that's what I would do."

Health Concerns

As with legalizing, people who experience resistance to eating what they want often attribute their resistance to health problems. "I really would love to eat chicken livers with fried onions," said one woman, "but they always upset my stomach." "I get incredible cravings for chocolate," said another, "but I know that if I eat it, I'll get a migraine."

When we suggest that you eat what your body craves, we are not suggesting that you ignore the feedback your body gives you when it receives these foods. In fact, some of our advanced demand feeders have suggested that you need to go beyond asking "What does my body crave?" when you attempt to make a match. You must also consider how your body will feel after the match has been made.

One New York participant named Parma showed us how this works. "I remember when you taught us to vote for our stomachs over our mouths when we make the match. That's no longer a problem for me. If my head wants ice cream but my stomach wants chicken salad, I have the chicken salad and, when I'm finished, I ask myself if I want the taste of something sweet. But now I go even further," said this experienced demand feeder, "and ask myself how I think I'll feel when I've finished eating whatever I'm eating. Sometimes I become aware that the food is too heavy, or too fatty, or too spicy, and I shift my choice.

"I can do this now," Parma continued, "because I'm no longer struggling with feelings of deprivation around food. If I choose not to eat something, it's not because I believe that I *shouldn't* have it, but because my body either doesn't want it or can't handle it. I make the decision to go with what my body craves because that's what feels good."

In light of our cultural emphasis on dieting and health, it is hard to believe that, left to our own devices, we would actually eat what our bodies require. We have seen, however, that people do end up choosing a wide variety of healthy foods if they allow themselves to legalize *all* food.

Some nutritionists have made the point that the foods we choose to eat are limited to foods we ate as children. The health and fitness department at Conoco, in Houston, Texas, which teaches their employees the basic principles of Overcoming Overeating, responds to this limitation by offering a Healthy Choices program in their cafeteria. Each day a "healthy" item that may be unfamiliar to the employees is offered along with its recipe. The idea is to expand people's culinary repertoire so that, when they attempt to figure out what it is their body is craving, they can choose from a wider range of possibilities.

Once you are accustomed to demand feeding and no longer eat compulsively, you will have the luxury of considering whether or not the foods you are eating naturally are consistent with your nutritional beliefs. At that point, you might entertain the possibility of expanding your choices and fine-tuning your matchmaking.

Relying on Formerly Forbidden Foods

Some people resist making a really good match by always opting for the foods that had once been forbidden. "What do I want to eat? A hot fudge sundae," comes the answer, reflexively, like a child who had been let loose in a candy store for the very first time after years of hearing her mother say, "NO CANDY."

This kind of reflexive choosing was a problem for Barbara, a participant in our Chicago workshop. "Sometimes I think hard about what it is that I'm hungry for and decide that I really want a salad. But even when I make the salad I'm craving, when I finish eating it, I often feel deprived. This has happened to me often enough so that, sometimes, when I crave a salad, I buy an order of french fries to go with it—just to avoid that feeling of deprivation."

Barbara, a veteran dieter, spent more than twenty years believing that eating a salad was good and that eating fries was bad. During those pre-demand-feeding days, whenever she ate a salad, she felt both virtuous and deprived. At this point, however, her head has not caught up with her stomach. She is no longer eating a salad to be good, but she still reacts as though that were the case.

Of course, there is always the possibility that Barbara may be playing a trick on herself. She may be choosing a salad because of some hidden agenda to diet. If that is the case, she will know soon enough, as her feelings of dissatisfaction only grow stronger.

"Rehearsing" in a Safe Place

This task of learning to match food with hunger is not an easy one. Our workshops offer a kind of camaraderie that many compulsive eaters find empowering, but even with the support of peers, people still have trouble giving themselves the foods they crave.

We wondered what would happen if people could spend a week in an environment that was entirely supportive of their efforts to demand feed themselves. What if you lived in a world where there was twenty-four-hour, on-demand food service? What if someone were available to prepare exactly *what* you wanted, exactly *when* you wanted it? Would you have any difficulties matchmaking in such an environment?

These "what ifs" became a reality in 1992, at Lake Austin Spa Resort during the first of what have become regular week-long Overcoming Overeating workshops. The spa provided the environment we envisioned for helping the sixty women who attended become attuned demand feeders. The women went into the week with high hopes and many trepidations; they emerged from it with new insights.

Each woman was given a list of all the foods available and told to add anything she thought she might need that was missing. There were no scheduled mealtimes. "Whenever you are hungry," we told the participants, "just go into the dining room and order exactly what you want." For starters, the women discovered that it was not necessarily easy to allow themselves to have things their way.

"When I walk into the dining room and the waitress asks me what I want to eat, I feel very uncomfortable," said Louise, "like I'd rather get it myself. I mean, why should someone be fussing over me?"

"There's something about being able to have anything I want that overwhelms me," said another participant. "At least in a restaurant you're limited by the menu. Here, there is so much to choose from that you're limited only by your imagination. I'm beginning to feel like I don't even have one. All I can think of are my usual few foods!"

"I asked for something this afternoon and, when it came, I realized it was the wrong match for my hunger," explained Ellen, who has been struggling with compulsive eating for nearly thirty years. "I sat paralyzed for a while, not knowing what to do. The truth is, I was afraid to ask for something else. Finally, I forced myself. After all, if not here, then where? But for the rest of the meal, I was sure the waitress was angry at me."

"I have a confession to make," said Sue, who had been very, very quiet. "This is our third day here and so far I've eaten only what has been available on the buffet table. I heard what was said about ordering exactly what you want, but I haven't allowed myself to want anything other than the fruit, salads, and desserts that are provided. I guess it's clear that I'm used to wanting only what's available."

The woman next to her responded. "Each time they ask me what I want, I feel like I'm dreaming," she said. "It's so hard for me to believe that someone really wants to know what it is that *I* want—and that I can just sit here and have people give it to me. It feels so . . ." She searched for a word and finally said, "It feels so *intimate.* I can hardly stand it. I've never experienced anything like this."

At this point, a participant named Rachel burst into tears. "I'm feeling so angry," she said finally. "Being taken care of in this way makes me so much more aware of my needs—and it forces me to recognize that my needs *can* actually be met. I can't stop thinking about how my needs weren't met when I was a kid and how I always assumed that it must be because something was terribly wrong with me."

Several people in the group said that they could identify with what Rachel was talking about. Finally, one of the women made a poignant observation. "For me, the problem goes further than that," she said. "Eating this way and being here in this nice place makes me stop and wonder why I don't do this kind of thing for myself . . . why don't I live like this?"

"That's a good question for all of us," said Rachel. "I guess because we continue to feel that we should just accept whatever is around."

By the end of the week, this group of women pledged to bring the environment of the spa home with them. They understood that this would not be easy. But, they also understood that they deserved this kind of nurturing environment—in fact, for most of them, it was long overdue.

Taking It On the Road

You will never be able to actualize your commitment to demand feeding until you have access to the foods you crave—and that includes at home, at work, in a store, as well as while you're shopping and while you're traveling to work, to home, or to the store. You never know when hunger might strike, and you never know for sure what you will want. Our motto, like that of the Scouts, is "Be prepared." But to be prepared, you must learn to provide for yourself, and as we observed earlier, self-care is not always easy for women. Although mothers of young children would never think of leaving home without packing a bag of supplies, (a diaper, a toy, a bottle, a cookie, and whatever else they know their baby likes) these same women balk at the suggestion that they do the same for themselves. Whether mothers or not, our recommendation is the same: Do for yourselves what you would do for a baby. Identify the foods you might possibly become hungry for on your outing and pack them in a tote bag.

The objections we have heard over the years to carrying a food bag are endless. For a moment, notice your initial reaction to this suggestion and write it down before you read on. Now continue reading as though you were a participant in one of our workshops and see where your response fits.

> *Participant:* I feel so silly carrying around a food bag! It's one thing to take home a doggie bag from a restaurant, but it's quite another to need to carry it with me constantly.
>
> *Response:* Why do we feel so silly carrying food with us? Many of us feel embarrassed by our need to eat (Chapter 8) and the food bag is tangible proof of this need. By carrying food we are announcing to ourselves and others that we have needs and that we will meet those needs. We are saying that we no longer value staving off hunger until someone else's predetermined mealtime.
>
> *Participant:* In the morning when I'm trying to get the kids off to school and myself ready for work, it takes too much time to try and figure out what I want to put in a food bag.
>
> *Response:* Aren't you worth the time and effort? You would not forget to pack the kids' lunches or, if you did, you would rush to school and drop them off—even if it meant risking being late for work. Everyone can count on you . . . except yourself. Isn't it time for you to be there for *you*?
>
> *Participant:* I don't carry a food bag because the food I want is either too messy or it will spoil if I carry it with me all day.
>
> *Response:* You can buy containers that preserve food and are easy to carry. Many people we know are using insulated bags to carry their food for the day. One woman, in partic-

ular, inspired us all. As far as she is concerned, every food can be made travel-proof. The day of our workshop she brought bean salad, carrot cake, cold soup, cheese, bread, an apple, crackers, a chicken dish and some cookies. She told us that her in-office hamper is even more elaborate because she has access to a small refrigerator and a microwave.

Participant: It seems to me that if I carry Oreos, I want to eat them—pure and simple. Why should I put myself at such risk?

Response: It seems to you that you are eating Oreos just because they are there. On some level you believe the old "out of sight, out of mind" argument left over from your dieting days. What you have forgotten is how obsessively you think about the foods you've removed from your reach. We are certain that you do not yearn for Oreos because you have placed them in your food bag. You yearn for them either because you have not yet really legalized them or because you are experiencing mouth hunger and would go in search of cookies even if they were not at your fingertips. To show yourself that Oreos are not the problem, bring many more of them than you could possibly consume in a day, along with a variety of other foods you like. Again, having food around in large quantities allows you to relax. If mouth hunger is leading you to the Oreos, then feed that mouth hunger in a caring, accepting way until it subsides.

Participant: The whole idea of packing a bag for myself feels obsessive and infantile. I don't want to spend so much time thinking about food. After all, isn't that my problem in the first place?

Response: It is true that thinking about food all the time has been an aspect of your compulsive eating problem. The focus we are talking about now, however, is different. We are urging you to focus on food in a way that works for you rather than against you. We want you to invest time, thought, and money in food in a way that will cure your problem. Making sure you have an ample supply of food available all day long is an investment. You are stocking the pantry so that you will be able to respond to your own needs. That response is long overdue.

Participant: The idea of a food bag seems terribly wasteful to me because at the end of the day, I have to throw away a lot of food.

Response: When you are doing well with our approach, you do eventually eat small amounts of food many times each day. That means you end up with leftovers that you do not use. Those leftovers in your food bag, however, are a sign that you are eating less. You are eating less because you feel more secure, and you feel more secure *because you have a surplus of food available at all times.* On one level, it is true that throwing food away is wasteful. But is it really more wasteful than eating foods you don't really need or want? Your body should not be a waste disposal. And what about the waste involved in years of buying diet books, gadgets, and food products that have all failed?

Participant: Carrying foods makes me feel cheap. It reminds me of the days I used to "brown bag" it because I couldn't afford to eat lunch out.

Response: You may not want to be reminded of the days you had to eat at your desk, but carrying a food bag does not have to mean poverty. Think of the food bag as a first aid kit. It guarantees that you will be cared for if you get hungry at a time when you cannot make it to your favorite restaurant. Carrying it does not mean you will use it. You can simply disregard it if you prefer to eat out.

The food bag addresses the issue of self-care in a very direct way. Those of you who carry a food bag have made a conscious decision to stop allowing your needs to go unmet, and, even though you may still resist that decision, the bag is there to remind you of it.

We asked veterans of our approach what made it possible for them to use a food bag successfully. They told us that as they became accustomed to the good feeling that comes from having a well-stocked house, they wanted the same comfortable feeling in their workplace and wherever else they were. In other words, the more accustomed you become to the comfort of having the foods you want available to you, the more willing you become to carry the food with you. This experience becomes so pleasurable that it overrides your resistance.

Remember that, in order to begin to carry the food bag, you first need to feel entitled to the kind of care and respect it implies. There will be times when you do not feel deserving of your own kindness or when you do not feel motivated to provide it for yourself. During those times, let your new internal caretaker support you. She will be glad to pack your food bag—she is always happy to fuss over you. She understands that you have mistreated yourself because, until now, you have not had the kind of inner strength you needed to do things differently. She also knows that it is easier to care for yourself when you are not alone.

A Day in the Life of a Prepared Eater

The idea of exploring a specific hunger in order to make a perfect match and carrying around a food bag sounds strange to most people. The fact is that, when you see the plan in action, it begins to make a great deal of sense. What follows is a glimpse into an average day of an attuned, prepared eater we'll call Iris.

Before Iris goes to bed, she looks at her calendar for the next day. One of her children is going on a school trip, which means that she must pack his lunch in a paper bag rather than in his usual lunch box. She goes downstairs, packs his lunch, packs lunch for her other two children, and sits down to think about what she might want to eat the following day.

It takes a while to become acquainted with your body's particular cravings. At the beginning, Iris would simply guess at what foods might do the trick. She would do the best she could to supply herself with what she thought she might want and, if she missed something, she would run out during the day and pick it up. At this point, she is quite skilled. Certain foods have become staples in Iris's food bag. Beyond these foods, she finds that her cravings tend to shift about once a week, and she adjusts the content of her food bag accordingly.

For example, she knows that this week, she has had cravings for salty, oily things. In a few minutes, she puts together her bag: Greek olives, cold chicken, salad (slightly soggy, just the way she loves it), pretzels, a few slices of bologna, some special tarragon mustard, celery, an apple, and three bags of peanut M&M's. She sets her bag in the refrigerator next to her children's and heads upstairs for bed.

Iris knows that she generally isn't hungry until about 10:30 A.M., but she makes a point of checking in with herself earlier, while she's feeding her children. They all leave the house with food bags packed for the day. Iris stops at a nearby Italian bakery to pick up a fresh, crisp loaf of bread. Sure enough, at about half past ten, Iris is hit with her hunger. This hungry feeling that Iris has come to recognize in recent months is most welcome to her. It is a signal that the time has come to care for herself in the attuned way that eventually will lead to the resolution of her compulsive eating. In fact, she says, "Oh, terrific. I'm hungry now."

She reinforces her commitment to her own good caretaking by eating as often as possible each day in response to stomach hunger. But before she eats, she stops for a moment and thinks about what food will best satisfy her need. The answer this morning: olives and bread. Salty, just the right weight, and available right in her food bag.

Throughout the day, Iris goes through a similar process each time her stomach signals her. Iris has a friend from our workshops who cuts sandwiches and unwrapped candy bars into small pieces and packs them in separate plastic bags so that she can get to them easily whenever she feels hungry. This kind of readiness enables her to take good care of herself. Another woman sometimes packs containers with goodies typically thought of as dinner foods specifically to avoid thinking about eating foods in traditional ways—for example, a sandwich for lunch, candy for snack, and steak and potatoes for dinner.

At lunchtime, a friend comes in to ask Iris if she'd like to join a few of their coworkers for lunch. Iris has just eaten but says she'd be delighted to join them. When they arrive at the restaurant, she orders a cup of coffee. "On a diet?" someone asks. "No," Iris explains. "I was hungry a little while ago and ate then. I'm just not hungry now." On the way back from the restaurant, she buys a bag of cookies at her favorite bakery to add to her food bag.

Over the course of the day, Iris thinks about eating experiences as being keyed to her stomach rather than to the clock. At about three, Iris feels hungry again. Once again she stops to think about what she wants. She isn't quite sure, so she imagines how various items would feel in her stomach and when she gets to bologna, she knows that's what she wants. She cuts a piece of the fresh bread, spreads it with the tarragon mustard she bought at a gourmet food store, and eats half of an open-face sandwich. About an hour later, she realizes that she is hungry again. This time she wants bread with a little salad.

On the way home, Iris shops for her family's dinner. As she walks down the aisles of the local supermarket, she makes a point to think about what each member of her family likes to eat. She shops with everyone's tastes in mind—including her own.

By six o'clock, Iris is home starting dinner. Her husband is working late and it's her night to cook. She helps her children with their homework and checks the rice and chicken she is preparing. "I don't want that," one of her kids says when he looks at the contents of the simmering pan. "I'm going to have a bowl of Cheerios instead." Iris nods, as her young son brings *his* dinner to the table. It's taken her a while to get used to the fact that everyone in her family is now eating on demand, but the system of having something available each evening for whomever wants it seems to be working. Although she was afraid to give up the notion of "balanced" meals, Iris has noticed that her children eat a wide variety of foods in the course of a week.

They all sit down shortly after seven. Iris realizes that she is not at all hungry and sips a glass of wine while she talks to her children about their day. Later that evening, when her husband comes in, Iris recognizes that she is ready to eat and she's delighted that the chicken she prepared earlier is exactly what she wants. The kids are all in bed when Iris and her husband sit down together.

"How was your day?" she asks.

"Just great," he says as he polishes off his dinner and pushes the plate back on the table. Then he adds. "I'm in the mood for a piece of pecan pie."

"Well," says Iris, "it just so happens that I've got it. I thought I might want something like that and bought a pie, but now it seems much too heavy to me."

Iris's husband cuts himself a piece of pie and calls to her, "How about some grapefruit sorbet?"

She thinks for a minute and then smiles. "Perfect," she says.

She's learning . . . and so are they all. Now, if she could only figure out a way to carry sorbet in a food bag!

Chapter 10

Knowing How Much Is Enough

We all begin life knowing perfectly well when we have had enough to eat. Watch an infant at her mother's breast. She'll begin suckling with great energy, focus, and enthusiasm, but after a while, her attention will wander. She'll push the breast away and smile up at her mother. She'll turn to look at someone who has just walked into the room. She'll play with the breast, rather than suckle.

An attuned mother recognizes and accepts this behavior as an indication that her baby has had enough to eat. It is not until babies are able to eat solid food that people begin telling them how much they *should* eat. It is not unusual for a child's simple declaration of "I'm full" to be met with an offer of membership in the "Clean Plate Club" or the proverbial injunction "Have one more bite for Grandma."

Long after the people in our program have managed to legalize food and eat when and what they want, many of them continue to struggle with the issue of *stopping* when they have had enough. Some compulsive eaters simply do not know when they are full, but many of those who are aware of when they have had enough to eat cannot stop eating until they reach an uncomfortable point way beyond satiety.

"Stopping when I've had enough is the most difficult part of eating on demand," said one woman. "Even though I know when I've had enough to eat, I can't imagine stopping before I finish everything on the plate." Admission to the Clean Plate Club is easy; getting out is not.

Why do we continue to eat when we are no longer hungry? Why are we unable to allow enough to be enough? In the course of our work, we have found many different sources of the resistance compulsive eaters experience when they attempt to eat only as much as they need. For example, in order to let go of the food on your plate, you must be willing to acknowledge that food is simply food, not magic. You must also be willing to admit that you have had enough to satisfy you, that your needs are not endless. You must feel comfortable saying, "No more." And finally, of course, you must be prepared to lose some weight.

The Quest for Magic

Learning to recognize when you have eaten enough is simple for anyone who thinks about food as a fuel. When your "tank" runs low, you fill it up, go about your business, and refill it when you run low again. For compulsive eaters, however, food is far more than fuel. They use food as a companion, a tranquilizer, a caretaker, and a talisman.

Compulsive eaters are able to use food to soothe themselves because food represents the love and caretaking of early childhood. The hungry infant cries and, magically, food appears. For almost everyone, in this early phase of life, food/Mommy makes everything all better. Each time a compulsive eater reaches for something to eat when she is not hungry, she is trying to recapture this early, magical sense of security. Because food symbolizes such a simple, pleasurable time of life, it can be difficult to say, "Thanks, but I've had enough."

As you legalize food and begin using it as the fuel it was intended to be, food loses some of its specialness and thus some of its symbolic power. Because food was so central to your earliest experience of comfort, however, it continues to retain what we call "blurring potential." In other words, in a pinch, you will always be able to use food's magical association—you snug in your mother's arms—to momentarily obscure a present pain. This blurring potential is at the heart of your resistance to stopping eating when you are full.

"It happens before I know it," said Ruth, a participant at a California workshop. "I start out eating from stomach hunger, but before I know it, I'm eating mechanically, way past fullness. I don't know exactly what happens to cause that shift from aware eating to mechanical eating. Maybe I start thinking about something that's troubling me and shift from stomach hunger to mouth hunger. Or maybe the food itself triggers the shift. Maybe I just get lost in the food the way I have for so much of my life. Sometimes before I start eating, I remind myself to keep track of what's going on, but very soon I lose track and eat until I'm too full."

The experience Ruth describes is familiar to compulsive eaters who are still struggling to stop eating when they are full. Her insights are good ones. It is not at all uncommon for an eating experience that was triggered by stomach hunger to slip into one that has more to do with mouth hunger, particularly if something is bothering you. When that happens, and when you notice that you have eaten beyond fullness, try to figure out, after the fact, what was bothering you. Ask yourself just what was on your mind, or what you were feeling, that led you to eat more than you needed.

It is also possible, as Ruth suggested, that the food itself may evoke all of your old desires to get lost in it or, in our terms, to get blurry. After all, you have spent much of your life using food to take you away from yourself, and it may take a while to change that response. Until that happens—until food has really lost its magic—it is likely that food-as-fuel will easily turn into food-as-love.

"When I'm eating," said Natalia, at a Boston workshop, "I just don't want to let go of the food. I know that I only need a little bit and that I can put the rest away to have again when I'm hungry for it, but eating actually feels cozy to me. The separation from food is very, very difficult. I like feeling very full. It makes me feel calm. I don't want to stop eating until I get that overly stuffed feeling."

Natalia is reluctant to let go of the solace that food has offered her for most of her life. She knows that she can get more food whenever she wants it, but the truth is that stomach hunger, and the eating that satisfies that hunger, is not the issue here. "What I want is that old feeling of getting lost in my food,"

Natalia explained, "and even when I'm eating from stomach hunger, I feel a yearning for the old sensations."

Natalia misses the magical blur that she once got from food. She always believed that food made her safe; what it really made her feel was "spaced out." What happened in the past, and what continues to happen today when she eats to the point of feeling stuffed, is that she feels uncomfortable, but less agitated—"spacey." The problems that led her to overeat are camouflaged. Now, they all boil down to one solitary fixation: "What am I going to do about my eating and my weight?"

It is also important to understand that when you cannot stop eating even though you have had enough, it may be that the presence of food elicits a longing in you to extend your boundaries and feel less alone. "When I eat more than I'm hungry for," said Kyra, a participant in our New York group, "it's almost always because I feel terribly lonely. The food represents someone who's there for me. When I see the food, I want to take it all in. I get anxious about whether I'll ever have it again. I know I'm the one preparing the food and I do feel committed to allowing myself to have as much of it as I want, but my feelings don't respond to logic. The idea of eating just a little bit of food leaves me feeling lonely."

Laura, another woman in Kyra's group, had a different take on the magical quality of food. "I'm sure you're right about attributing magical powers to food," she said. "But when I can't stop eating, all I'm aware of is how much I love the taste of the food in my mouth. I don't want to stop because I don't want to lose that delicious sensation."

Many compulsive eaters talk about not wanting to relinquish the delicious taste of food in their mouths, but that conviction conflicts with the simple fact that the deliciousness is significantly diminished once you continue to eat past the feeling of fullness. The wish to hold onto a delicious taste, even after you are feeling full, is a wish to forestall a return to yourself and your reality. When you feel yourself about to overeat in an attempt to hold onto the food's good taste, you need to stop and ask yourself, Do I really need to lose myself in this taste right now, or can I allow it to fade and leave me with my feelings?

When we talk about eating to satisfy your hunger as opposed to eating as a quest for magic, it is important to become attuned to what it takes to leave you feeling satisfied. Different people are satisfied with different degrees of fullness. Ask yourself, Do I like having just enough food to satisfy my hunger, or do I prefer to feel a bit more full?

Kate, from a Texas workshop, told us that she once asked her husband, who had no history of eating problems, why he had stopped eating a particularly delicious appetizer. "I want to eat the rest of my meal," he said, "and I hate feeling stuffed." Nell, a participant in Kate's workshop, responded to this story with a laugh. "I have no trouble eating from stomach hunger," she said, "and I have no trouble figuring out just what I want to eat. But the stuffed feeling that your husband says he hates is exactly what I go for. I love everything about eating, and for me that includes the chewing, the swallowing, and the feeling of having food in my stomach. I associate that feeling with satisfaction, and it's hard for me to settle for anything less."

It is important to respect your preferences around fullness. However, many compulsive eaters discover that their old desire to be very full conflicts with their new desire to eat often during the day in response to stomach hunger. As they become more attuned to their hunger signals, they often start questioning their ideas about fullness and satisfaction.

Voting for Satisfaction

Over the years, we have thought a lot about how to help people stop eating when they have had enough. There are a number of steps you can take to make it easier to stop eating when you are full. For example, allowing yourself access to more food than you could possibly eat helps greatly when it comes to stopping. When you are cooking pasta, make sure that the pasta bowl is large and filled to the top. When you reach for a cookie, see to it that your cookie jar is full. When you pack your lunch, include three sandwiches instead of just one or two. And when you open up your freezer door in search of ice cream, make it a point to have several gallons of your favorite flavor.

Jane, a participant in our New York workshop, told us that she "dequantifies" food in order to avoid eating defined portions. She takes sandwiches and cuts them into quarters and does the same with doughnuts, muffins, candy, and all sorts of things. She also empties most packaged foods into large bowls and containers so that she is never thinking about prescribed measurements.

Having a surplus of all of your favorite foods relaxes you. Surplus reminds you that, if you are hungry again in half an hour, you can have more of whatever is tasting so good at the moment. Unfortunately, no external measures, such as keeping your house well stocked or dequantifying food, get to the heart of the problem that makes you overeat.

If it is pleasurable for you to pursue eating after you have had enough, there needs to be something equally pleasurable about putting down your fork. For a compulsive eater, that pleasure comes from feeling that *you,* rather than food, are in control.

Most compulsive eaters do not know the satisfaction of eating only as much as their stomachs desire, but it is indeed a genuine satisfaction. "I can't believe how good I feel when I walk away from the table having eaten not one morsel more than I wanted," said one woman who, for the first time in her life, is leaving food on her plate.

We call this process of gaining control "voting for the inside." It involves the recognition that what is happening inside you is more important than what is happening outside. In other words, the fullness or emptiness of your stomach takes precedence over the fullness or emptiness of the plate. The good feeling that comes from respecting what is happening within you eventually replaces the illusory satisfaction of eating more than you need.

As you approach the experience of "voting for the inside," it is important to distinguish between feeling that you *must* stop eating as soon as you have had enough and feeling that you would *like* to stop eating as soon as you have had enough. There is no more certain route to failure for compulsive eaters—who already have a long history of rebelling against rules regarding food and eating—than to turn "voting for the inside" into a rule. Any such rule or command will be met by immediate resistance, and, before you know it, you will be back in the Clean Plate Club. You can stop eating beyond satisfaction if you *want* to—but you will never stop eating beyond this point if you feel that you *have* to.

As you attempt to gain release from the magical hold that food has on you, it is also important to recognize that the ability to stop eating when you have had enough develops gradually as part of the process of discovering who you are as an eater. Stopping when you have had enough is linked to eating often in response to stomach hunger; and all the components of demand feeding—the when, the what, and the how much—strengthen your sense of security and lessen your need to use food as magic.

Pam, a workshop participant from Indiana, talked about this unfolding process. "I've always had trouble leaving food on my plate," she said. "It has helped me to remember that I'm stopping as soon as I've had enough because I want to eat again as soon as I possibly can. In *Overcoming Overeating*, you talk about the fact that each time you eat in response to stomach hunger, you are making a deposit in a bank account labeled 'Good Caretaking.' If I 'vote for the inside,' the chances are I'll get hungry again soon and can make another deposit; it's very clear to me that the more times I feel stomach hunger each day and eat, the more relaxed I feel."

Tess, from Atlanta, talked about the pleasure she feels when she stops eating because she is full. "Before I eat anything," she said, "I ask myself, *How hungry* am I? That helps me hone in on what I want to eat and alerts me to the issue of *how much.* I want to know when I'm full. It's the same as wanting to know when I'm hungry, and wanting to know what my body is craving, and wanting to know what I'm feeling if I find myself thinking about food when I'm not hungry. I like the feeling of 'voting for the inside.' Eating just as much as I'm hungry for makes me feel authoritative. The other night in a restaurant the waiter saw the food I'd left over—which, incidentally, I did without thinking about it—and he asked if anything was wrong. In fact, nothing was wrong, and everything was right. I felt terrific. For the first time in my life, *I'm* in charge, not the food. It may sound crazy, but the kind of satisfaction I get from that is really much more pleasurable than eating those extra few bites ever was. I feel like I have myself back."

Satiation, Separation, and Identity

Before you can expect to say "I've had enough," you have to have a strong sense of just who "I" is. Beyond that, however, you have to believe that no one knows your "I" better than you do. This issue is a difficult one for compulsive eaters who have generally spent their lives believing that everyone knows more about what they should eat, when they should eat it, and when they should stop eating than they do themselves.

"I carry a bag of muffins around with me every day," said Julie, who attended one of our Chicago workshops. "I know that I'm supposed to eat as many of them as I want, but I always want two. Somehow, in my mind, two muffins is an appropriate portion, and I can't get beyond that."

Another woman in Julie's workshop responded, "I do the same thing in restaurants. I'm served a portion and I finish it because it seems like I should. It's as if someone in that kitchen knows the *right* amount that a person should eat."

This notion that others are better able to determine when we should stop eating is often at the heart of resistance in this final stage of demand feeding. One woman in the Chicago workshop nailed the issue when she said, "It's almost as though I'm breaking a rule when I don't eat what other people lay out for me . . . or when I want to eat more than is there. My mother always said, 'Can't you finish just that little bit?' and 'What a pity to throw this out.' She also rarely cooked more than our allotted portions, so you couldn't have more if you wanted it."

Each time you say "I've had enough" while there is still food on your plate, you are actually asserting that you know your capacity better than whoever defined your portion. And each time you finish the portion when you really do not want to, you are asserting the opposite: that whoever dished out your food knows what you need more than you do. "I now think it out before I eat," said Jess in our New York workshop. "I remind myself that the chef really doesn't know what I need. Only I know. And then I go further and remind myself that I want to know. I like the feeling of voting for the inside. It makes me feel full of myself."

There was a time, early in our lives, when we felt completely merged with our mothers. During that time, we all believed that our mothers knew everything that was going on inside our hearts, minds, and stomachs. Part of normal development involves a process that psychoanalyst Margaret Mahler called "separation-individuation," in which children recognize that their mothers are one person and they are another. At some point, each of us discovered that our thoughts and emotions were our own until we chose to share them—and so was our appetite. Saying "I don't want anymore" was yet another signal that you were an individual, separate and apart from everyone else, including your mother.

Compulsive eaters, as we've said, use food as a reminder of the time when they felt merged with their mothers. It is not surprising, then, to learn that they may have ambivalent feelings about this issue of their separateness. Many compulsive eaters are acutely aware of not wanting to be separate from food and all it represents.

"I have lots of trouble with endings," said Alice in a California workshop, "so it's no surprise to me that stopping is my Waterloo. I'm just not comfortable being alone. Saying good-bye to food, even when I've had enough to eat, feels too much like an ending to me. When I push the plate away, it means that I'm in one place and the food, and all it represents, in another. I hear other people say that they are exhilarated by their ability to stop eating when they've had enough, but for me, stopping feels like a loss."

Zeda, a woman in that same workshop, was able to answer Alice. "I also have a lot of trouble with good-byes," she said, "but I've been focusing on the fact that if I stop as soon as I'm full, I'll get to eat again fairly soon. Now, instead of feeling sad when I'm full, I start to feel excited about what I'll eat the next time I'm hungry. I pack my food bag carefully and take it with me wherever I go. I carry empty plastic bags with me so that I can pick up extra things that I crave during the day. More often than not these days, I finish eating, look at my plate, and notice that there's still food on it. I can't begin to tell you how powerful that makes me feel!"

If acknowledging the fact that you are a distinct human being with unique needs, desires, and boundaries makes it difficult for you to stop eating when you have had enough, it may help to practice your matchmaking. Making the right match, as we said earlier, is a way to identify yourself. You will have an easier time stopping when you have had enough if you eat what you want in the first place.

In one discussion about stopping when you feel full, Jody raised an important issue. "I've noticed," she said, "that I have a hard time stopping even when I don't like what I'm eating. My kids have no trouble saying 'I don't like this and I don't want anymore,' but I do. The more I think about it, the clearer it becomes that the difficulty I have in acknowledging that I don't like something is by no means limited to food. I'm always worried about saying no and hurting someone's feelings.

"Obviously, a casserole isn't going to feel rejected," Jody continued, "but I still have a hard time pushing it away. Instead, I hang onto it, pretending I like it. It's as if I'm afraid that if I don't stay with what I've got, I won't find anything else. Maybe if I could begin to say no to food when I don't like it, I'd have an easier time saying no in other parts of my life as well."

Food and Satisfaction

It's hard to say "I'm satisfied" when you feel that there is, or always has been, a great deal lacking in your life. Nancy, a woman in California, expressed it well. "If I feel satisfied, but haven't eaten very much, I don't trust it. Are two bites really enough? Can that be all I need? My mother always used to say, 'Nothing is ever enough for you.' Now, when I eat more than the few bites I need, it's as though I'm confirming what she said. 'You're right, Mom,' I'm saying. 'Nothing you gave me was enough.' And do you know what? It really wasn't. My mother had a hard time giving to herself and a harder time giving to me. But the extra food doesn't take the pain of that away."

Nancy's story is not unusual. People often tell us that, not only are they shocked to discover how little food they really need, but also they are disturbed by that discovery. They always thought of themselves as being insatiable around food and now they see that they can be satisfied by small portions. When food is simply food, we do not need very much of it. On the other hand, when food is used to express how needy we feel *and* how bad we feel about needing so much, no portion is ever big enough.

Myra, a participant in a Texas workshop, expressed her problem this way. "I know exactly when I'm satisfied," she said, "and I just go right on eating. My problem is that I've been rebelling for so long by eating compulsively that I'm confused about who I'm eating for and who I'm stopping for. Whenever I feel satisfied by a small amount of food, I worry that if I stop eating, I'll be submitting to all of those voices who have been telling me that I eat too much and that I should lose weight. So I keep on eating. If I'm in a restaurant and in the mood for a small salad, I'll eat it and feel all of these approving eyes on me—and then rebel with a huge dessert—even though I really feel satisfied by the salad."

Part of what concerns Myra is the possibility of losing weight; we will talk about the issue of body size in depth later. For now, however, it is important to understand that until Myra is clear that eating less and losing weight have nothing to do with succumbing to the lifelong pressure she has felt to diet and be thinner, she will not be able to stop eating when she has had enough. As long as she remains embroiled in her old conflict, she will continue to eat beyond fullness.

Myra would have an easier time disengaging from this conflict if she made it a point to always put more food in front of her than she could possibly eat. Esther, who had a similar problem, put it this way: "I have to have enough food in front of me so that I don't think about portions. The more concretely I show myself that there is absolutely no limit on what I can have, the better able I am to distinguish exactly how much I want."

The issue of self-caretaking is at the heart of eating beyond the point of satisfaction. Until you have convinced yourself that *you* will never deprive yourself in the way you were deprived, or in the way you have deprived yourself in the past, you will continue to eat more than you need. Not only do you have to give yourself permission to eat as much as you want, but you also have to permit yourself to need whatever you need in other areas as well, regardless of whether or not your needs are met. There is no such thing as needing too much, whether it is food, love, compassion, or comfort. Unfortunately, many compulsive eaters feel ashamed of their needs.

Andrea is one such person. "In the three years since I began doing this eating work, I've noticed that my problem with stopping when I've had enough is always related to my job situation. As soon as I'm unhappy in a job, which has happened too many times in the past few years, lunchtime is when I attempt to make up for it.

"I've been at this long enough to know what I'm supposed to do," Andrea continued. "I go out and stock up. I always have plenty of food at my desk and I always try to buy more than I can eat. But even if I don't eat it all, I certainly go way beyond fullness and end up feeling stuffed. I try not to yell at myself about it, but I feel so uncomfortable that it's hard not to get down on myself. It's frustrating because outside of the job, this doesn't happen anymore.

"The same thing happened two years ago when I was in an unhappy job situation," Andrea explained. "I decided to go back to school for more training and, when I finished, I found a job that turned out to be disappointing. I started eating beyond fullness. Finally, I got my present job, which I thought would be better. But this job is also unchallenging and unsatisfying, and here I am again eating way beyond the point where I feel full. Am I supposed to revamp my life every time I notice that I'm eating too much?"

Andrea is unhappy with her job, starts eating more than she's hungry for, and ends up saying, "Why am I eating so much?" What she really means is, "Why can't I ever be satisfied? Why do I always want more?" The drama she is enacting with food is actually about something being wrong with her for wanting more from a job or with her job because it does not offer her enough. However, as long as she believes that *she* is the problem, she will continue to eat too much. Once she gets to the point at which she can acknowledge her dissatisfaction and not judge herself for it, she will not have to displace her struggle onto food. Andrea wants more professional satisfaction—not more food.

The Issue of Weight Loss

People often notice that when they are able to stop eating as soon as they have had enough, they begin to lose weight. As soon as they make this connection, many people try to hasten the weight loss process by unconsciously turning their new ability to stop when they have had enough into a diet.

We all know what happens when we go on diets. As soon as "I've had enough and I *want* to stop eating" turns into "I've had enough and I *should* stop eating," any bona fide compulsive eater will feel compelled to rebel . . . and eat, and eat, and eat. Even if a compulsive eater does not turn stopping when she has had enough into a diet, she will still sabotage her progress as a demand feeder if she gets too invested in weight loss.

On one level, every compulsive eater longs to be thin enough to match cultural ideals, but each time a compulsive eater binges out of a diet and gains weight, she is protesting the very same cultural standard she longs to meet. In order to lose any weight, compulsive eaters must first make peace with the possibility that they may never lose weight. They must grant themselves the acceptance that the world withholds.

Harriet, from a Philadelphia workshop, fell into the trap we have just described. "I felt like I was really sailing along with my demand feeding," she said. "I surrounded myself with what I wanted, I ate when I was hungry, and I was really getting good at figuring out exactly how many bites of food it took to satisfy my hunger. My whole focus was on the process of demand feeding, until I suddenly realized that I was losing weight. The weight loss thrilled me. Here I was feeling great, doing something to finally end my compulsive eating, and I was losing weight, too! What could be better?

"But somehow," Harriet continued, "very shortly after I began to think about my weight loss, my focus shifted. I began to challenge myself to eat less and less so that I would continue to get thinner. That was the beginning of the end of demand feeding for me. I began to inhale food. I'd start out feeling hungry, eat until I felt satisfied, then sail right on past my feeling of satisfaction and eat until I was absolutely stuffed."

In order for Harriet to rediscover the feeling of fullness, she needed to develop a motivation other than weight loss. She decided to remind herself—each time she felt satisfied by a small amount of food—that what mattered most was to be true to herself as an eater. "I learned to disassociate my eating from my body size. The important thing has become what's going on inside my body—how empty or full I feel—as opposed to what's going on outside my body—how thin or fat I look."

Some people who are careful to focus on their eating rather than their weight still feel uneasy when they lose weight and, once again, start eating more than they need.

"Each time I eat, I eat a little more than I really need," said Stacy one night in a New York workshop. "I've gone over everything and I know that there's nothing particularly troubling on my mind when I eat beyond fullness. My house is always filled with a wide variety of the things I love to eat, and I'm not at all focused on losing weight. Of course, I wouldn't mind at all if I did lose weight—I do live on this planet with the rest of us—but I can honestly say that I have come to accept my body just as it is. But having said all of that," Stacy went on, "I continue to overeat and I don't have the foggiest idea what to do about it. It's almost as if I want to feel big and stay big."

Stacy's story is not unusual. Many compulsive eaters hold onto eating beyond fullness despite the fact that their demand feeding is going very smoothly. Many of them, like Stacy, recognize that in saying "I don't want anymore," they are saying "I am willing to become smaller." And many of them, like Stacy, conclude that, for one reason or another, they are more comfortable staying large.

Many compulsive eaters have associations to thinness that interfere with the natural weight loss that is often a by-product of attuned demand feeding. You will learn that the associations you have to thinness have more to do with emotional issues than with body issues. For example, many compulsive eaters consciously believe that it would be great to be thin, but they unconsciously associate thinness with weakness and vulnerability. We will talk about these issues in depth in Chapter 15. For now, it is important to recognize how the fear of weight loss can interfere with your ability to stop eating when you have had enough.

Some compulsive eaters make the decision to hold onto their weight indefinitely. Others, like Betty, eventually decide that they now feel comfortable about losing some weight. "It took me a long time before I was ready to lose some weight," Betty explained when we asked her what she thought had made it possible for her to stop eating when she was full. "Probably, the most important thing for me to understand was that becoming a demand feeder—and I mean an absolute, complete demand feeder—was a very gradual process. I knew that I was really there when I decided to stop worrying about it. After all, what was my hurry? I had all the time in the world. I wasn't aiming at losing weight for summer anymore; all I cared about was taking care of myself and making myself feel comfortable. As it turns out, I've lost weight. It's nice to be thinner, but that's not what I wake up every morning feeling good about. The thing I really feel good about is that I no longer feel addicted to food."

A Final Clue About Demand Feeding

Sometimes, people have a particularly difficult time with one aspect of demand feeding—either the "when," the "what," or the "how much" of eating. If that is the case for you and you are sure that you have paid careful attention to the mechanics of demand feeding—keeping a well-stocked house, carrying a food bag, stopping your self-castigation—it may be time to look at your problem with demand feeding in a slightly different way. It is possible that one particular area of this process is difficult for you because it relates to some issue in your life or some aspect of your character that gives you trouble.

One of the things we have discovered in our workshops is that the ways in which women talk about their specific problems with demand feeding, the words they use, provide clues as to why one specific area has become a stumbling block for them. If you have trouble knowing what to eat, for example, do you say, "I don't know what I'm hungry for?" or do you say, "I can never get it right?" In this case, examining the words you choose may help you discover what underlies your particular problem with identifying what foods your body craves.

Consider the following transcript from an advanced group in which six women managed to move beyond their specific stumbling blocks by examining the words they were using to describe their problems with demand feeding.

> *Shauna:* I had trouble making the correct hunger/food match while I was on vacation, which surprised me because usually I'm very good at it. At some point I noticed that I was eating lots of foods that were high in fat and I began worrying. I worried about why I wasn't eating healthier foods and I worried about how long this fatty-food eating would last. As I see it, I was in the good foods/bad foods trap again. At some point during my vacation, I must have stopped viewing all foods as equal. In retrospect, I'm sure that my obsession with fatty foods versus healthy foods must have interfered with my ability to make accurate food/hunger decisions.
>
> *Group:* What do you think was going on during your vacation? Where were you?
>
> *Shauna:* My father has a house by the shore. I decided to meet my sister and her family there for three weeks and vacation with them. On the whole, my sister and I get along very well, but there is usually some tension when we live to-

gether again for a while. This time, though, the vacation was remarkably tension-free. I can't think of anything specific that happened that I could link to my problems with making a good food/hunger match.

Group: Was there anything in general that was bothering you?

Shauna: [*thoughtfully*] Well, although we were getting along quite well, I couldn't help but be aware of the fact that my sister has lost a lot of weight this year and, as you know, I've regained the weight that I had lost on my last diet. It's one of the few times in our lives that she's been smaller than I am. I guess you could say that she became the "good" one this summer. All my life I did the right thing and tried to please everyone. I was always the favorite. Now I don't fit that picture. My sister is married, has a home and children, a good job, and now she's even thin. I'm single, live in an apartment, I was recently laid off, and I'm bigger than ever.

[*At this point, Shauna paused and the group was quiet.*] I think I'm beginning to see why I had such trouble making the match this summer. In my mind, my sister and I had traded places and I just didn't match up to my old image as the family's "good" little girl.

Sara: Let me try my hand at making sense of where I'm stuck. I'm having trouble again figuring out when I'm hungry. It's hardest for me when I'm on the road and, since my job involves lots of traveling, I really need to deal with it. I've always been nervous about traveling. In fact, I have a recurring dream about traveling in which I'm going to Europe, but I forget to bring my passport.

Group: What comes to your mind about your dream?

Sara: Well, I obviously need a passport to get out of the country. The passport is my identity paper; it describes who I am and it makes it possible for me to move around. Without it, I'm not officially recognized and I can't really go freely from place to place.

My mother was a very anxious person. When she was upset, there was no way to get her to pay attention to us. Forgetting my passport is like forgetting myself. I guess what

I'm saying is that when I travel, I often leave myself behind. Not being attentive to my hunger is one of the ways I do that. When I'm on the road and feeling anxious, I neglect myself in very much the same way that my mother neglected us when she was anxious. If I could remember this the next time I travel, maybe it would help. If I could stay connected to my hunger, it would ground me in my own caretaking abilities and I'd probably be a less anxious traveler in the long run.

Anna: I've been doing this work for years, but I still have trouble stopping when I'm full. I can't seem to drop out of the Clean Plate Club. The other night I asked myself a question I had never asked before. Why is it, I wondered, that I always have to eat what's dished out to me?

All my life I've felt that I had to be grateful for what I got. My parents always told me how good I had it compared to my friends. My mother worked full time because we needed the money, and when she brought home a dress she thought I would like, I never told her if I didn't like it. In fact, I focused so much more on her feelings than on my own that I would wear it to school the very next day—even if I hated it—just to make her feel good.

I think that eating beyond fullness is like wearing the dress that I don't really like. I still feel that I have to accept what's given to me, whether I want it or not. I'm always struggling with this issue of not being able to say no, but this is the first time I've actually connected it to being unable to stop eating when I've had enough. When I'm tempted to eat beyond fullness, I need to remind myself that I'm entitled to take in only what I really want.

Marion: I still don't know what I want to eat when I'm hungry—and I can't stand not knowing.

Group: Is there anything going on in your life right now in which you are confronting the issue of knowing and not knowing?

Marion: When you say it like that, a bell goes off. I'm furious with myself because I can't decide if I want to stay in my very lucrative job or leave it and look for something that's more fulfilling. It took me a long time to get to where I am today. Everyone thinks I'd be crazy to quit. But lately, I haven't been all that happy. I've been thinking about leaving my field altogether.

I hate my indecision. I can see that my issue with food is symbolic of where I am in my life—not knowing what I want to do with my life and not knowing what I want to put in my stomach. Realistically, it's going to take a while before I can figure out the job issue. In the meantime, while that's cooking, I'd like to give myself permission to respond to my food needs.

We've often talked in group about how our food problems can be resolved before our other problems have been worked through. I'd like to get in touch with what it is I want to eat and, maybe, once I'm less anxious about that, I'll be in a better position to be clear about my other needs as well.

Edith: No matter how much I think I've legalized food, I realize that I keep certain foods *slightly* forbidden. I bring them into the house, but I don't open the packages. I'm afraid that once I start, I'll never stop. It seems crazy to me, because I've come so far with this approach, but I can't seem to get over this.

Group: What else are you afraid you'll never stop doing once you start?

Edith: As you say it that way, I think of my feelings. I must still believe that, if I let myself go, my feelings would overwhelm me. It's like, if I start crying, I'll never stop.

When you look beneath your particular demand feeding problem, as these women did, you will come face-to-face with an aspect of yourself that needs attention. Giving yourself this attention will help you become increasingly comfortable with demand feeding and will focus your awareness on what is really troubling you. It is always important to keep in mind that *your resistances to demand feeding are simply signals warning you to proceed with caution.* They are indications of your reluctance to abandon a way of dealing with problems that, on some significant level, has worked for you in the past.

Part Three

RECLAIMING YOURSELF

Chapter 11

MOUTH HUNGER

IT'S NINE O'CLOCK IN THE EVENING. YOU'RE CURLED UP IN BED WITH A good mystery when suddenly you start thinking about getting something to eat. You stop and ask yourself whether your impulse to eat is physiological or psychological. In other words, are you having stomach hunger or mouth hunger? You determine that what you are feeling is, in fact, mouth hunger, and you decide that it must be satisfied.

In the past, you would have berated yourself for this kind of driven, compulsive eating, and to escape your self-reproach, you would have resolved to start dieting the very next day. But you have given up dieting. And it is our hope that you have also stopped yelling at yourself for needing to satisfy your mouth hunger.

If you have been using this approach for a while, you understand that having mouth hunger means that while you were reading, something made you uncomfortable. At the heart of this kind of understanding is the awareness that mouth hunger is a signal. When you want to eat even though you are not physiologically hungry, it means that something is up. You went to food for comfort because you did not know what was troubling you, or because you could not comfort yourself in another way, or because you had a feeling from which you felt compelled to flee. If you were in physical danger, you would turn on your heels and run. If you are a compulsive eater and you sense that you are in some kind of emotional danger, you turn and run to food. But now, however, you also trust that the time will come when you will be able to deal differently with your discomfort, and you are sympathetic to the fact that, at the moment, you need to eat.

In *Overcoming Overeating* we explained that you reach for food when you are in trouble because food symbolizes love and comfort. Food welcomed you into the world and now, each time you reach for it when you have mouth hunger, you are trying to return to a time when you felt welcomed and safe.

Perhaps you first used food for comfort during a time in your life when you were very anxious. Or perhaps you started reaching for food for reasons other than physiological hunger in response to your first dieting experience. Diets put many foods off-limits, and once those foods are "forbidden," they take on magical healing powers as well. Feeling tense? Have a cookie. Feeling sad? Have some ice cream.

We also explained in our first book that compulsive eaters translate whatever is bothering them into simpler, food- and fat-related terms. Your problem, though, has nothing to do with the kinds of food you eat or what you weigh. Compulsive eaters have a problem calming themselves when they are upset and are often reluctant to let themselves know the truth about what is disturbing them at any given moment. Food is not an effective solution for what actually are problems in self-soothing and in truth-telling. As a compulsive eater, you need a solution that will help you "sit" with some of your feelings, comfort yourself, and learn to think through what is genuinely bothering you.

As you know, we believe that demand feeding is that solution. Each time you feed yourself when you are physiologically hungry, you offer yourself a kind of nurturing reparenting that makes you feel more secure. The more secure you feel, the more able you will be to deal with the feelings you now attempt to avoid by eating.

Think of it this way. Each time you reach for food when you are not hungry, you are looking for a caretaker. You end up searching for a caretaker in the refrigerator because there is no one at home—no presence within you at that moment—to do the job of soothing. Our goal is to help you develop a soothing presence within yourself. Each time you feed yourself when you are hungry, you are demonstrating that you can take care of yourself. Just as a parent demonstrates that she or he can care for a child by feeding her or him in an attuned way, so, too, are you demonstrating your self-care abilities by feeding yourself on demand.

You are beginning to care for yourself in other ways as well, by dressing differently, by looking at yourself with delight, and by talking to yourself in a tender, gentle way. You are also attempting to understand your problems rather than yell at yourself about them. Hopefully, you are becoming a reliable self-caretaker, increasingly attuned to your own needs.

How does the comfort you now offer yourself stack up against the comfort you once sought from food? Eventually, *you* will come out ahead of food as caretaker-of-choice. Each time you feed yourself in response to stomach hunger, your credibility as a caretaker is reinforced. Ah, yes, you say to yourself, I can be trusted.

You must allow time for this trust to develop. The day will come when it will not even occur to you to eat unless you are hungry. Until that day arrives, however, you must learn to handle your inevitable urges to eat in response to mouth hunger. This transition to eating from stomach hunger rather than from mouth hunger is a gradual one. With that caution in mind, let us discuss the four stages in the handling of mouth hunger.

Stage 1: Full Permission

When you first use our Overcoming Overeating approach, you handle mouth hunger quite simply. Each time you want to eat, you ask yourself, "Is this stomach hunger or mouth hunger?" If the answer is mouth hunger, you ask yourself a second question: "Can I wait to eat until I feel stomach hunger?"

When you first begin to question whether or not you can wait for stomach hunger, your answer is likely to be no. After all, you've been eating in response to stress for many years now. It is your way of attempting to help yourself and it makes sense to reach for what you know, particularly when you are feeling desperate. If your answer is that you cannot wait, you must go ahead and eat—*but,* if at all possible, give some thought to what it is you choose to eat. Your body is not craving anything at that moment, but you can be selective about which food would best satisfy your mouth hunger. If you want chocolate, for example, do not reach for an apple.

Before you eat from mouth hunger, address the stress you are experiencing in a caring way by saying something like the following: "I'm sorry that I am feeling so upset right now, and I'm particularly sorry that giving myself food is the best way I know of to calm myself. I am going to eat something, and I hope that doing so will help me. But I will not say one reproachful word to myself after I've eaten, or later if I feel full, or tomorrow when I look at myself in the mirror."

You deserve to be treated in this kind, caring, humane way. After all, as a participant in one of our workshops said, "If I saw a person banging her head against a wall, I wouldn't yell at her or call her bad." Logically, eating when you are not hungry makes no more sense than banging your head against the wall, but both acts are extremely meaningful and both bespeak a great deal of underlying pain.

What happens when you stop yelling at yourself for eating from mouth hunger? You eat less and are less inclined to binge. Yelling is the centerpiece of the compulsive-eating ritual. Food and eating are essential parts of that ritual, but it is the yelling that ultimately punishes you and distracts you from whatever it was that sent you to food in the first place. It is the yelling that completes the translation that we discussed earlier. By the time you finish your yelling, you are convinced that your problem is your eating and your weight—a problem, you tell yourself, that you can solve by dieting.

At this stage, if you need to eat from mouth hunger, then you should simply go ahead and do so. Tell yourself that the next time you eat, perhaps it will be in response to stomach hunger. Of course, understanding that you should allow yourself to eat from mouth hunger without yelling at yourself—and actually doing so—are two entirely different matters. Following are some examples of the obstacles people encounter when they try to give themselves full permission to eat in response to mouth hunger.

The Obstacles to Granting Yourself Full Permission

Living with a lack of control

"I've been moderately successful in terms of going with my mouth hunger," said Judy in a Chicago workshop. "I tell myself, 'Okay, you're having mouth hunger. Can you sit with the feeling and wait to eat until you're hungry?' Then I listen for the reply. 'No, I really want to eat now.' So I say, 'Okay. Enjoy the food as much as possible.' "

As a result of granting herself this kind of permission, Judy has gained some new insights. "I realize that when I give myself permission, I become a mother to myself. But I'm not just *any* mother . . . I'm a mother who allows her child to eat and who stays with her child while she's eating," she said. "When that happens, it's great and I don't eat nearly as much. I also feel much less alone than I usually do when I eat compulsively."

At other times, however, Judy will look back at her day and feel bad about having eaten from mouth hunger. "I'll get down on myself," she told the other members of the workshop. "I'll say, 'This is not going anywhere. I'm never going to lose weight if I keep giving into mouth hunger. It's self-indulgent. I ought to be able to wait it out. At least I should try harder.' "

We urged Judy to think about those times when she yells at herself for eating from mouth hunger. Why is it, we wondered, that there are times when she yells and other times when she does not yell? What accounts for the difference?

"It's like a bad body thought," Judy answered. "It just comes over me. I think it probably has to do with how my day has gone."

In fact, at the time we spoke, Judy was going through a particularly difficult period. "I'm unemployed," she told us, "and it's hard for me to stay optimistic about finding a job, given how bad the economy is. Some days I feel motivated and write lots of letters or make a whole bunch of phone calls. Other days I just can't hack it. I probably have about the same amount of mouth hunger on any given day, but on the days I'm really working at finding work, I treat myself more sympathetically. The days I'm sloughing off, I think I find it harder to be forgiving, and that's when I get down on myself for eating from mouth hunger."

What precisely does Judy mean by "getting down" on herself? "When I yell, what I'm really saying is, 'Don't be such a wimp. Can't you make a success of anything?' " she explained. "I'm yelling at myself for having eaten when I wasn't hungry, but I know it's about more than that. It's hard to accept that I'm doing the best I can to find a job on a day that I haven't done much."

Although Judy has no trouble making the connection between her bad feelings and her mouth hunger, it is still difficult for her to treat herself with kindness. "It's really hard to give yourself permission to eat from mouth hunger," she confessed. "It means accepting that you don't have as much control over yourself as you'd like to think you have. I guess it's pretty much the same when it comes to looking for a job. Some days I can work hard at it and other days I just can't do as much. I was raised to think that you should force yourself to do certain things whether you liked them or not. So when it comes to mouth hunger and the job search, I can't help feeling that I should just get over my problems."

Judy was upset with herself for not working equally hard each day to find a job. Ostensibly, she turned to food to allay the anxiety of her job search, but, more significantly, she turned to food to escape her harsh judgments about her alleged lack of effort. For Judy, however, harsh judgments proved inescapable. Instead of berating herself for needing time off from the frustrating and emotionally exhausting endeavor of finding a job, she berated herself for needing to eat.

Like Judy, we all find it hard to accept our need to eat in a driven way. Most of you would like to exercise more control over yourselves—with regard to food and everything else as well. When you yell at yourself for eating from mouth hunger, you are expressing distress at your lack of control. It *is* distressing to recognize that you are not in charge of yourself as much as you would like to be; but it is also distressing that you cannot simply acknowledge your lack of control in a more consoling way.

When we yell at ourselves for eating compulsively, we are doing something we have been taught to do. We have all learned two *un*-golden rules: that it is "wrong" to eat too much, and that it is "right" to yell at ourselves when we do something wrong. Most of us believe that self-criticism inspires change and that, as Judy said, we should simply force ourselves to change our ways. This "pick-yourself-up-by-your-bootstraps" mentality, which suggests that having control over oneself is simply a matter of will, is rooted in the notion that lack of control is just plain, old infantile. Yet nothing could be further from the truth.

You do not choose to have mouth hunger and you cannot simply *will it away*—but you *can nurture it away* in time. We assure you that your mouth hunger will diminish as you become more secure through feeding yourself on demand. Judy, for example, may continue to have trouble coming to grips with what she sees as her lack of productivity. But, if she manages to stop yelling at herself about eating, in time she will no longer need to eat over these concerns.

Remind yourself that if you could be more in control, you would be. Take heart that someday you *will* be.

Judy's story underscores the need for patience as you make the transition from eating in response to mouth hunger to eating in response to stomach hunger. Even when Judy called her problem an "eating problem," the disguise was a thin one. She knew all along that she was anxious about finding a new job and that she was unhappy with herself for not being more consistent in her efforts. Knowing what she was feeling, however, did not make her feel less compelled to eat.

At this stage of her work with demand feeding, Judy needed to accumulate more experiences of eating from stomach hunger before she could feel secure enough to sit with her feelings without eating. Although she had insight into her problem, insight was not enough. The idea that if you know what is bothering you, you will stop eating compulsively, is a common misconception. Actually, as you will see in the next example, compulsive eaters often use this idea to attack themselves.

Facing the fact that knowledge is not enough

"I read your book a year ago and for several months did quite well," said Sandra in a San Diego workshop. "When I ate from mouth hunger, I was okay with it. What surprised me most, however, was what a hard time I had with my memories as I brought more and more of my formerly forbidden foods into the house."

What Sandra remembered was the association she had made as a child between food and emotional nurturing. "When I was ten years old, I was sent to live with my grandmother. It was a very hard, lonely time for me, and I wound up gaining seventy pounds. In the process of stocking my house with food, I discovered that certain foods, especially particular kinds of cookies, evoked memories of that very painful time in my life. Legalizing food turned out to be unexpectedly painful."

In the course of trying out these formerly forbidden foods and retrieving painful memories, Sandra put on weight. "I was forced to do a lot of long overdue emotional work," she said. "Now I feel that I know much more about that traumatic time in my childhood, but I'm still eating from mouth hunger. I've worked incredibly hard, but I'm not seeing the results. I always know that I'm feeling lonely or abandoned or hurt when I go for food, but that doesn't stop me from eating."

As Sandra spoke, her impatience with herself was evident. From her perspective, something did not make sense. If discomfort with feelings was at the heart of mouth hunger—and Sandra had done considerable work on her feelings—why hadn't she reaped some reward for her labors? If she knew more now about her feelings from childhood, why did similar feelings in the present still drive her to eat?

Many people who work with us raise this question. Sandra continues to eat in response to certain feelings because she is not yet psychologically secure enough to take a chance on experiencing those feelings without the cushion of food. She has not yet accumulated enough stomach hunger experiences to be able to do things differently.

When we probed further about what had been happening with Sandra and her eating, we discovered that she was no longer carrying a food bag and that her supplies at home had dwindled. Sandra had been focusing more on her feelings and less on the mechanics of her eating.

It was extremely important for Sandra to focus on her feelings in this way and to work through the traumatic events of her childhood. We are in no way discounting that work. It is important to keep in mind, however, that eating in response to stomach hunger—*even more than understanding yourself*—is the fundamental cure for mouth hunger.

Each time you recognize stomach hunger and satisfy it, you are demonstrating to yourself that you are on the road to becoming a reliable and attuned self-caretaker. Eventually, your self-attunement will make it possible for you to sit with your painful feelings without reaching to food for protection. At this stage, Sandra needs to understand that she is turning to food not because she is being obstinate or contrary, but because she does not yet feel strong enough to be there for herself in a truly loving way. She may have done a lot of emotional work, but she has not yet done enough of the mechanical work of feeding herself in response to stomach hunger.

Imagine how terribly difficult these feelings must have been for her as a child if, as an adult, she still feels so frightened by them. Beyond accumulating lots of experiences feeding herself from stomach hunger, Sandra needs to develop patience and compassion for those times when she eats from mouth hunger, for she will need these qualities in order to confront her fears head on, without using food as a buffer.

Relinquishing the piracy of overeating

Grace, from Denver, had an interesting perspective on the issue of giving herself full permission to eat in response to mouth hunger. "It's as though you're asking me to give up piracy," she said emphatically.

What, we wondered, does giving yourself permission to eat from mouth hunger have to do with piracy?

"When I eat from mouth hunger," Grace explained, "I'm on a stealing, rampaging expedition. I drive to the store impulsively, buy all my binge foods, start eating in the car, and keep going when I get home. I don't stop until I've made my way through everything I've bought. Then when I'm finished—and after I've awakened from my stupor—I get into a rage with myself for being so bad . . . so disgusting . . . so dreadful. After I've said everything I can possibly say that's awful about myself, I feel purged and ready to go straight, to give up my piracy and begin 'clean living' again. Your approach means giving all of that up—giving up my looting, giving up all my awful accusations, and giving up my oaths to live a good, clean life. That's an enormous loss for me. I *want* to feel wild and 'bad!' And then I want to feel purged."

Grace continued. "If I calmly tell myself that I'm going to eat from mouth hunger and not even yell at myself for doing it, what's the point?" she demanded. "I've tried it and I actually feel a little ridiculous doing it. I go to the kitchen, where, incidentally, I now keep twice as much of any binge food as I could possibly consume in one night of the worst kind of binging. No more jumping in the car, no more stealth—it's all right there. Then I take out exactly what I want. I even put the ice cream in a dish the other night instead of eating right out of the container. What a joke! It's like slow motion. I feel like I'm walking through water or something. Last night, halfway through an assortment of goodies, I put everything away and went back to the living room. Do you know the song 'Is That All There Is'?"

Grace is definitely on target about how difficult it is to give yourself full permission to eat from mouth hunger. Without the sense of illegality and self-loathing, mouth hunger loses its bite. The piracy metaphor that Grace used is well taken. No one runs for carrot sticks to satisfy mouth hunger. Even experienced nondieters have to "delegalize" certain foods at moments of mouth hunger in order to make them "special enough" to offer comfort and "forbidden" enough to merit punishment.

Beyond the Obstacles: Full Permission

Someone in a workshop once said, "Eating from mouth hunger and then yelling at yourself about it is like taking an incredibly negative vacation. The point of it is to get away from it all. Speaking gently and calmly to yourself as you eat chocolate that you have fully legalized makes it impossible for you to escape your troubles in this way. The more compassionate you are with yourself about eating in response to mouth hunger, the sooner you become aware of what is troubling you."

It is important to understand that giving yourself full permission to eat in response to mouth hunger strikes at the heart of the ritual of compulsive eating. You eat to soothe yourself; then you yell at yourself for eating in order to lose yourself in self-reproach. If the idea of calmly and compassionately watching yourself eat at the very same time that you want to lose yourself in self-reproach sounds like a contradiction, it is. And that is precisely why it is so difficult to do.

As you attempt to be gentle with yourself when you eat from mouth hunger, you can count on losing your patience from time to time. Remember, however, that even when you feel unable to confront what is upsetting you without the buffer of food, you can still recognize that you are in trouble—and you can offer yourself support. Janet, in New York, put it well when she said, "If you are coping with a difficult feeling, you have two opportunities to be a good caretaker to yourself. The first opportunity comes the moment the feeling strikes. But, if you can't deal with what you're feeling and need to eat something, you can take care of yourself later by being sympathetic rather than reproachful."

Whenever you are having a lot of mouth hunger, you need to reinforce your support systems by doing any or all of the following:

- Bring in supplies to remind yourself that all foods are legal.
- Make sure that you are wearing comfortable clothing that you really like.
- Remind yourself that mouth hunger eating will diminish the more accepting you are of its presence.
- Keep careful track of how you are talking to yourself. Are you being as loving, patient, and gentle as you can possibly be? Your mouth hunger is a sign that your caretaker was not up to the task of soothing you. You need to summon her back to work.

As you become more sophisticated in this approach, you will undoubtedly notice that when you unconsciously cut back on your supportive activities, mouth hunger often follows. Conversely, mouth hunger is usually diminished when your cupboards are bulging, you have a plentiful food bag by your side, you are wearing comfortable clothing, and you are talking to yourself gently.

Even knowing this, however, from time to time you will find yourself slipping, cutting back on your supportive activities and eating more from mouth hunger. Do not be shocked or dispirited. *Slipping is part of the process.* As much as we all want to change, it is also part of our human nature to resist change. Painful as it may be, it is often easier to stay lost in food than to examine disturbing feelings.

Stage 2: Naming Your Problem

Once you have gotten the hang of giving yourself full permission to eat in response to mouth hunger, you are ready to greet your mouth hunger with a new response: naming the feelings and thoughts that trigger it.

As we have said, knowing what is bothering you may not stop your mouth hunger, but it is a step toward its eventual resolution. If you do not know what is prompting you to eat at a specific moment, promise yourself that at some point after you have eaten—possibly hours or even a day later—you will look back and try to identify what was disturbing you.

Think back to the situation you were in when your mouth hunger struck. What might have been troubling you at the time? The trigger for your eating is not always complex, so pay attention to the first thought, image, or feeling that occurs to you, even if it seems trivial. You do not need to *do* anything about the feeling or disturbance you uncover. For now, it is enough to know its name.

As you investigate what triggered your mouth hunger, you need to appreciate that "naming," like giving yourself full permission, can be a difficult process because it runs counter to the purpose of compulsive eating. Compulsive eating is a method of soothing, but it is also a method of disguising the truth under the all-purpose label *fat.*

The Obstacles to Giving your Problem a Name

You know by now that you are not alone in your efforts to hide many of your problems under the generic heading of "eating and weight." There is tremendous cultural pressure to eat less and lose weight rather than focus on the real problems that confront us—real problems none of us are supposed to have. According to the media barrage, if we would only eat right and exercise, we would all live happily ever after in disease-free families with two parents, two children, and plenty of money. The fact is, we all have lots of problems. Everyone grapples with stressful situations and unpleasant feelings, and we all confront dangers, both real and imagined.

As we grow older, presumably we learn to cope with our problems more successfully than we did as children. Unfortunately, however, we are not always able to distinguish between our adult selves and our more vulnerable child selves. When we feel more vulnerable—more childlike—we attempt to protect ourselves from the problems that frighten us by reaching for food. The more we feel unable to cope, the more likely we are to attempt to sidestep our problems by translating them all into the single issue of food/weight. As one woman in a Texas workshop said, "It's a lot easier to have a food problem than a personal problem."

Giving up the disguise

Earlier, when we discussed legalizing, we used the example of Martha, who had an erotic fantasy about an attractive stranger while she was at a party with her husband. As the party progressed, Martha could not stop eating and later berated herself for being so out of control with food. It was easier for her to think about having eaten forbidden food than it was for her to think about her forbidden fantasies.

Now we must try to understand why Martha was unable to name her problem correctly. Why couldn't she look at what was happening and say, "I'm anxious right now because this fantasy I'm having feels forbidden"? Even if she still felt too anxious to do anything but eat, why couldn't she have said later, "I ate because I felt frightened by feeling turned on to that man"? Why did Martha say instead, "It's disgusting that I ate so much"?

The answer is familiar to all of us. Do you remember ever hiding your eyes during the scary part of a movie? (Maybe you still do.) Do you remember ever wetting your pants, long after you were toilet-trained, then pretending it hadn't happened, hoping against hope that no grown-ups would notice? What about when your mom or dad began drinking, but no one said anything about the rages that followed? Or the time when your latest heartthrob moved on to someone else and you told yourself that you never liked him or her that much anyway? Or the time when . . .

We all try to disguise or deny what is happening to us when we feel that we cannot handle or tolerate the consequences. We fear that we will be overwhelmed with fear, guilt, shame, depression, and/or helplessness. In the example above, Martha felt both frightened by her feelings of attraction and guilty about having them. Rather than confront these feelings as a problem-solving, compassionate adult, however, Martha ate. She never gave herself the chance to distinguish between deeds and thoughts or feelings, to recognize that whatever fantasy she entertained about that man would have no impact anywhere except inside her own head. She had not, after all, hurt anyone.

Martha's inability to distinguish between thoughts and

deeds—and the harsh judgments with which she greets her thoughts—are a relic from her childhood. *Some* children are taught that thoughts are equivalent to deeds, but *all* young children feel that their thoughts and wishes are very powerful. Martha knows that no one can read her mind and that she will not actually be punished for her thoughts. She fears, however, and rightly so, that she will punish herself for being attracted to another man. To avoid her own moralistic self-reproaches, she eats and ends up punishing herself for that. The "sin" of eating has a well-known atonement—it can be dieted (absolved) away.

Anne Marie told the following story about disguising the truth from herself. "I had dinner out with a friend the other night and when I got home, I wanted to eat. Before I knew what was happening, I was eating ice cream, so I just went with it and concentrated on not yelling at myself. The next day I tried to think about what could've upset me. I really struggled with it, because on the surface, nothing extraordinary had happened at dinner. It finally dawned on me that I must've been feeling uncomfortable while my friend was detailing the latest crisis in her relationship. She's always in a crisis with her lover and I bend over backwards to be supportive, but I guess that the discussions are very reminiscent of my childhood. My mother constantly complained to me about my father, but she could never make up her mind to leave him. I think I was enraged at my mother for dumping on me like that, but I never spoke up or even allowed myself to know that I was angry. I don't actually feel burdened by these conversations with my friend, but evidently they stir up old angry feelings that I judge as unsympathetic or disloyal. To tell the truth, now that I'm talking about it, I think I was also feeling envious of my friend—at least she has someone to complain about. No wonder I was eating!"

Telling the truth isn't easy

Truth-telling, which is the key to living without mouth hunger, is complex. In order to let yourself know the truth about what *really* propels your eating, you must be clear about two areas.

First, you must be clearly committed to a new kind of independent thinking that requires reevaluating much of what you have learned in your life. Now that you have had some experience questioning your firmly entrenched ideas about food, dieting, and weight, it is time for you to move on and question the more general rules you have internalized about what is good, what is bad, what is right, and what is wrong. Knee-jerk, judgmental responses to your feelings and thoughts give rise to mouth hunger—and it is time to rid yourself of them. We will be discussing this issue extensively throughout this section of the book.

Second, now that you have some experience in responding compassionately when you eat from mouth hunger, it is equally important that you make a firm promise to treat yourself with compassion as you face your inner issues. The truth is not nearly as frightening when you do not have to worry about condemning yourself for it. If Martha had had a more relaxed and compassionate attitude toward herself, she would not have had to disguise her feelings from herself. In the next chapter, we will discuss the skills required for this kind of self-caretaking in detail. That discussion begins, however, with the next stage in handling mouth hunger.

Stage 3: "Sitting as Two" Rather Than One

Let us say that you have been using our approach for a while. Your stomach hunger experiences have been building; you have not been yelling at yourself about eating; you have been naming your feelings; and you have been trying to intercept your bad body thoughts. What happens next?

At some point you have an impulse to eat, but you realize that you are not hungry. You ask yourself if you can wait for stomach hunger and are surprised by your response. Rather than a clear yes or no, you sense a maybe. What do you do with *that*? Consider the experience of a woman in our New York workshop.

"I wanted to eat," Anne said, "but I knew very well that I was agitated, not hungry. I had just gotten off the phone with an old friend of mine. She and I have been arguing a lot recently. I caught myself halfway between the phone and the refrigerator and began to talk to myself. 'Let's go sit on the couch for a while,' I said. I thought if I could just sit there, my mouth hunger might pass. I was interested to see what would happen. Lo and behold, after about five minutes I felt much calmer and I no longer felt like eating."

Anne was able to "live through" her agitation without turning to food because she had accumulated many, many experiences of feeding herself in response to stomach hunger. The end result of all of those experiences was her realization that she might actually be able to sit for a while and watch her agitation pass.

Think, for a moment, about the way Anne talked to herself when she felt mouth hunger. She actually said, "Let's go sit on the couch," as though she were engaged in a dialogue: *Let's* means *let us.* Anne was not alone with her agitation. She had the company of a gentle and patient caretaker. We describe this process that Anne discovered as "sitting as two" rather than one.

Often, when you reach for food to help yourself out of a difficult moment, you are trying to become more than yourself. In other words, you are adding something—food—to yourself in order to cope. Think of eating from mouth hunger as an attempt to become bigger or more substantial in order to handle whatever is happening within you at that moment.

Of course, when we eat from mouth hunger, we are not simply adding to our bulk. As we know, food is highly symbolic for all of us. It stands for mother, love, comfort. When we run to it, we are, in effect, attempting to run home, to go back to a time when we felt part of a unit rather than on our own. We want to become more than our solitary selves.

Eating in response to mouth hunger is like holding a rabbit's foot for luck or dancing a ritual dance. We hope that by putting the food inside of us, we will gain power and strength. When we have jokingly suggested that, rather than turn to food, we all carry magic charms and touch them whenever we are anxious, our workshop participants have been quick to tell us that charms and amulets simply do not do the trick. They are, of course, correct. Food and eating are so embedded in our earliest experiences of being cared for that they carry a particular power and emotional charge.

Anne was able to "sit as two" rather than one because she had reparented herself by feeding herself on demand. She now possessed the internal magic of having cared for herself; she had that warmth and comfort inside her head and heart.

Perhaps Anne's new efforts to address her eating and her body differently had rekindled a lost sense of security. Or, perhaps she was giving herself a kind of support that had been missing earlier in her life. In either case, Anne was now present for herself in a new way. She was attached to herself and, at least during this particular experience of mouth hunger, that attachment was more effective than attaching herself to food.

One woman in a Virginia workshop said, "Eating food when your body doesn't want it is like being attached to something that's not attached to you." By this she meant that, when she was in trouble, she went to an inanimate object—food—because she could not turn to herself or anyone else. "Sitting as two," on the other hand, means sitting with yourself, providing comfort, soothing, reassurance, and problem solving. Sometimes, you can simply hold yourself or sit quietly as you watch your feelings wax and wane; other times you may want to think through what is distressing you and see if you can come up with a new perspective or solution.

You do not need food when you have yourself. Moving from food to yourself, however, is not without its challenges.

The Obstacles to "Sitting as Two"

Becoming accustomed to depending on food

As with all aspects of curing compulsive eating, "sitting as two" has a built-in contradiction that inspires resistance. You have spent years running to food because you felt you needed outside support. (Remember that food has been the habitual stand-in for your missing internal caretaker.) When you are able to sit and think about a problem rather than eat about it, you are demonstrating to yourself (and to anyone else who might notice) that you feel considerably more capable than you did before. In other words, you no longer need to disguise the truth from yourself or make yourself bigger to handle a difficult feeling. You have created a caretaker within yourself who is quite capable and who, as a result, encourages you to tell the truth. The paradox, however, is that while being able to nurture yourself in this way feels good, it can also heighten your feelings of loss.

Karen, a participant in San Francisco, reported that she feels strange when she is able to sit with herself and watch her feelings go by. "I don't quite know myself," she said. "After a few days in which I experience mouth hunger but don't need to eat, I get edgy. I've been eating mostly from mouth hunger for twenty years. Who is this person who doesn't need food in that way? When I stop eating from mouth hunger," Karen continued,

"I feel like I'm agreeing to be normal and something about that doesn't sit well with me. I feel like I'm losing out on something."

Unfortunately, Karen doesn't just stop there. "What often happens is, after I've noticed how 'well' I'm doing, I sabotage myself and start eating from mouth hunger again. I don't yell about it, so my mouth hunger only lasts for a few days and then disappears, but it has become a definite pattern."

Karen's experience is not at all unusual. Why do many of us get frightened or disturbed when we realize that we can provide for ourselves without using food? There are a number of possible reasons for this kind of reaction, which we will discuss in subsequent chapters. For now, however, let's consider just one of them: Karen's reluctance to be what she would call "normal."

Wishing for an outside caretaker

Compulsive eaters like Karen often consider themselves to be self-sufficient. They do not see themselves as needing a lot from other people. Their eating, however, tells a different story.

When you are not hungry but reach for food, you are doing so because you need help. Compulsive eaters are people who chronically reach for help from food rather than from other people. It is important to keep in mind that, even though food may be a symbol of the early caretaking you received, it is not an effective stand-in for a real confidante.

When you eat in response to mouth hunger, you may well be making a statement that you need a lot, but that you are forced to fulfill your needs as best you can by yourself. Taking care of yourself by eating may allow you to feel self-sufficient but, deep down, you may resent always having to take care of yourself.

If someone asked you, as you were eating, why you felt that eating was your only alternative, what would you say? If you were to answer honestly, you might respond with resignation or resentment. "That's just how it is. Who else is going to do anything for me?"

There are, of course, a host of understandable and upsetting reasons why you have come to rely more on food than other kinds of care. It is important to recognize, however, that, although eating compulsively has been your way of taking care of yourself, you have also probably resented it. When, like Karen, you discover that you can sit with yourself and watch your feelings go by, it is a sign that you—and not the circumstances of your life—have changed. No one has come along and made up for all of the things that may have been lacking in your life. Yet you no longer need to turn to food. You have become your own best caretaker and, as a result, you now feel sufficiently well nourished to be able to weather your feelings without eating.

The day you can say, "Maybe I can wait," is a great day. On that day, however, *you are also acknowledging that you are no longer waiting for someone else to care for you.*

Hopefully, there will be many people in your life with whom you can share your feelings and on whom you can depend, once you have provided some basic kinds of care for yourself. It is understandable, however, that you may feel somewhat ambivalent about having to become so responsible to yourself. As one woman in a workshop said, "It's a lot of responsibility taking care of yourself. I'd rather give the responsibility to ice cream!"

Stage 4: Facing the Issues That Prompt You to Eat

Throughout this chapter we have stressed the fact that as you accumulate experiences of feeding your stomach hunger, your mouth hunger will eventually fade. As your mouth hunger becomes less intense, you can use the techniques we have been discussing to facilitate the process of turning to yourself rather than to food.

As you work with our approach, your goal is to get to a point where it does not occur to you to eat unless you are physiologically hungry. However, many of you have told us that although you reach a point where you no longer experience much mouth hunger, it still lingers, particularly in certain situations or in response to certain feelings. Somehow, no amount of cajoling seems to get you over the hump at these times.

Workshop participants have summarized the problem this way:

"You say that mouth hunger will just decrease and then disappear. But it doesn't happen that way. It decreases, and decreases, and decreases—but it never seems to disappear. At certain times, it is not only present but *tenacious.*

"It is true that the more I eat out of stomach hunger, the less mouth hunger I have. The more self-caretaking I do—stocking the house, carrying the food bag, wearing comfortable clothes, intercepting bad body thoughts, working with the mirror—the less mouth hunger I have. And, if I have more mouth hunger than usual, and I increase my vigilance about stocking the kitchen, not yelling at myself, and all the rest, my mouth hunger subsides . . . *until* a certain feeling or situation starts everything rolling again. It seems as if there are always going to be certain issues that I need to camouflage with food."

The principle that mouth hunger fades as you become a better and better demand feeder does seem to have an outer limit. Once you reach that limit, you need to face the issues that trigger your mouth hunger more directly.

We do not count ourselves among those who urge you to take a bubble bath when you feel bad. Sometimes it is possible to resolve an unpleasant feeling by changing your activity or your locale. Often, however, when you feel distressed about something, you simply feel too bad to distract yourself. What do you do when you have the kind of bad feeling from which you cannot be distracted? We are convinced that there are some feelings about which there is nothing to do. Some bad feelings simply need to be felt. Only after you begin to feel them will you be able to find enough inner comfort to address them.

It has become clear to us that, in order to fully extinguish mouth hunger, you must be able to supply yourself with the help that you once sought from food. In other words, if you are going to tell the truth about your concerns and feelings, you must be certain that you can handle it.

In order to deal more directly with the issues that trouble you, you will need to understand more about the dynamics of mouth hunger. What have you been running *from* when you have run toward food? As we answer this question in the next chapter, hopefully you will become clearer about how to become a better caretaker of yourself.

Chapter

12

TAKING OVER FROM FOOD: BECOMING A SELF-CARETAKER

LET'S ASSUME THAT YOU HAVE REACHED A POINT AT WHICH YOU ARE eating more and more in response to stomach hunger and less and less in response to mouth hunger. Let's also assume that you are no longer yelling at yourself about how you eat or the way you look and that you are dressing comfortably. Because of these changes, the quality of your life has improved considerably. Of course, you do still experience mouth hunger. Sometimes you eat in response to that mouth hunger without yelling at yourself about it, and sometimes you ride it out without reaching for food. On the whole, food and bad body thoughts are no longer uppermost in your mind the way they were for most of your life. You feel better, more energized . . . And you find yourself wondering, what next?

The next step in our approach is a difficult one. At this point, we suggest that you actually confront the feelings that trigger your mouth hunger and explore them with the help and support of your inner caretaker.

WHY BOTHER?

Before we discuss how you can learn to cope with the feelings you have avoided for so long, it is reasonable for you to ask why you need to do this at all. After all, you are feeling good. Yes, you have mouth hunger, but is that such a problem? What's wrong with just continuing to do what you've been doing? Why investigate your mouth hunger any further? Why open what might be a Pandora's box? Why not leave well enough alone?

We are continually amazed by the courage of the women in our groups who are willing to lift the lid on the feelings that prompt their mouth hunger, even though it is frightening for them to do so. What compels them to push on? This is what one of them said.

"I recognized that confronting the feelings that triggered my mouth hunger was something I had to do to conquer mouth hunger once and for all," said Dorothea in a Dallas workshop. "At first, I wanted to get rid of my mouth hunger because I knew it was the only way I'd ever lose weight. But I realized that I was just playing games with myself. I know very well that as soon as I make weight loss a goal, I'm as doomed to failure as I was back in my diet days."

Dorothea is right. If you think about working on your mouth hunger because you want to lose weight, you are back in a diet mode and, sooner or later, you will rebel.

"What it came down to for me," Dorothea continued, "was that I just hate feeling *hooked*, which is how I've always felt about my relationship to food. When I first read *Overcoming Overeating*, the idea that I could get to a point where I wouldn't think about food unless I was hungry—well, I'd give anything to have that freedom."

This question of why bother to work so hard at understanding the feelings behind mouth hunger was the primary topic of discussion one evening in our New York workshop. Sasha began.

"You know," she said, "sometimes I get sick of asking myself why I've had an episode of mouth hunger. My weight is not what I'd want ideally, but I'm living with it just fine. I'm sure that even normal people occasionally eat when they're not hungry. On the whole, my eating is so radically different from anything I could ever have imagined, it makes me wonder why I need to make so much more work for myself?"

Another participant, Wendy, responded. "I keep trying to understand my mouth hunger because the fact that it's there at all tells me that I'm out of touch with something about myself.

On the surface, my food intake is out of synch with my hunger, but I know that mouth hunger involves a more important kind of being out of touch. That's what makes me probe. I think of eating from mouth hunger as 'leaning on food.' I don't get angry with myself anymore for needing to lean on something, but I'd much rather figure out *why* I need to lean at all, so that, someday, I'll be able to stand up on my own."

Wendy's comments triggered a response from Elinor. "I've been struck by the idea that I'm a mystery to myself," she said. "Last week, I told you that I had been eating a lot from mouth hunger but didn't know why. You helped me figure out that I was anxious about a business trip I'm about to take. It hadn't occurred to me that this trip was more meaningful to me than other trips I'd taken. Our discussion made me realize that a lot goes on inside of me that I don't pay much attention to. I don't want to hide from myself like that anymore."

"I have a similar feeling," said Shira. "When I funnel everything through food, my life becomes very narrow. The less mouth hunger I have, the wider and more open everything is. I'm not as afraid of my mouth hunger now because I see it as a route to getting in touch with myself in a deeper way. I learn from it."

By this time, everyone in the group was eager to talk. "I've actually reached a point where I feel kind of silly eating from mouth hunger," said Rebecca. "I want to figure out what my mouth hunger is about so I can provide for myself in ways that are really effective."

In one way or another, each person in the group that evening alluded to the rewards of facing the feelings that trigger mouth hunger head-on. What are those rewards? Rebecca summed it up by saying, "Working on mouth hunger is about learning who you are and getting your life back."

The women in this group share our conviction that compulsive eating is a detour, a way of sidestepping thoughts and feelings, that costs us dearly. Not only are we miserable living "in translation"—suffering from what we think are food and weight problems—but we also keep ourselves from growing emotionally.

We have said that mouth hunger is our response to anxiety and that anxiety is a signal of danger. *What dangers does your mouth hunger signal?* Although specific answers to this question vary from person to person, there are enough similarities to talk in general terms about the roots of our anxiety.

The Roots of Our Anxiety

Marcia, a woman in an advanced workshop, told us of a recent encounter with mouth hunger that she handled with humor.

"I started feeling extremely anxious at work the other day," Marcia said, "and I really wanted to eat. At the same time, I could tell that I didn't absolutely have to eat, so I decided to have a little talk with myself instead.

" 'Okay,' I said, 'you have a deadline and it's making you tense. But a deadline doesn't mean that you'll be dead if you don't meet it. Your client may get angry if you miss the deadline; you might even lose the account; and, if you keep missing deadlines, you may end up losing your job. If you never find another job, I suppose you could end up alone and poor—but that's the worst of it! You still won't be dead!' "

Everyone laughed in response to Marcia's anecdote. We laughed because we all identified with this common experience of bringing an extreme level of panic to an issue that, clearly, was not life-threatening. Why do we experience things as life-or-death issues when they are not? Where does this inappropriate level of anxiety originate?

Marcia responded to a work deadline as though her life actually depended on it. She found relief from her anxiety by reminding herself that her life, in fact, was not at stake. Why the overreaction? For most of us, death is our most elemental fear. There are many things, however, that can feel like mini-deaths to us on the continuum of fears. We fear losing the people we love, we fear losing our physical well-being, we fear losing love, and we fear losing our self-esteem.

These fears are part of the human condition and stem from one of the distinguishing characteristics of human development: the fact that children are completely dependent on their parents for survival for a very long time. For an infant, the loss of the people on whom she depends *is* tantamount to death. Although Marcia knew that she would not die, her soliloquy reflected this early concern about being separated from parents or caretakers.

She imagined herself severed from her job/parent, her source of financial support.

As children get older, the fear of actually losing their parents changes into a fear of losing their parent's love. "What if I am *bad*?" they wonder. "What if I disappoint my parents? Will I be punished? Will I be hurt? Will I be cast out?" Marcia's anxiety about disappointing her clients was related to this fear of loss of love. She worried that if her clients were not happy with her, they would leave her. Would anyone else "love" her enough to hire her? Her panic mounts. If no one else hires her, will she end up on the streets, alone and unloved?

The good news is that Marcia was able to maintain enough distance from her panic to keep some perspective . . . and to not eat. But we can see from her story that even though Marcia is no longer a dependent child, the fear of losing love and being deserted continues to fuel her anxiety. These childhood fears haunt all of us as adults. On a rational level we may recognize that if one person doesn't love us, someone else will; if one job doesn't work out, another one may be better. But on an emotional level, we often forget that we are no longer entirely dependent creatures. When that happens, we respond with a disproportionate amount of fear. We panic and become overwhelmed by anxiety—and if we are compulsive eaters, we reach for food.

Unfortunately, even if we do not feel dependent on our parents (or our partners) for our survival, we can still panic at the prospect of falling short of ideals and standards. At some point in development, our parents no longer need to tell us what to do; we have internalized all their rules. We pick up where our parents left off and continue to talk to ourselves about whether we are "good" or "bad." Just as we once worried about being punished by our parents for not meeting their standards, now we worry that we will punish ourselves for falling short of the expectations we have internalized. When we punish ourselves, we feel shame and guilt—and we feel like reaching for food.

How did Marcia manage to get through her anxiety without eating? When she decided to talk to herself rather than to eat, she let herself know, in a humorous and loving way, that whatever transpired, she would not abandon herself. Even if everyone else in the world left her, she assured herself, she would continue to love herself. This kind of assurance—this unconditional self-love—is the key to learning to handle anxiety without reaching for food.

All of us eat from mouth hunger in an effort to sidestep the fear of loss that is so deeply rooted in childhood: loss of life, loss of love, and loss of self-esteem. In particular, you may fear being alone and abandoned; you may fear being punished or scorned; or you may fear feelings of shame or guilt. But although these fears each present themselves differently, they all reach back to our childhoods and they are all about loss. Our greatest fear, after that of bodily harm or actual death, however, is the loss of self-love. Without it, we are unbearably alone.

Feelings we have as adults often trigger this primal childhood fear of loss. As adults, we are likely to turn to food when some feeling or thought in the present has resonated with some feeling, thought, or event that caused us anxiety when we were children. When that happens, we respond to our feelings with an intensity that has more to do with the past than with the present.

Suppose, for example, that you feel very envious of a colleague. Rather than simply experience your envious feelings in a straightforward manner, something about the feelings makes you so uncomfortable that you find yourself reaching for food.

Why does your envy trigger such intense anxiety? Because something in your past, which you associate with the envy you are experiencing right now, was very frightening to you. Perhaps, as a child, you wanted to be rid of your baby sister so that you could occupy her enviable position. The intensity of your "bad" wishes frightened you. Children have a difficult time differentiating between what occurs in their minds and what is real and they often fear being punished for their "bad" wishes and thoughts. Today, when you envy a colleague, you may feel more like the frightened little girl you once were than the professional adult you actually are.

What is the reality of your current fear of envy? The woman you envy probably has no idea what you are feeling, and even if she knew you were envious of her, she might be flattered rather than threatened or angry. After all, we generally envy people we admire. It is conceivable, of course, that this particular woman might feel uncomfortable with your envy and in response, opt to keep some distance from you. The distance she would create, however, probably would be something you could live with and in no way would reflect how the next person you envy will react.

Unfortunately, you do not give yourself the opportunity to think about how this woman might react to your feelings of envy. You reach for food and avoid these feelings and thoughts altogether. But in reaching for food, you also become judge, jury, and defendant. You find yourself guilty of a crime you believe you committed a long time ago. In colonial times criminals were punished by having hundreds of pounds of stones piled upon their chests until they were crushed to death. You are somewhat kinder as you force yourself to bear up under a heavy burden of food-induced guilt and shame.

What are your alternatives? To begin with, you might look your envy in the face and reevaluate it. As a child, you were convinced that wishing could make it so and that your sister might indeed disappear. As you look at it now, is your envy really so dangerous and reprehensible? Can you live with it and, perhaps, use your envy as a guide to what you might like for yourself?

We understand that it is extremely difficult to make the transition from thinking in terms of your past to thinking in terms of your present. At this point, your reactions are on automatic pilot. Learning to intervene and take control requires expertise. And that expertise can come from the caretaker within yourself.

The first job of this caretaker is to bring you into the present where you can realistically reevaluate the dangers that your mouth hunger signals. Are you really going to get into trouble if you let yourself know what you are feeling or thinking? And if you do get in trouble, will you be there to help yourself through it? In the past, food has been your talisman to ward off danger. In the future, being a good self-caretaker will prove much more effective.

Think about it. If you could develop an inner caretaker who would continue to care about you no matter what, how would that affect your anxiety? Imagine it. She would *never* abandon you. She would be there for you, no matter what happens and no matter what anyone else thinks. Her arms would be strong enough to hold you and she would be capable of helping you deal with your feelings. The great advantage to being a grown-up is that you really can develop the capacity to take care of yourself.

From Food-Reliance to Self-Reliance

Let's assume for the moment that you want to rid yourself of your reliance on food and hire yourself to care for yourself. What qualities would be required for the job? What qualities would be most necessary in a caretaker whose job it is to help you learn to sit with feelings that, until now, have been too threatening? What qualities would help you feel that you are on firm, safe ground? We recognize that you deserve the very best care you can get. Think about what qualities are necessary to guarantee that kind of care.

More than anything else, in order to take proper care of yourself you need to develop compassion, patience, and understanding. These three qualities come under the heading of *unconditional self-love.* Lacking this kind of unconditional self-love, you used to worry that you would do or think something that would make you feel ashamed or guilty. Your worry was not unfounded. When you are under the control of a stern, withholding, judgmental caretaker, it is reasonable to feel like you are walking on eggs. Once you can trust that you will be there for yourself, no matter what, you no longer have to worry about where you put your foot down.

A self-caretaker also needs *courage to feel deeply and to become an independent thinker.* If you have worried about being overwhelmed by your feelings, you need to know that with the support of an inner caretaker, you will be stronger and more able to weather your storms. If you have felt troubled by guilt and shame, you need to know that, not only will you never condemn yourself, but you will reevaluate the "rules" by which you have struggled to live. Remember, a courageous caretaker always asks, "Who says?"

Finally, a caretaker needs to be a patient and *creative problem-solver* who knows when to work and when to let go. In order to confront the "dangerous" feelings that you have been avoiding by eating, you need to demonstrate to yourself that you can think through situations; you need to prove to yourself that you are committed to working on the problems that distress you for as long as is necessary.

Let us examine each of these qualities in more depth.

Unconditional Love

Ella Sharpe, a British psychoanalyst, wrote that the patient in psychoanalysis must "externalize in thought and feeling the inner drama." In order to facilitate this process, the analyst, with great tolerance and a lack of anxiety, welcomes all the characters in a patient's play onto the analytic stage. To begin working on the problem of learning to calm yourself, you must adopt a similar nonjudgmental stance. You need to find a way to welcome all of the characteristics that combine to make you who you are.

The truth is, no one has an easy time confronting each and every aspect of themselves. We all have internalized family and cultural beliefs about how we should feel, think, and behave, and we all fall significantly short of these ideals. Aware of it or not, we all yearn for a wise, kindly person to embrace us with a soft smile and open arms. Instead, our stern internal caretakers stand, watching, with their hands folded across their chests, shaking their heads from side to side, tsk-tsking with disapproval. Of course, we shrink away in fear, preferring to hide. Without those wide open, loving arms, it is impossible to face the truth about who we are, and until we face that truth, we will remain captives of our mouth hunger.

The kind of unconditional self-love we promote is very much like the profile of the accepting parent typically described in parenting books. As parents, we are urged to focus any disapproving comments on our children's behavior rather than on their character. "It makes me angry when I ask you to clean up your room and you ignore my wishes" is different than "You're such a slob!" The first message conveys your feelings about a particular behavior; the second makes a sweepingly destructive generalization about the child's core being.

As you attempt to develop an accepting, unconditionally loving stance within yourself, it is helpful to keep in mind that there is a difference between *accepting* your thoughts and feelings and *liking* them. We are not advising you to tell yourself that you like those characteristics about yourself that you do not really like. Accepting yourself means that you are willing to stop condemning yourself, lay down your weapons, and welcome yourself in all of your unevenness. Unconditional love means trusting that what you feel, think, or do has validity even when you don't immediately understand your feelings, thoughts and actions.

The idea of granting yourself permission to know yourself fully, *without* judgment and *with* love, is a tall order. All of the trips you make to the refrigerator when you are not hungry are testimony to the difficulty you have had establishing a truly accepting internal caretaker. Each trip into the kitchen for food means that something is stirring within you that feels shameful and uncomfortable, something from which you must turn away.

"I don't have nearly as much mouth hunger as I used to," said Lenore in a Denver workshop, "but when it hits, it *hits,* and at that point, I can hardly remember to ask myself if it's my stomach or my mouth that wants food. I just *have* to eat."

The difficulty we have creating a caretaker who accepts us unconditionally is not surprising. Many of us are starting from scratch, without role models. The rules we all learned as children about who we should be and how we should act—which reflect everything *but* unconditional love—continue to have a profound hold on us. Many of us were told that we were loved in spite of our shortcomings, but such declarations were not always convincing. How can a child believe she is loved unconditionally when her mother says "Mama loves you so much *when you're nice* like you were today." Or, "Stop crying—you have no reason to be so upset!"

Earlier in this book we urged you to legalize your body and to legalize food. In the preceding chapter, we urged you to begin legalizing your thoughts, feelings, and actions, whatever they may be. You may not measure up to some abstract ideal—neither yours, nor someone else's—but you still deserve to live with yourself compassionately and patiently.

Consider the example of Nina, a participant in our New York workshop, who has been working at naming her feelings and struggling with developing a genuine sense of self-acceptance.

"Last weekend I was eating up a storm," Nina reported, "and even though I had a general idea about what was upsetting me, it took several days for me to figure out exactly what was going on."

Nina had talked to the group in the past about feeling

closely identified with her younger daughter, who reminded Nina very much of herself as a child. "My older daughter is usually brave and outgoing," Nina explained, "but my little one, Beth, is timid and shy the way I was as a girl."

The day before Nina began eating from mouth hunger, Beth was upset. She told Nina that her best friend had excluded her from a sleep-over party to which she had invited two other girls. "The three other girls were talking about their plans on the playground," Nina said, "and Beth heard the tail end as she approached them. She was heartbroken and incredibly embarrassed and ashamed."

Nina tried to be comforting and loving when she spoke to Beth about the incident and made it a point to let Beth have her upset feelings, but it wasn't easy. "I know that what's important is to let Beth know that we love her deeply regardless of where she stands with friends. But, wow, was it hard for me."

Why was it so difficult for Nina? "I remember being very tuned into who was invited to what party and who had the most friends when I was ten and eleven," Nina said. "I used to lie in bed at night and count the number of friends I had, as if having enough friends proved that I was all right."

Beth's situation transported Nina back into the insecurity of her own childhood. "On the one hand," she explained, "I felt all of the pain of my own childhood in the most immediate sort of way. Plus, I felt that special stab of anguish a mother feels when her child is unhappy."

As the weekend progressed, however, Nina began to believe that there was yet another layer of meaning motivating her eating. She started to understand her reaction more deeply when she told her husband about Beth's experience. He was sorry to hear about his daughter's unhappiness, but, much to Nina's surprise, it did not affect him in the intense sort of way it had affected her.

"My husband thinks that Beth is absolutely wonderful and he's confident that she'll overcome her shyness and be just fine. He had a few good suggestions about how we might help Beth by talking openly about how friendships happen and work, but the whole situation didn't alarm him the way it alarmed me. Obviously," said Nina, "my husband doesn't equate worth with social acceptability. He thinks that Beth's problem is that she gets hooked on one person and that, when she learns to be comfortable with a variety of people, she'll have all the social life she wants."

Nina's talk with her husband was revealing on a number of levels. First, the fact that he did not have the same kind of emotional response to the situation that she had underscored how much Nina identified with her daughter. Beyond that, Nina found it comforting to see that her husband did not think there was anything really "wrong" with their daughter.

As Nina was talking with her husband, she was startled by the realization that she actually had felt that there was something wrong with Beth. "It was very painful for me to face it," Nina said, "but a part of me really believed that those girls must have excluded her for a good reason. Maybe she was unpleasant to be around. Even though I was loathe to admit it, I felt disappointed in Beth for being unpopular," Nina said, "and that made me align with the girls who had hurt her."

Long ago, whenever Nina felt excluded by her peers, she assumed something was wrong with her. Now, she caught herself making the same assumption about her daughter. "No wonder I kept eating!" Nina said. "I couldn't bear to watch myself reject my own child." Everyone in the group was quiet when Nina added, "And I couldn't bear to think about how disappointed my own mother must have felt in me when I was excluded by friends."

Nina had reached a point at which she was willing to be gentle with herself about her eating. This time, however, she was able to go beyond that gentleness and both confront and accept parts of herself that she did not like. She did not like the hostile feelings she had felt toward her own daughter, but she understood their origins and allowed herself to have them.

Learning to welcome your feelings is not very different from learning to handle your bad body thoughts, which required that you stop the self-abuse and learn to accept those parts of your body you had previously condemned. Now the time has come to accept *all* your thoughts and feelings in the very same way.

The Courage to Feel Deeply

Most of us are creatures of habit. As a rule, we like things the way they are, simply because that is the way they always have been. Even if we are not happy with things the way they are, it sometimes seems easier to live with that unhappiness than to tolerate the jarring process of change.

Compulsive eaters, who have spent years eating to avoid the intensity of their deepest feelings, need to summon up a great deal of courage when they attempt to confront those feelings in a head-on way. Nina, for example, was frightened by the very strong, negative feelings she had felt toward her daughter.

One of the reasons these feelings were so frightening is that they had been bottled up for so long. Feelings always fester and become more intense when we stifle them with food. Ultimately, Nina had the courage to face the fact that, on some level, she felt aligned with the very people who had made Beth feel so excluded.

In order to give yourself permission to discover what is prompting your mouth hunger, you need to reassure yourself that no matter how "bad" a feeling is, it is *only* a feeling. Most of us learned early that certain feelings should always be avoided or modified. "Don't feel so bad," we were told. "It's nothing. Have a dish of ice cream." The truth is, we can survive any feeling *as long as we allow ourselves to experience it without judging it.* In order to learn what is prompting your mouth hunger, you need to develop a reassuring inner voice that says, "Feelings are feelings; they may feel forever and unbearable, but they always pass and you will survive them."

The Courage to Think Independently

In addition to providing us with the courage to feel deeply, a good caretaker must also offer us the courage to think independently. Nina, having reached a point at which she could acknowledge her disappointment in her daughter's lack of popularity, needed to move on and question her ideas about the importance of popularity. She also needed to question her ideas about being a good mother.

Nina's husband, who had grown up with an entirely different set of standards, reacted very differently to Beth's situation. His reaction helped Nina recognize how relative her response was and that she had options. Rather than simply pass on to her daughter a set of standards she had learned from her own mother—standards conveyed by worried looks and anxious words—she could rethink the rules she had internalized.

It is true that Nina failed to offer her daughter the kind of genuine support she would have liked to feel, but Nina, like all parents, is nothing more or less than a person who is struggling to do the best she can for her kids. The fact that she was finally able to face the anger she felt toward Beth and forgive herself for it meant that she had created the possibility of feeling differently the next time a situation like this arose. Who says, for example, that parents should *never* have hostile reactions to their children? And who says that we will not make the very same mistakes that our own parents made? Where did Nina get the idea that any parent could always be loving and accepting? Where did she get the idea that parents should be able to overcome their own difficulties at a moment's notice?

Nina's ideas about how parents should behave stem, in part, from promises she made to herself as a little girl—promises about how she would do things differently from her own mother. Her ideas are also shaped by the general ideas she has internalized about "good" behavior, about how she should feel and think to win her parents' love and approval. We are all shaped by these early learnings and values. As adolescents, we challenge many of these lessons by experimenting with new ways of doing things as we venture into the world beyond our immediate families. Early teachings run deep, however, and are difficult to challenge in any lasting way.

From the outside, our lives look very different from those of our parents or grandparents. But if we delve more deeply into our thoughts and feelings, how different are we really? Are we still having trouble with the same "rules" that plagued us as children and that plagued our parents as well? Are we as anxious? As guilty? As unhappy? As frightened? When people go for counseling or psychotherapy, they are often struggling with the rules they acquired as children. They may not be aware of that struggle, but they are aware of its repercussions. They complain of feeling anxious, depressed, or stuck. Underlying these feelings are the tyrannical unconscious rules that make it difficult for them to mourn, love, work, and grow.

To feel free enough to *not* reach for food when you are *not* hungry, you must learn to question. You have already asked many important questions in your efforts to cure your compulsive eating. First you asked, Why should I diet? Then, Why should I lose weight? Now, the time has come to ask:

Who says I should feel one way rather than another way?
What's wrong with thinking this way rather than that way?
Why should I be one way rather than another way?

In her efforts to develop an independent stance, Nina needed to question many of the rules that governed her feelings: Who says that being popular makes you a good person? Who says that I must never have a disloyal feeling? Who says that I must never act like my mother?

Until now, much of your compulsive eating has been a reflex reaction to thoughts or feelings that did not fit your cultural standard. The buzzer sounds *wrong thought . . . wrong feeling . . . unsafe idea . . . bad move.* Usually, you make these judgments unconsciously and notice nothing more than the fact that you are headed for the refrigerator.

When you stop to question whether you must eat from mouth hunger or whether you can wait for stomach hunger, you are really asking yourself if you can stop, look, and listen to your thought or feeling without condemning it. *Can you welcome it instead?*

The more you accumulate experiences of eating from stomach hunger, the more likely you will be able to answer that question in the affirmative. Beyond that, your answer will depend upon what kind of an atmosphere you, with your internal caretaker, have created. How compassionate are you? How independent a thinker have you become? Someone has to jump in there at the moment of mouth hunger with a loud "who says?" Who says I can't handle this thought or feeling? Who says that what I'm feeling or thinking is "bad"? Are my conclusions based on experiences from childhood, or are they based on my adult, independent evaluation?

This notion of becoming an independent thinker is sometimes confused with becoming irresponsible. Where do right and wrong come into it? you may be wondering. As you begin to question your rules and values, you need to remind yourself that, for the most part, you struggle with thoughts and feelings, not actions. There are, of course, laws that govern our responsibility to others. Parents who do not care for their children, for example, are guilty of neglect. But parents who don't spend every moment of their time caring for their children are guilty of nothing. And parents who sometimes feel resentful of the pressures involved in caring for children are guilty of being human.

Peggy, a participant in our New York workshop, addressed these issues one evening.

"I've reached a point where I do most of my eating from stomach hunger," she reported. "But, every night after I put the kids to bed, I have trouble. I know what it is, but I haven't been able to do anything about it.

"The problem is that I have a running list in my head of all the things I need to get done. By the time I tuck my kids into bed, I'm usually exhausted. But rather than just relax and zone out in front of the TV, I always start eating. Sometimes I do some of the things I feel I should be doing, and sometimes I don't—but I *always* eat."

There is no law that says Peggy should work from dawn to midnight—except the one in her head that says something to the effect of "A good person is one who accomplishes a lot each day." Or, "The devil makes work for idle hands."

Where did Peggy's unconscious rule originate? Perhaps she learned it while watching her own mother work with boundless energy. Or she may have developed it in reaction to watching her mother flounder around without ever getting anything done. She might have picked it up in church, or, in a more general way, from the culture around her that prizes productivity above all else. Or maybe Peggy developed the need to work, work, work as a way of avoiding uncomfortable thoughts and feelings.

Whatever its source, Peggy is now stuck with a rule that offers her only two options: work, or eat to avoid feeling guilty about not working. If she wants to find another option, Peggy will need to question the rule that guides her behavior. She will need to ask herself why her need to relax reflects negatively on her value as a person: Is this really a moral issue? Who says that being productive every minute is such a great thing? Am I a bad person if I don't accomplish everything I'd like to accomplish in a day? Can I accept my need to relax without judging it?

Then she has to continue with more questions: Would it be dangerous for me to just sit and watch TV or, for that matter, just to sit? Will I be able to manage it if I begin thinking about something that's troubling to me? And she will have to remind herself that a thought is only a thought. "Even if it makes me anxious," she will need to say, "I can just sit with it and still be safe."

The results of this kind of internal dialoguing are very exciting. All kinds of things began to cross your mind. For example, Peggy began thinking about all of the things that used to give her pleasure. "It occurred to me that I might actually enjoy sitting around and doing nothing in the evenings," she said. "And then I began to think about sex. Maybe my sex life with my husband would improve if I didn't always feel the need to be so busy. I was raised to believe that sex was something a woman tolerated, not that it was something to be enjoyed. I don't think I bought into that until my kids were born. Once the kids came, I began to feel safer with less sex and more work. I think it's time to reexamine some of this," Peggy concluded triumphantly.

Each of us is charged with deciding how we want to live our lives. We cannot make a conscious decision, however, until we make ourselves examine the rules by which we have been living. The chances are, you will accept some of those rules and toss others out. The more you question the rules that govern your thoughts and feelings, the less likely it is that you will continue to eat from mouth hunger.

Solving Problems and Letting Go

Once you have reached the point of confronting your thoughts and feelings and accepting them, without judgment, you are ready to call upon your internal caretaker for help in solving problems. You have busted your old system of thinking wide open and, as a result, you have room for all kinds of new perspectives.

The first step toward solving your problems involves recognizing that not all problems have practical solutions. Sometimes the best solution is acknowledging that some things cannot be changed, that the best solution is to allow yourself to mourn what you have lost or what you never got, and then to move on.

Such was the case for Susan, a participant in our New York workshop. Susan had a very difficult childhood. Both of her parents were alcoholic, and her mother was obsessed with dieting and thinness. "She used to give me skim milk in my bottles," Susan told the group, in an effort to emphasize that she truly had spent her entire life on diets.

Susan has had to struggle with her family legacy in many ways. An alcoholic, like her parents, Susan had managed to give up drinking a few years before joining our group. And recently, she had arrived at the point at which she could begin to look at her bouts with mouth hunger for clues to her emotional life.

Although these accomplishments mean a great deal to Susan, she told the group about ways in which they have left her feeling sad. "For a long time after I stopped dieting, I felt very lonely and depressed," she said. "Finally, I realized that diets and drinking represented my most fundamental tie to my mother. Without them I felt very separate from her, and that was painful. I'd deal with the pain by returning to all of the old bad body thoughts that used to connect us. Now I can't do that anymore, and the more separate I feel from my mother, the more clearly I see her for what she is. That makes me very sad."

As Susan began to confront the feelings behind her mouth hunger, she realized that, more often than not, she was inclined to reach for food whenever she felt a kind of angry churning inside her. After focusing on the feeling, which she associated with being "trapped," she recognized it as something she felt often when she was with her parents. Once she made that association, Susan began to make some headway.

"My whole family came into town last weekend to attend a cousin's wedding," she said. "Usually, in situations like that I have a lot of mouth hunger. This time, even though I was eating more than I needed, I didn't really eat from mouth hunger."

What made the difference? Susan believes that she used to eat and drink around her parents to blur the very unpleasant reality of who they were. "It's amazing the things you hear when you don't eat or drink," she told the group after this last visit. "I heard, loudly and clearly, that my parents are not very nice—to each other or to anyone else. They're nasty and sarcastic and generally rude.

"Beyond that," Susan continued, "they're so involved with themselves that they don't really take notice of anyone else. I was eager to tell them about a promotion I'd just gotten at work, but they barely responded. My news just rolled off their backs. When that happened," Susan concluded, "I began to feel very angry . . . the same kind of anger I feel when I reach for food. I didn't reach for food this time and my anger soon turned into a very deep kind of sadness. I see that when I don't eat, I'm left with real feelings about real events. And where my parents are concerned, I feel very sad, and angry, and deprived."

When Susan was a child, she began eating in an effort to dull her pain. Now, as an adult, Susan recognizes that she has other options. She no longer drinks to blur the pain; and little by little, she is no longer using food to cover things over. She cannot change who her parents are, but she can recognize the pain she feels when she is with them and make it a point to spend as little time with them as possible.

"Of course, avoiding my parents doesn't solve my problem either," Susan added. "Even when I'm not with them I encounter situations that trigger the same feelings in me. I don't like those feelings, but I realize that if I'm aware of them, I have the option of doing something about them. It would be a big step for me to say, for example, 'This conversation is making me feel uncomfortable,' or, failing that, if I could simply give myself permission to leave the room."

Another woman in the group identified with Susan's situation. She also had parents who simply were not able to be there for her and she, too, struggled with mouth hunger most when she felt angry. "I've heard you talk many times about the need to mourn things," she said, "and I never really understood what you were getting at until now. I can see why I've always been so frightened by my anger. Acknowledging my anger meant acknowledging my deprivation—and also acknowledging the fact that there isn't a damn thing I can do to change that. I guess you're right," she said as the group came to a close that night. "Some things are simply sad and there's nothing much to do about them, except feel sad."

Of course, some mouth hunger is triggered by conflicts that we can attend to more directly. Zoe told the following story.

"For some time now, I haven't had much mouth hunger. Yet almost every evening I eat past the point where I'm full. I've started wondering if there's something I'm trying to block out by having such a stuffed feeling every night. It's become a chronic problem."

We asked Zoe if there were some other "chronic" problem in her life, and she responded immediately that she has been unhappy about her job situation for a number of years. She "fell into" a particular line of work and although she's learned to do her job well, it holds no great interest for her. It became clear from the discussion that Zoe eats too much at night to avoid thinking about her future. She does not feel up to the task of making a career change. As we talked further, Zoe told us that she thought some of her problem stemmed from the fact that no one in her family had much ambition. "My parents and my sisters don't know why I'm complaining," she told us. "They think I should be grateful to have such a good job. I really can't imagine making a change."

Zoe has turned to food to avoid confronting what some part of her feels is an irreconcilable conflict. How could she be a better caretaker to herself? As a good self-caretaker, she would have to take all of her distress seriously, both her unhappiness at work and her anxiety about wanting more than she thinks she should want for herself. She would have to challenge the ideas that constrain her, and she would have to be extremely patient with herself as she slowly explored some alternatives. Problem-solving requires determination, patience, and an ability to understand that obstacles must be appreciated before they can be overcome.

Clearly, Zoe's path will not be an easy one. She is bound to have objections to most of the career suggestions she makes to herself or that she hears from other people. Her doubt about whether she is entitled to have more out of life is a serious obstacle and one that will be at the core of many of these objections. However, as a good self-caretaker, she will accept her doubts but not be deterred. She will also seek out whatever professional help she needs to overcome both the real and self-made obstacles.

We pointed out to Zoe that she has already proven herself to be a top-notch problem solver. After all, she is well on her way to resolving her problem with compulsive eating, a problem that only a few years ago she would have sworn was impossible to overcome. If she and her caretaker are as determined to solve her career problem as they were to solve her eating problem, the future looks promising indeed.

Patience, compassion, and understanding; permission to question and break the rules; problem-solving and mourning—these are all important qualities and capacities to develop. With a good caretaker inside, you can feel safer exploring the feelings that trigger your mouth hunger. It's no wonder that one of the women in our New York group suggested that we design bumper stickers and T-shirts that read "A Good Caretaker—Don't Leave Home Without Her!"

Chapter

13

STRONG FEELINGS/ FORBIDDEN WISHES

YOU ARE WORKING TO DEVELOP QUALITIES WITHIN YOURSELF THAT WILL make you a reliable self-caretaker so that when mouth hunger strikes, you will be prepared to respond to it in ways other than eating. Janice, a participant in our weekly workshop in New York, told us that she now sees mouth hunger as an opportunity to flex her developing caretaking muscles. "When I feel mouth hunger," she explained, "I know there's an issue brewing that I haven't yet addressed and I almost look forward to exploring it."

We are going to discuss a number of situations in which compulsive eaters typically experience mouth hunger. Before we do, however, it would be useful for you to recall the last time you experienced it. Try to recall exactly what you were feeling when mouth hunger last struck. Where were you? What were you doing? Who were you with? What was going through your mind? What was happening in your life in a more general way? Keep your own experience in mind as you read the next two chapters.

In the course of our work, we have found that mouth hunger is generally triggered by one of three situations: (1) when we feel in danger of being overwhelmed by our feelings; (2) when we feel the guilt that follows "forbidden" feelings or thoughts (the sense that we have broken a taboo); and (3) when we feel like a failure in any context. The more familiar you become with these triggers, the better equipped you will be to respond to them with something other than food.

Feeling Overwhelmed

Sometimes you eat from mouth hunger because you feel too overwhelmed, anxious, or depressed by what is happening within you to stop, look, and listen to your feelings. You feel swamped and reach for food the way a drowning person might reach for a life preserver.

Although the specific situations in which we feel overwhelmed are different, we can usually relate to each other's experiences and generalize from them to our own. Consider the following two situations with this in mind.

Toni and Her Three-Ring Circus

"Last month, I was getting my family ready to go on a two-week camping trip," Toni reported. "It was hectic, but in my family, things usually are." Toni, who works full time, has three children, and is married to a man whose job requires that he work long hours, is extremely well organized and generally very good at managing her family. This time, however, she felt as if she were coming apart at the seams. "I reacted to the chaos with an upsurge of mouth hunger, the likes of which I hadn't had in years.

"I've been doing this eating work long enough to know that it's never the outside hassle that makes me eat—it's what's going on inside. But it wasn't until we were finally on the road that I could get some perspective on what was going on for me," said Toni. "Incidentally," she continued, "packing a great food hamper for the trip calmed me down a lot. That's what made me feel safe enough to explore what had been going on."

Once Toni began her exploration, things began to fall in place. "My father died a few weeks before our summer vacation last year," she said. "He'd been sick for a long time, so his death was expected, but even when you're expecting it, it's very hard to lose your last surviving parent."

As Toni thought about her father, she remembered what he was like whenever a big family event was in the making. "He was a fairly anxious guy," she explained, "and he dealt with his own anxiety by attempting to be in control of everything. Whenever we were planning a big party or trip, he'd run around yelling at everyone, telling them what to do. The more I thought about it, the more I could see that, in the last few weeks, I had been behaving just like him. As weird as it may sound, I think I was acting like him in an attempt to be closer to him on the anniversary of his death. It was as though I allowed him to inhabit me."

Toni is an old hand at this approach—old enough to know that had she been able to sit quietly with herself and provide herself with food even sooner, she would have had her insight sooner as well. But Toni, like all of us in these situations, felt pulled in two directions. On the one hand, she knew that she needed to provide herself with caretaking. On the other hand, she was reluctant to face the depth of her sadness on the anniversary of her father's death. Experiencing that sadness meant acknowledging the reality of her loss. Rather than do that, she ate and, through her behavior, found a way to keep her father alive within herself.

Later that evening, Toni thought of something else that had contributed to her upsurge of mouth hunger. "As I think about it now, I realize that I was very angry with myself for being overwhelmed. I take a lot of pride in my ability to handle my three-ring circus—to remain calm in the midst of chaos—but the flip side of that pride is that I judge myself very harshly when anything slips. As a kid, I decided that I'd never act 'crazy' like my father," Toni explained, recalling how unpleasant his behavior would become when he felt anxious. "Maybe when I was being so hard on myself about my mouth hunger and about feeling overwhelmed, I was really feeling angry at my father for having been so anxious much of the time."

Toni knows that good caretaking means unconditional self-acceptance—no yelling about eating or anything else, for that matter. But as we have pointed out, when we fear being overwhelmed by our feelings, we find ways to avoid them. We are always struggling with contradictory impulses—wanting to grow, yet wanting, simultaneously, to avoid pain. Toni's insights about her mouth hunger, however, leave her one step ahead in her struggle.

Lydia, another group member, had a different experience that stemmed from having felt overwhelmed by her feelings.

"I Eat Doughnuts Because I Hate My Job."

"I hate going to work because my job is so boring," said Lydia. "When I have a day off, I never reach for food unless I'm hungry. But when I'm at work, I feel much better when I have something in my mouth. It mollifies my rage if I chew something or eat sweet things like doughnuts. It's my reward for the unpleasantness I have to go through. I'm trying to change my life," Lydia concluded, "but until that happens I feel too frustrated at work to just sit with my feelings."

It was clear to everyone that Lydia, like many experienced nondieters, had slipped with regard to legalizing food. She was once again seeing food, particularly sweets, as a reward. Everyone agreed that Lydia's impulse to reward herself was a good one, but it was clear that she needed to find a reward other than food.

Lydia was interested. "I often promise myself that I'll play more," she told us, "and I've been treating myself to more special things lately, but somehow those treats only help a little bit. At the moment I'm eating, I really want to be screaming, ranting, and raging," Lydia continued. "It doesn't help to tell myself that I'll go to a movie in six hours."

Lydia needs some good caretaking. What would that entail? What has to change within Lydia so that she will not need to reach for food when she is unhappy at work? We put these questions to the group.

"If Lydia were a child in a lot of distress at school and I were her caretaker," said Allison, one member of the group, "I would make it absolutely clear to her that I would do all I could to help remedy her school situation. But if I discovered that the situation was beyond fixing, I would get her out of there and into a different school. Lydia says that she wants to change jobs, but does she really believe that she has the power to do that? For example, how much time does she spend job-hunting?"

Lydia was about to reply, but we thought it best to get everyone's ideas on the table first. Lynne, another group member, picked up where Allison left off.

"Everyone in my family eats when they're upset. I don't think that they even realize that there are other ways of dealing with bad feelings. The lesson of my childhood was very clear. If you're angry, frustrated, or feeling bad, the thing to do is *eat.*

"At this point, I'm very angry that my options were so limited as a child," Lynne continued. "I'm angry that we never discussed anything. Home was a stifling place. Feelings were always pushed down and numbed with lots of eating and lots of TV. Now I've come to see food as a very limited reward. I deserve much more than brownies or cookies when I'm feeling overwhelmed by frustration or unhappiness!"

"I know that my ability to deal with frustration has increased a lot since I started using this approach," said Barbara. "Now, as soon as I realize that I want to eat because I'm having a tough time, I immediately reinforce all the basics of demand feeding. In fact," Barbara continued, "I think Lydia needs to carry a great big food bag with a lot more in it than doughnuts. It also helps to start each day working in front of the mirror and dressing yourself very carefully. If I spend time getting comfortable with my body and then dressing accordingly, I'm in a much better frame of mind for the day. I'm also careful about giving myself exactly what my stomach wants when I'm hungry. I always find that very reassuring."

"If I were Lydia," said Joanne, another member of the group, "I'd go on a campaign to take care of myself in style. Not only would I be careful about stocking the house with food and dressing myself well, but I'd up the ante on all my caretaking. Like Allison said, I'd be looking for another job, big time. But I'd also be taking a taxi to work, planning to meet friends for lunch, reading a wonderful novel, seeing lots of good movies. I think if I were feeling generally well cared for, I'd be more convinced that I was actually going to change the things in my life that made me miserable."

When you are unable to cope with an intense, unpleasant feeling, you need to take a few steps back in order to look at the larger picture. You become more able to cope with intense feelings when you have built a foundation of caretaking experiences starting with demand feeding and moving on to more general aspects of self-care and nurturing.

As we began to wind down, Lydia confessed that her efforts to find another job had been only half-hearted. She also recognized that she had been feeling too demoralized to do nurturing things for herself with any consistency. Her intense frustration at work was actually a sign of general neglect. She had deserted herself when she most needed her own support. No wonder she turned to food.

We urged Lydia to take better care of herself in the ways the group was suggesting. She would then see if this good caretaking enabled her to better weather the frustration at work without turning to doughnuts for the very limited relief they offered. If she could not provide herself with the caretaking she needed, some counseling might then be in order.

Forbidden Feelings

Children have an uncertain sense of their own boundaries, of where they end and where their parents' begin. As a result, they often assume that their parents know everything that is going on in their minds. Consequently, for them, a "bad" thought is just as dangerous as a "bad" act.

Beyond making the assumption that their parents can read minds, children make no distinction between their own feelings and the feelings of their parents. When a child feels angry at a parent, for example, she often fears that her parent is angry at her.

As we grow older, we learn that we can keep our thoughts and feelings secret if we wish. We also come to understand that, often, when we are worried that someone is angry at us, it is because we are angry at them. Our worry is the result of our guilt.

Much mouth hunger is triggered by "forbidden" thoughts and feelings. Even though we are no longer children, we live in two time zones simultaneously: in the past, as the children we once were, and in the present, as the adults we have become. When we experience a thought or feeling that we once considered forbidden, we continue, as adults, to feel vulnerable and frightened. We worry that if people knew what we were thinking, they might not love us as much; or, if people knew what we were feeling, they might punish us.

The reality is that this drama of crime and punishment plays silently, within our own heads. We are not punished by others for what goes on in the privacy of our minds and hearts; instead, we manage to do a bang-up job of punishing ourselves. We monitor out thoughts and feelings continuously and we condemn ourselves much more harshly than would an audience of our peers. We experience this self-punishment as guilt.

As compulsive eaters, we eat to escape our own wrath, but our self-condemnation proves inescapable. In the end, we still feel guilty.

Phoebe, from Houston, recounted the following story: "I went home to visit my aging father and had a huge upsurge of mouth hunger. It finally dawned on me that I was sitting on years of unexpressed rage toward him. Instead of dealing with those feelings that are so 'undaughterly,' I ate and ate and yelled and yelled at myself for needing so much food." Clearly, Phoebe's mouth hunger was triggered by the angry feelings she considered forbidden. Rather than suffer guilt about those feelings, however, she reached for food and *then* felt guilty about having eaten. By eating, Phoebe tried to avoid thinking through her situation.

You and your inner caretaker have a lot of work to do when it comes to your so-called transgressions. You need to accept yourself unconditionally and stringently question the codes of conduct you have always accepted as givens.

One participant in an advanced workshop we held in New York observed that the feelings most of us think of as forbidden bear a marked resemblance to the seven deadly sins: Anger, envy, lust, avarice, sloth, gluttony, and pride. Evidently, people have worried about these feelings for a very long time. It is time for you, however, to reconsider the concept of *forbidden.*

Beyond the rules that are essential to maintaining law and order, we each make our own decisions about what we regard as moral and ethical behavior. Part of that evaluation includes deciding whether or not there is such a thing as an illegal or immoral thought or feeling, as differentiated from an illegal or immoral act. Mouth hunger often signals our inability to make this distinction.

As important as it is to recognize the right we all have to think and feel *anything*, it is also important to understand that it is not the end of the world when we do, occasionally, act wrongly. "Deeds are usually not irrevocable," said Lianna, a participant in a Texas workshop. "We can always apologize and make amends if we do something we feel is wrong. After all, when we're eating from mouth hunger, it's not typically because we've killed someone!"

Lianna has a point. Compulsive eaters deal much too harshly with themselves in reaction to their so-called crimes of thought, feeling, and deed. Our mouth hunger signals danger, danger that comes from having violated some childhood taboo. Our real protection from this danger lies in our ability to treat ourselves with kindness. The kindness we are advocating involves thinking about what has happened, possibly reassessing the standards by which we judge ourselves, and if we continue to feel we have been "wrong" and want to "improve" ourselves, approaching the task with the kind of understanding, acceptance, and gentleness that fosters change.

Let's look at some examples of how this process has worked for group participants who have experienced mouth hunger in response to forbidden feelings.

"As a mother, I should not want to work, too."

"I didn't have an eating problem until after I started having kids," said Babs, a participant in a California workshop. "I never lost the weight after my first pregnancy, and I retained some of the weight from my subsequent two pregnancies as well."

Babs, who has been using our approach to compulsive eating for a while, is distressed because she feels that her mouth hunger is increasing rather than decreasing. "My oldest child is in kindergarten," she says, "and the other two are at home. I feel incredibly grateful to be able to be home with them, but basically I'm at home eating all day long."

It did not take long for the group to help Babs get a handle on her problem. Before she had children, Babs had a job she loved. She'd been a designer for a manufacturer of children's clothing. She and her husband both had working moms, however, and they had decided before their children were born that it would be better for everyone involved if Babs could be home with the kids while they were young.

Unfortunately, the decision they made before the children were born was based on theory rather than experience. Babs and her husband were in a financial position that enabled her to stay at home. The problem was, Babs discovered that being home full time with three children did not make her happy the way she had thought it would. She just was not cut out to be a full-time mom, but she felt too guilty about leaving her children and changing her plans to return to work. So instead, she stayed home, experienced lots of mouth hunger, and ate.

Babs had not been able to talk to her husband or her friends about her unhappiness. "I feel ridiculous complaining about a life that so many people would envy," she explained. "I mean, who am I to feel unhappy when I have so much?"

Bab's guilt infiltrated every aspect of her life. For example, she had the money to hire babysitters, but never allowed herself to use them unless it was "absolutely necessary." It would have been good for Babs to give herself some relief, but instead, the more she wanted to be out of the house, the more rigid she became about staying home. And, of course, the more rigid and judgmental she became, the more her mouth hunger increased. She used food and her preoccupation with her body to distract herself from her true feelings.

How might Babs have been a better mother to herself as well as to her children? She might have allowed herself the opportunity to reassess her decision to stay home. After all, what works for Mary Jane across the street may not work for her. From there, Babs might have gone on to challenge her childhood fantasy that her life would have been perfect if only her mother had been home all of the time. The truth is that some mothers are better mothers when they are around full time, and others are betters mothers when they work outside the home. It is clear that there are no absolutes in this regard.

Babs' guilt about her real desires kept her at home and made her feel angry and resentful toward her children. Rather than face up to her resentment, she sidestepped it with food and unwittingly prolonged her misery.

Guilt, like anxiety, is a red flag. It warns us to stop what we are doing and try to figure out exactly what is going on. Once an issue demands our attention, it persists in one form or another until we confront it and think it through. Anger is another red flag, particularly for women.

"I should not feel as angry as I do."

Sally, a participant in a Chicago workshop, described her experience. "My brother-in-law called the other day and I noticed that as soon as we had finished talking, I began chewing my way through a bag of bagels. I was really biting those bagels with a vengeance." Sally said, "and I knew that I wasn't hungry. I'd just eaten an hour or so earlier, but I kept stuffing those bagels into my mouth and screaming at my brother-in-law in my head. Later, of course, I felt completely stuffed and disgusting."

We discovered very quickly that Sally's family was in a crisis. Her father had died recently and her conversation with her brother-in-law concerned a dispute about the will she and her sister were having. "The problems with my father's estate will take a long time to resolve," Sally said dejectedly, "and if I continue to eat at this pace, I'll be a blimp by the time we're finished."

Although Sally has been working with our approach for several years, she has had an ongoing problem with mouth hunger. "I got to the point where my mouth hunger was only occasional, but I never felt completely free of it," Sally explained. "Then when my father died and the dispute over the will began, it came back full force."

One of the ways Sally had successfully dealt with her mouth hunger was to treat herself kindly. When her father died intestate, however, and she and her sister began to dispute their joint inheritance, Sally's kind and gentle caretaker abandoned her. "All of this business with the will has left me feeling overwhelmed by guilt," she said. "My sister and I were never allowed to fight when we were kids. We weren't even allowed to feel angry at each other. If my father knew about these battles, he'd be miserable."

During their childhood, Sally's sister was sickly. The fact that Sally was prohibited against even feeling angry at her sister was exacerbated by the fact that her parents expected her to care for her sister as well. "Everybody took care of her, even after she recovered," Sally said with resentment. "To this day she expects extra special treatment—even in the will. And to this day she gets it. That's why I'm fighting with her about the will. I want her to know that I deserve exactly the same kind of treatment that she does."

Sally sounded determined. The fact that she was eating from mouth hunger and feeling disgusted with herself about it, however, told us that despite her apparent resolve, she was feeling like a "bad" girl. Ostensibly, she felt disgusted with herself for eating and for gaining weight. In fact, she felt disgusted with herself for being angry and for violating the "love thy sister" rule.

Sally and her inner caretaker need to do two things. First, they need to cuddle up with each other. Sally is in pain. Her father has just died. In addition, she is reexperiencing all the struggles that clouded her childhood—rivalry, rage, and envy. She needs to be held, nurtured, and comforted.

Once Sally has managed to offer herself some succor, she will be in a better position to explore her feelings, think them through and hopefully proceed with some independent thinking. For starters, she and her caretaker need to question the rules that are triggering Sally's mouth hunger: Who says that all sisters should love each other? Who says that sisters cannot be angry at each other—even if they actually *do* love each other? Who says that years of being ordered to take care of someone not much younger than yourself do not take their toll?

As a child Sally was told to not feel what she was feeling. More than that, she was forced to act in a way that was directly opposite what she was feeling. What could Sally have done back then? If she rebelled, she would have been punished and would have felt guilty. But when she did as she was told, she felt guilty anyway, for being insincere. Beyond that, she also worried about being "found out."

As an adult, Sally has more options. In the heat of her conflict, however, she does not see them; that is why she eats and tries to turn away. Sally can challenge the rules she learned about what constitutes "goodness" in people, particularly in sisters. She can also develop sympathy for the plight she endured as a child and mourn the freedoms she should have had but didn't.

Sally might discover that her anger toward her sister diminishes as her own self-compassion increases. The two girls clearly occupied very different positions in their family, and there may be more to her sister than her parents allowed either of them to see. Of course, it is also possible that Sally's exploration will clarify how much she really does not like her sister. Whatever the outcome, Sally's rage is very real and deserves her respect and consideration.

When our mouth hunger is triggered by anger, as it was for Sally, we are presented with a paradox. As a rule, eating from mouth hunger is regarded as self-destructive. "If only she didn't eat all the time, she wouldn't be so fat," people say as they shake their heads in judgment. "Why do I do this to myself?" you berate yourself with the same judgmental tone, after you have finished eating something you weren't really hungry for.

We have repeatedly emphasized that the impulse to sidestep feelings and use food as a calming agent is a good one, deserving of respect. However, when we eat in response to a forbidden feeling—particularly the forbidden feeling of anger—there is a dual dynamic at play. When we eat in response to anger, we are actually turning our anger inwards, and that is self-destructive.

Although this connection between anger and self-soothing is somewhat confusing, it can be traced back to our earliest feeding experiences. As an infant, pleasure is centered around the mouth. Sucking is comforting. However, sucking is only one part of this early phase of development; biting is the other. Eating always contains these two qualities which exist in various combinations at different times—the soothing quality of sucking and the more aggressive one of biting.

Whenever you eat in response to mouth hunger, you are trying to help yourself. Sometimes, however, you seek that help with a vengeance. This vengeance with which you turn to food may actually be an unacknowledged vengeance you feel toward someone else but are afraid to experience or express. Or you may simply be furious with yourself for getting angry in the first place. You feel self-destructive at these moments because you are turning your anger against yourself at the same time as you are attempting to soothe yourself.

There are times when we eat in a way that feels self-destructive, even though we are not aware of feeling angry. These are times when we are disappointed, hurt, or feeling abandoned. We turn to food at times like these to avoid a sense of isolation or the feeling that we are unloved. However, there is a way in which anger plays a part in these situations as well. Part of our fear of abandonment is the anger we feel about being abandoned. At times like these, eating feels self-destructive because it is contaminated with anger that we have turned against ourselves.

Anger is intricately enmeshed in our eating because it is very difficult for many of us to live comfortably with our anger—and anger often leads compulsive eaters directly to the refrigerator door. Women, in particular, have a very difficult time learning to deal with anger. We have found that with this issue, more than any other, women need the help and support of their inner caretakers to question precisely what it is that "nice girls" are permitted to feel. Can we feel angry? Can we raise our voices? Can we protest when we are treated badly? Are we allowed to make demands? Do we want to fight back when we are hurt? All of these questions need to be answered with a strong, resounding YES. We recommend that you read *The Dance of Anger* by Harriet Goldhor Lerner to educate your caretaker in the care and handling of angry feelings.

What about those times when your eating has very little to do with anger, but still feels self-destructive? Let's go back to our workshops for some examples.

"I'm not sure how I feel about success."

In our weekly New York workshop, Adrienne told us the following story.

"I came home from work last night and I thought I was feeling fine. Then suddenly I started eating. I felt like I was shoving food into myself in a driven, angry way—as if I were *determined* to make myself fatter. My eating felt very self-destructive."

Adrienne went on to tell us that she had not been having much mouth hunger for quite a while. During the last few weeks, however, she had noticed herself eating in this driven, angry way several times. When she began talking about what was going on in her life, Adrienne mentioned that the business she had started a few years back was booming for the first time. Although she was exhilarated by her success, it was soon clear to everyone in the room that something about her accomplishment also made her feel anxious. Adrienne recognized her anxiety but had not really thought it through. In fact, she probably ate in the evenings to avoid thinking about it.

What was it about success that compelled Adrienne to eat in a self-destructive way? "No one in my family has ever been a big success," she told us. "I'm thrilled about what's happening, but it also scares me because it somehow feels very aggressive to move ahead of all of them. What if I'm a huge success? What if I become very rich? Will I still feel like a part of my family or will I become an outsider?"

Adrienne ate in an effort to weigh herself down, to slow

down her success. Eating from mouth hunger was an old behavior that seemed out of place in her new situation. This sense that our overeating is anachronistic or out of place is often what we mean when we say that we are eating in a self-destructive way. As we take one step forward, eating in this old, driven way expresses our impulse to take two steps back—it is a response to a new-found sense of freedom.

One could say that such "regressive" eating is self-defeating. To do so, however, obscures the fact that eating in this way is an attempt to keep ourselves safe. Mouth hunger, at these times, warns us that we are going either too fast or too far for comfort. Although we may not be aware of it, chances are that we are punishing ourselves for violating some internal prohibition and alerting ourselves to the presence of an unexamined rule.

Adrienne needs to think about why she is uncomfortable being more successful than anyone else in her family and just which taboos she is breaking with her success. Perhaps, as a child, she entertained an aggressive wish to be more powerful than her parents. She may equate her current success with the fulfillment of that wish and it may make her uncomfortable.

When your mouth hunger feels particularly aggressive, it may be a sign that you need to stop and catch up with what you are feeling. Think through carefully what is happening. What taboo have you violated? How do you view this taboo today from your adult perspective? Do you still consider it a rule worth obeying? Would setting it aside be as dangerous as you thought it would be when you were a child?

Even if the taboo that continues to frighten the child inside of you does not feel realistic to the adult you have become, it is important to respect your fear and move ahead at a comfortable pace. You can decide to change the rules that govern your behavior, but your feelings usually proceed at a much slower pace. If your actions carry you further than your feelings can sustain you, a conversation with your caretaker will provide you with better ballast than food.

"Don't think you're so grand."

Our discussion with Adrienne triggered recognition in Linda, another member of the group. "I've made a lot of progress with my eating," Linda said, "but I noticed recently that I still eat from mouth hunger at least once toward the end of each day.

This evening eating has become a ritual for me. I don't feel anxious beforehand, but it's almost as though I can't go to bed until I ritualistically clobber myself on the head.

"When Adrienne was talking, I realized that I've been treating myself very well lately. Just last week I bought the lap-top computer I'd been coveting. I've also been giving myself all the food I want and a lot of nice clothing."

Linda had grown up in a very frugal family. As she spoke, it became clear that beyond being frugal, her family actually regarded self-deprivation as a virtue. "I was just like them until things started changing with my eating this past year," Linda said. "Adrienne felt guilty about being more successful than everyone else in her family, and I bet that, in a similar way, I've been feeling guilty about giving myself things. That's probably why I have to clobber myself every night—as punishment for allowing myself to have things. It's as if I'm saying to myself, 'Who do you think you are? Don't think you're so grand!' "

"Just the thought of breaking a taboo makes me nuts."

Several women in the group were eager to participate in this discussion. Fran said that she had clobbered herself with food a few nights earlier in response to the advances of a married coworker.

"It's bizarre that I would punish myself because a married man came on to me," Fran said. "After all, it's not as though I came on to him. In fact, we were having lunch together when he made his move and I handled it all very calmly. I said that I liked him very much—which I do—but that I wouldn't get involved with a married man, first, because I don't approve and, second, because I'm not a masochist.

"When I got back to the office, I was anything but calm," Fran said. "I ordered myself another lunch and ate it furiously with my office door locked. I might as well have been plastering myself with food at that moment. I just wanted to be huge."

Why was Fran punishing herself? We talked for a while and Fran acknowledged that even though she declined the proposition, there was a part of her that found it tempting. "But that wouldn't account for how absolutely terrified I felt," she said. As we talked more, we kept coming back to the irony of the situation: The man made the pass, which Fran declined, but Fran is the one who ends up feeling guilty. "I guess just feeling attracted to this guy was enough to send me into a frenzy," Fran said. "I know it's ridiculous. I mean, he doesn't even know that I felt tempted. But *I* know, and that was enough to send me to food."

On some level, Fran believed that her attraction to this man had caused him to approach her. She therefore assumed responsibility for the come-on and judged herself at fault. This notion that her feelings had caused this man to act in a certain way indicates that the situation was triggering some guilt in Fran left over from her childhood. It is children, after all, who believe that their thoughts and wishes have great power.

We could not help but think of all the little girls who, at some point, declare their intention to marry their daddies. Imagine what a tailspin it would cause if Daddy declared that he had exactly the same feelings and planned to leave Mommy and marry his little girl?

In healthy families, there are boundaries between adults and children regulating all kinds of behavior, including sexual behavior. These boundaries give children all the space they need to have the fantasies that are necessary for the development of their self-esteem. When adults violate these boundaries by abusing children sexually, the children feel that their fantasies and feelings caused the abuse. They loved their daddies, and their daddies loved them back; they assume the burden of guilt for having "bad" feelings in the first place. To do otherwise would leave these little girls even more exposed to the reality of their situations. They are, in fact, helpless and completely at the mercy of the abusive adult who is supposed to be protecting them.

As far as we know, Fran was not an incest survivor and her anxiety probably stemmed from quite normal fears about her childhood fantasies. Fran's reaction, however, is not unusual. It is not at all uncommon for women to feel guilty about advances made towards them—and not only because of their girlhood fantasies. Fran's anxiety, in no small measure, is the result of her awareness that women are often blamed for the transgressions of men. "She asked for it," is the catch-all justification for anything from pinched behinds to brutal rapes. Not surprisingly, the discussion that followed was about sex and sexual taboos.

"Isn't mouth hunger really about breaking sexual taboos?"

Sophie, a member of this same group, responded to Fran's story by saying that she had noticed a definite cycle with regard to her eating and her sense of herself as a sexual person. "As soon as my eating gets organized around stomach hunger, I have much less mouth hunger and I begin to feel thin," Sophie said. "I probably have not actually lost any weight, but eating from stomach hunger all the time, to me, is the same thing as being thin . . . it's the feeling of being in touch with myself."

Sophie went on to say that as soon as she begins to feel in touch with herself in this way, she begins to feel more sexual. "It's a real transformation," she said. "I feel more alive as I walk down the street and more aware of my body, particularly in relation to other people's bodies. Whenever I'm in this state, I start looking at bodies a lot and I start noticing other people looking at mine."

This state of heightened sexuality does not last long for Sophie, however. "Invariably, not long after enjoying these feelings, I start having lots of mouth hunger," she explained. "I eat, then I feel full, then I shut down on all these nice feelings. I don't yell at myself about the mouth hunger. Eventually, I surround myself with my favorite foods and do lots of mirror work until I get myself back on track with my stomach hunger. Then the cycle begins again."

Heads were nodding all over the room as Sophie talked. Apparently, lots of women in the group knew exactly what she was talking about. But everyone had a hard time coming up with a solution. "Maybe we should all consider celibacy," Susan suggested wryly.

"It's really astounding," said someone else. "I know Susan's joking, but it's hard to think of another way out. I actually think that if I knew I was going to be celibate for the rest of my life, my mouth hunger would decrease considerably. How is it possible that we are all still so uptight about sex? Granted, for centuries the rules against female sexual pleasure were pretty stringent, but are we still operating by those old rules? Are we still intent on being old-fashioned *nice girls*?"

We suggested putting the problem in the framework of caretaking. What would we have to provide for ourselves in order to feel more comfortable with our sexual interests and pleasures? After all, we go to food because we don't know what else to do about our sexual anxiety or guilt.

Michelle had a difficult time thinking about providing herself with anything that would diminish her sexual anxiety. She had an easier time, however, thinking about what she might want to offer a daughter, if she had one. "When I was a child," she said, "the only thing I ever heard about sex was that it was wonderful *if you were married.* The message was like a broken record—sex and marriage, sex and marriage. When I masturbated as a preteen, I knew I was being sexual, but I certainly wasn't married. By the time I was making out with boys, I was really hysterical about it. And when I slept with someone for the first time, forget it. I promptly gained twenty-five pounds. Talk about wearing your guilt on your sleeve. I actually gained so much weight that I looked pregnant!"

What would Michelle want to tell her daughter about sex? "I'd want her to know that her body was there for her to enjoy. If guys look at her, let them look. And she has eyes for looking, too. I so desperately want to feel free about all of this," Michelle concluded. "It makes me furious to hear that all of us are still so incredibly messed up about sex."

"You may have heard that you're supposed to be married when you have sex," Natalie, a participant in the group, said in response to Michelle, "but I *am* married and I still have exactly the same anxiety whenever my mouth hunger begins to fade. I've been married for twenty years. What am I afraid of? What do I think is going to happen if I'm more in touch with my sexuality?"

Natalie went on to answer her own questions. "I suppose I could worry that I'll have an affair," she mused, "but that doesn't seem likely. I'm still nuts about my husband and he'd be delighted if I felt sexy more often. It's hard to believe that I could still feel inhibited, but I think there's a part of me that never really grew up. I don't think I've ever felt I had the right to my own sexuality. I may be married with children, but there's a little girl inside me who feels that sex is for Mommy—not for me. I guess I need to provide myself with an inner caretaker who will encourage me to explore my adult privileges."

"I felt fine about sex once I came out as a lesbian," said Anne, another participant in the workshop. "I actually lost weight at that point—from relief. As soon as I got involved in a live-in relationship, though, I felt less interested in sex again and I gained weight. The same thing happened in my marriage years ago."

Like other members of the group, the less Anne experienced mouth hunger, the sexier she felt; but as she began feeling sexier, she also began experiencing more and more mouth hunger. "Sex is so intimate," she said, by way of explanation. "Maybe the closer I feel to my partner, the more frightened I feel about the possibility of losing her or losing myself."

This suggestion that intimacy triggers feelings of vulnerability—and that vulnerability triggers mouth hunger—sparked a great deal of interest among other group members. "What would you need in order to feel more reassured?" we asked.

"Well," Anne began, "I guess if I'm afraid of the consequences of being sexual—the vulnerability, the guilt, or the dependency—I need to face my fears more openly and reassure myself that *I'll* take care of myself, no matter what happens. Basically, I need to give myself what the eating gives me: It slows me down. I need to remember that sex is a complicated business for me. I need to give myself the time and space to think through my feelings about it."

What else can you do for yourself so that you do not have to turn to food when you have sexual feelings? First and foremost, it is important to reassure yourself that you will never act in ways that overwhelm you. For example, you will not say yes when you mean no, and you will speak up if a partner does something that makes you uncomfortable. Historically, women have been pushed into the sexual act and pushed into someone else's idea of "proper" or "improper" sexual feelings. When we turn to food in response to our sexual feelings, it is often because we are trying to blot out our hesitations. We are pushing ourselves the same way we have felt pushed in the past. No woman has an easy time taking her concerns about sex seriously.

Next comes the real issue of recognizing your own sexual feelings and responding to them with sensitivity and kindness. (We will have more to say about this when we discuss women's fears of losing weight.) When mouth hunger strikes in response to sexual feelings, it is very important that you stop, look, and question what you have been taught. Remind yourself that everything you have learned about female sexuality evolved from a culture that subordinates women. Be bold! Ask questions! Who says that nice girls *do*? Who says that nice girls *don't*?

You and your internal caretaker have to formulate answers to these questions that feel comfortable and right for you. We have no doubt that your caretaker is in favor of a lot of self-exploration. We have no doubt that she wants to help you find out what feels good to you. She is pro-pleasure, but she also wants you to feel safe at all times. Who knows where the two of you will go? The important thing is that you go there *together.*

Let's sum up this topic of eating in response to forbidden feelings.

First, remember that you eat in an automatic way whenever something feels forbidden. You need to replace that automatic reach for food with an automatic pause. Once you learn how to stop and think about the rule that is making you anxious, you'll feel more in control and less driven to eat. You may even discover which rules make you feel most anxious—and that they no longer have a place in your life.

Second, reassure yourself that you are now committed to becoming a much more benevolent self-manager than you have been in the past. You are not going to reject yourself and you will make every attempt to regard whatever you are thinking, feeling, or doing with understanding and compassion.

Third, bear in mind that daily life events inevitably stir up aggressive feelings within you. These aggressive feelings are not inherently bad. We all have them as part of the human condition. What you need to do, however, is stop attempting to cover your aggression with food.

Finally, remember that even when something feels good—like sex—it can still make you feel anxious, particularly if it violates an old taboo. What can you do about your anxiety other than reach for food? You can have a meeting with your caretaker, talk about what's causing your anxiety, and decide just how, and at what pace, you wish to proceed.

Chapter

14

REEVALUATING STANDARDS

WE ALL HAVE STANDARDS BY WHICH WE JUDGE OURSELVES, OTHERS, and the circumstances of our lives. When one of these does not measure up to our standards, we feel a sense of disappointment, shame, even loss. Mouth hunger often signals these feelings.

When you felt this kind of disappointment in the past and ate in response to it, you yelled at yourself for needing food. Consciously, you were disappointed in yourself for eating in what you viewed to be an infantile manner, thus remaining unaware that your real distress was about not living up to some other standard entirely.

Once you learn to stop yelling at yourself for eating in a "regressive" way, you can move on to explore the real feelings of disappointment that produce your mouth hunger. You can begin this exploration by asking yourself two questions:

What are the standards by which I measure success?

What, for me, constitutes failure?

You have learned to ask, Who says I should *look* any particular way, *eat* any particular way, or *feel* any particular way? Now you need to wonder why you should *be* any particular way.

Challenging the shoulds that you have always taken for granted and relinquishing your unrealistic expectations will lead to a decrease in your mouth hunger. As you read on, you will see exactly how these challenges helped those participants in our workshops whose mouth hunger was triggered by failing to measure up to certain standards.

Challenging Unrealistic Standards

"I should be stoic."

Vivian told us the following story in a Texas workshop.

"I've been having a lot of trouble with my knees lately. I've already had surgery once, and I'm going to have it again, but I'm often in a lot of pain. In the evenings, when I'm sitting around at home in pain, I eat."

Vivian's eating makes her panic. "I'm afraid to gain any more weight, because that makes my knees worse, so I get very down on myself when I eat," she explained. "I know that eating is not going to help me and I certainly know by now that yelling at myself only makes matters worse. Most of the time, I'm pretty good about not getting down on myself for eating, but I'm having a tough time around this pain thing in the evenings."

Clearly, Vivian's pain upsets and perhaps frightens her. She turns to food for the comfort, or mothering, that she is unable to provide for herself. The fact that Vivian is so upset about eating, however, suggests that her situation is more complicated. We reminded her that the reprimand "I *should not need* to eat" is usually a cover-up for "I *should not need* something else." The reach for food is a way of trying to escape this conflict.

As we talked, Vivian told us more. "When my mother was a young child, she was in a very bad accident that left her disabled. As an adult, she suffered from severe arthritis and was always in a lot of physical pain. She never really complained though," Vivian said with pride. "Everyone always commented on how she rose above her difficulties. She always had a smile on her face. I have so much less to cope with than she had. I feel like a baby for folding this way just because of pain in my knees."

The conflict that Vivian was trying to sidestep was a conflict over standards. As a little girl, she had learned to equate stoicism with virtue and, today as an adult, she still considers it a weakness to acknowledge pain. No wonder Vivian has to eat! She has to cope with the pain in her knees as well as the pain of her self-condemnation. Have you heard the expression "Never hit a guy when he's down?" Vivian apparently has not. She is seizing the moment of her pain to bludgeon herself with recriminations: "You should not give into this pain." "It's not so bad." "Why are you sitting here like this?" Rather than defend herself against her own assault, she reaches for food.

Vivian, or Vivian's inner caretaker, needs to challenge the lessons of her childhood and develop an independent point of view. Who says that stoicism is such a good thing? she needs to ask herself. Maybe there are better ways to manage pain than to deny it. After taking this step, Vivian's caretaker needs to rush in with a great deal of compassion and gentleness. Once Vivian has had more than her fill of tenderness, she will be able to think more clearly and find ways to manage her pain without denying it.

The notion of "rising above" one's circumstances is more suitable to angels than to real flesh-and-blood women. Stoicism generally carries too high a price tag for comfort. "My mother died young," Vivian told us, "and it was unclear what exactly caused her death—she kind of faded away. It's true that she was very determined, but I think that she was also quite depressed."

"I should be more independent."

Monica, from California, told us that she had only recently moved there from the Midwest. "It was very hard for me to move here," she said. "I had met someone I liked a lot, but we were not ready to make any decisions about living together. When we met, I was in the process of searching for a new job and I knew that I had to let the quality of the job offer, and not its location, be the deciding factor. We talk on the phone a lot and we've made a commitment to see each other at least once a month and for longer stretches over holidays. If, after a while, we still want to be together, one of us will make a move.

"What I'm concerned about is that, every night since I've moved here, I've been eating my way through the evenings. I'm not eating large quantities at any one time, but I'm eating constantly. It's become a ritual. Before I moved here, I'd gotten to a point where I felt mouth hunger only sporadically. I'd even started to lose some weight. But this night eating has me over a barrel."

Monica had already attempted to deal with her mouth hunger by packing a good food bag each day and filling her pantry with everything she craved. "I tell myself that it's okay to eat from mouth hunger if I have to. I'm also working on getting used to the fact that I've gained some weight by wearing comfortable clothing and looking in the mirror in an accepting way. But I'm surprised and concerned about this ritual of night eating. I hate to admit that eating through the evening actually does make me feel better."

Monica was surprised by the fact that eating in the evenings brings her comfort, but we were not. Food is highly symbolic and, as long as Monica does not yell at herself for eating, the food probably does make her feel calmer. The fact that she feels calmed by food, however, does not mean that she is not in trouble with her feelings. By continuing to reach for food every night, Monica distances herself from what is really on her mind—and that is precisely what she needs to explore. When we asked Monica how she thought she would feel if she were not eating throughout the evening, she replied, "I'm not sure. I know that I feel lonely here, but I'm generally pretty good at amusing myself. I've lived in lots of different places in my life, so I know that it takes time before you begin to feel at home. Whenever I want company, I call my friends back home."

Monica's experience with this move, however, was different from moves in the past. "I feel some terror underneath my eating that I don't understand," she said. "I'm a little embarrassed to say it, but I feel like I did when my parents first started letting my sister and I stay home alone without a babysitter. I'm living in a very secure building, so it isn't really my physical safety that I'm worried about. But somehow I still feel unsafe."

We went back and forth with Monica until we got clearer about her feeling of being unsafe. It did seem peculiar that, after all her moves, she was having such a hard time with this one. Finally, it dawned on us that although this move was similar to other moves Monica had made in the past, Monica herself is quite different from who she was before. Specifically, she no longer has a major eating problem. When she moved to California, Monica's eating problem was as much a part of her past as the home she left behind.

As Monica thought about it, she realized that what we were saying was true. She had never before experienced a fear of new places because she had always eaten her way through difficult times. Here she was in Los Angeles with all her feelings on the surface. No wonder she was trying to resurrect the comfort she used to get from food.

Monica is trying to cope with both an unfamiliar place and unfamiliar feelings, feelings she had always buried under food. She was concerned. Would these feelings overwhelm her? Would her arms be big enough to hold her? Monica is more independent and self-reliant than she has ever been before, but this move is something of a maiden voyage for her, and maiden voyages can be as frightening as they are exciting.

Monica is also eating from mouth hunger because she feels that her identity as an independent, self-reliant person is being challenged by her fear. Even though she has a great deal invested in this identity, it is not something she has ever really explored. What does it mean to be independent? Can you feel as frightened as she does now and still be independent? Ultimately, Monica will have to redefine her idea of independence so that it accommodates, even embraces, human frailty. She will need to recognize that the fear she feels does not make her less independent; it only makes her human. Monica left her eating problem behind when she moved, but she forgot to bring along her nurturing caretaker, who understands that feeling scared and tentative is part of moving on.

"I should be able to accomplish what's expected of me."

Jill, a participant at one of our New York workshops, reported that she always eats from mouth hunger when she feels that she cannot finish all her work.

"All day long people come into my office and ask me to get something done for them," she said. "I'm the low person on the totem pole and I work for a number of people, so the buck stops with me. At this point, I'm working ridiculous hours and I barely have time to come up for air. When I look around at the other people in my office, I can't help but notice that no one seems as overwhelmed as I. They work late a few nights a week, but not *every* night, the way I do. And not only do I stay late, but I stay and work *and eat.* I don't yell at myself about the eating anymore, but I know that I'm eating from mouth hunger."

Jill believes that she must satisfy everyone who makes demands on her. Understandably, the idea of satisfying everyone makes her feel anxious and, rather than think through her anxiety, she turns to food. How could Jill make food irrelevant in this situation? Again, the internal caretaker must come to the rescue. If Jill were certain that her love for herself did not depend on her performance, she would be in much better shape. She could relax a little, and with the help of her caretaker, think through this issue of demands.

Jill's caretaker might help her see that it is as important to assess the demands being placed on her as it is to assess her performance. Maybe Jill is being asked to assume too much. Maybe the demands are unreasonable. Jill needs to be able to step back from her situation, reassure herself that she's there for herself—whether she finishes the work or not—and begin to take her breathless feeling seriously. If she's running to catch up, maybe there really is too much work to do!

What steps could Jill take if she discovers that her workload is too big for her to handle? Perhaps she needs to talk with colleagues about how they handle similar situations. Perhaps she needs to talk with her supervisor about how best to prioritize the work on this particular job. She should certainly read *Janice La Rouche's Strategies for Women at Work.* There are all kinds of things Jill can do to help herself, but she cannot do any of them until she and her caretaker work together to ease some of her pressure. Eating in response to that pressure simply puts the problem on a back burner.

As the group talked more about Jill's situation, it became apparent that she has always had a problem accepting her limitations. "I come from a family of high achievers," Jill said. "Everybody made a big deal about doing your best and coming out first. I think I get very alarmed if I feel I'm not going to be the best at something. You're right that I don't stand back and look at the situation realistically. I just eat and keep pushing."

A number of people in the group that evening related strongly to Jill's story and spoke about situations in which they have mouth hunger for similar reasons.

"I should be able to work, no matter what."

"I went to work sick the other day," said Carole, "and I ate all day long, even though I wasn't hungry. I knew what was happening. In fact, I kept pointing out to myself that I wasn't feeling well and that I wasn't hungry, but it didn't help. I had a very tight deadline to meet and I just kept right on working and eating.

"By lunchtime I was ready to drop. Then I had an idea. I called my mom and said out loud, 'I'm coming home to be taken care of.' I haven't done that in years," Carole admitted. "As a matter of fact, I get irritated with her when she offers to do things for me. But, do you know what? I stayed in the office for another hour or so and although I still felt awful, I was much calmer and I didn't need to eat. If I had acknowledged how sick I really felt in the morning and had stayed home, I'm sure my eating would have been just fine."

"I had a similar experience," said Lucy, after listening to Carole's experience. "Yesterday with my boyfriend, I made a big deal about the fact that I couldn't have dinner with him because I had to work on a paper that's due next week. I wanted to see him, but I really did have to work. So I stayed home, but it took me forever before I could sit down in front of my computer in a serious way. Finally, at around eight o'clock, I began to work. I worked well for a few hours, but then I started thinking about eating and watching TV. So I ate a little something—I don't think I was really hungry—and I told myself that I'd watch TV for half an hour.

"I kept thinking that I should get back to work, but I felt too tired. The more I struggled with myself, the more I ate. I remembered all the talks we've had here about these kinds of struggles and I finally said, 'Okay, you don't have to work anymore tonight.' But I felt guilty about it and I kept eating until I went to sleep."

Lucy anticipated our response. "I know what you're going to say," she continued. " 'Too little, too late.' It's true. If I'd listened to what I knew to be the case—that I'd gone as far as I could go on the paper that evening—I'd have respected my fatigue and gone to sleep. I might have watched a little TV, but I wouldn't have needed to eat. Well, maybe next time."

The Battle between "Less Than" and "More Than"

Why are we so dissatisfied with ourselves? Why does the fact that Jill cannot do all the work that is put in front of her leave her concluding that she is somehow "less than" she ought to be?

Why does Carole think that she should be able to work even when she is sick? And why does Lucy think that she should be able to concentrate even when she is exhausted?

We believe that all three of these women ate in an effort to become "more than" they were; or, in reverse, they ate to avoid a confrontation with their limitations. They did not want to feel that they were "less than" they should be.

It is difficult to give up the omnipotent fantasy that we can have it all, be it all, or do it all. There is something exhilarating about stretching our limits and pushing to go one step more. This sense of exhilaration explains why some people are motivated to climb mountains, leap ever-higher and wider across the stage at the ballet, or jump out of airplanes. We understand the very human urge to be all we can be . . . and then to push past that to be just a little bit more. But there is a difference between *stretching ourselves* and being *disrespectful of our limitations.* When we are disrespectful of our limitations like the three women described above, we are usually attempting to compensate for old feelings of inadequacy.

The sources of these inadequate feelings are different for each of us. Some of us did not receive enough of the right kind of attention when we were children. Others received attention only when we did something outstanding. You may feel that your "true" self—with all of your ups and downs, strengths and weaknesses—is not enough. Each time you feel as if you are falling short of some inflated standard, you get upset and then probably eat to make yourself "big enough" to meet these standards.

What is the antidote to mouth hunger that stems from a feeling of not being big enough? As we've said before, nothing is more effective than learning to challenge the standards by which you judge yourself and learning to accept yourself *as you are* without any conditions. You must learn to ask, "Who says that tiredness, illness, a slow pace (fill in whatever you consider to be your weakness) makes me less of a person?" The goal is to feel lovable *with all of your transgressions and limitations.*

Until you can learn to accept yourself in this unconditional way, you will continue to pay a very high price for your unrelenting demands. You will exhaust yourself and your problems will continue to grow. D. H. Winnicott, a British psychoanalyst, coined the term "false self" to describe the self some people feel they must create early in life in order to gain acceptance from their families. You will never see the end of your compulsive eating as long as you believe that only your false self is deserving of recognition and acceptance. Robyn Posin, the therapist we mentioned earlier, has created a set of cards with messages that model a more nurturing way of relating to yourself. One message that is helpful in establishing the kind of self-acceptance we are talking about reads, "Go only as fast as the slowest part of you feels safe to go."

Supporting Yourself in Style

Barbara, a participant in that same group, had been able to do precisely what we've been talking about and was eager to share her experience.

"I always eat more from mouth hunger before I get my period," she said. "This month, I decided in advance that during that week, I was going to cut myself some slack. I was going to be as nice to myself as I could be, and I did just that.

"I made time in the middle of each day to read," Barbara said. "Also, since I know that I usually feel unattractive the week before I get my period, I decided to take the time and make the effort to dress carefully. I even wore jewelry a few days." Barbara also made it a point to take stress vitamins and to remind herself each day that she did not have to accomplish everything she set out to do.

Barbara's approach was very successful. "I did crave sweets more than I normally do," she said, "and I ate them when I was hungry, even if they were not quite what my stomach would have chosen, but I didn't feel any mouth hunger at all." Recognizing her special needs the week before her period, Barbara made it a point to support herself in style—and she reaped the rewards.

Challenging the Values Underlying Rejection

Barbara's story of self-acceptance and self-love compelled another group member, Ruth, to speak up. "I understand what everyone's saying about having to accept who you are and maintaining love for yourself no matter what," she stated, "but I have a problem with it. I *don't* love myself the way I am."

Ruth went on to talk about some serious disappointments

she had recently experienced with men. "Two weeks ago, I had a second date with a guy who'd responded to an ad I placed in the personals," she said. "I had a very nice time; he seemed to have a very nice time. But then he just didn't call me again. Last month, same story. That time, I had three dates in the course of two weeks with a guy and then he just disappeared. With him, I did a lot of the calling and I sent a cute note after our third date. I know I have a tendency to get overly involved too fast and to do too much, so this time I'm not pursuing. The problem is that instead of pursuing this new guy, I'm eating up a storm and feeling terrified about gaining back the weight I've lost. I know that I'm supposed to feel loving and supportive of myself, but the truth is, I don't. I don't love myself and I don't see how I could when men reject me all the time."

Everyone felt for Ruth who, at this point, was terribly upset. She had been a champion dieter and had fought hard to give up dieting and work with us on her compulsive eating. Everyone in the group remembered how difficult it had been for Ruth to legalize food and how much fortitude it took for her to accept life at a weight that was so much higher than her goal weight had been. Ruth worked in a fashion-conscious, diet-obsessed industry and, as someone who had never been comfortable bucking the tide, her new stance took a great deal of courage.

We also knew, however, that Ruth was unusually sensitive to how people viewed her and that this sensitivity had long been a source of her mouth hunger. Everyone hates rejection, but for Ruth, rejection really felt like death. She had married young mostly because being married made her feel acceptable. The marriage was a mistake and soon ended.

Not surprisingly, Ruth's mother is also inordinately concerned about appearances and acceptability. "How did he like you?" her mother asks on the phone the day after a date, never, "How did *you* like him?" Inquiring about her work, Ruth's mother will ask, "How do they feel about you at work? Are you making a good impression?" never, "How do *you* like your job these days?"

Ruth eats because she is upset and because there is a confrontation she is hoping to avoid. It is the confrontation between a value system she learned from her mother, which does not work well for Ruth, and a new system of values that she is only beginning to formulate for herself.

When Ruth abandoned diets, it was the first time in her life that she had actually said, "No more." That experience worked out very well for her. In fact, it worked out immeasurably better than all the years she had said, in essence, "Yes, Mother, my body is disgusting and I deserve to be punished and deprived of food."

Now, however, Ruth must confront another self-punishing way in which she says, "Yes, Mother." Based on what Ruth told the group, she is saying, "Yes, Mother, you are right. If a man does not call me for another date, it means that *there is something wrong with me.*"

Ruth's mother is not the issue here. Rather, the issue is the system of values that her mother and all our mothers have handed down to us and that we fail to challenge. Most of our mothers had no choice but to say, "Yes, sir, I will train my daughter to be what you want." This kind of acquiescence was the cornerstone of accepted female behavior. Children gain a sense of self-worth by receiving approval for those who have power—and girls are encouraged to continue seeking approval in this manner into adulthood.

Why does Ruth run to food when a man does not call? Because, rather than face her feelings and think them through, she allows the man's response to determine whether or not she is lovely and lovable. The truth is that there are many, many possible reasons for the man not calling Ruth back—and none of them has anything to do with Ruth's worth.

Perhaps he met someone he likes better. Perhaps his dog died. Perhaps he's impotent and never goes out on more than two or three dates with any one woman. Or perhaps he decided that Ruth was just not a match for him and he did not know how to say that to her directly. Maybe the man goes for six-foot blondes and went out with Ruth as an experiment to see if he could get excited about a five-foot redhead.

Our mothers may have led us to believe that, if we contorted ourselves enough, we could please everyone. How long are we going to hold onto that belief? Does everyone we meet please and interest us? Most of our mothers taught us, directly or indirectly, that men determine whether or not we are lovable. Now many of us, like Ruth, turn to food to calm ourselves when we feel rejected by a man's disinterest. How long are we going to measure our worth in this way?

In addition to looking to men for self-validation, Ruth also relies on the approval of her mother, the original source of her values, to feel loved and lovable. Clearly, Ruth feels that her mother's love hinges on her "success" in the outside world—with work, with men, and with friends. Is it any wonder that Ruth, whose sense of self is quite dependent on acceptance from others, feels so devastated by any response that even remotely resembles rejection?

Ruth needs to make a distinction between what her mother believes and what she believes. Is she lovable separate and apart from her mother's response to her and from some man's response to her? She may feel disappointed or angry or sad if someone she likes does not feel the same way about her, but does this lack of reciprocity mean that she is unlovable? Learning to make such distinctions is what we mean by thinking independently and granting yourself unconditional self-regard. Disappointment becomes devastating only if you reject and abandon yourself.

We were optimistic that Ruth would solve this problem. She had come a long way toward changing her eating and we knew that, little by little, she would start challenging some of her other ideas as well. This discussion of disappointment reminded us of a discussion in a Chicago workshop about what happens when, rather than feeling disappointed in yourself, you feel disappointed in someone else or in your life in general.

Facing Up to Disappointment

Marie had been using our approach for almost two years and she felt that her life had improved significantly as a result. "I'm eating much less than I used to and I feel completely free of the obsession with food," she reported. "But I never have a day when I don't have some mouth hunger. I'm almost at the point of saying, 'That's how it's going to be for me.' But as I listen to people talk today, I realize that I don't often ask myself if I can wait until I feel stomach hunger. Usually, I just eat if I feel I have to. I gather from what you're saying that if I want my remaining mouth hunger to disappear, I'll have to address it more directly."

When we asked Marie to tell us something about her life, she began by saying, "I've been keeping busy, but my life hasn't been great for the last five years or so. My job is great—I have my own public relations business—and I have a lot of friends. But my marriage broke up five years ago and my only child, my daughter, moved to New York last year. I'd have to say that things have not turned out the way I expected them to."

Marie sought professional help after her divorce to resolve some of her rage. "I thought we had a really good relationship," she said, "but after twenty-five years of marriage my husband decided that he had never had a chance to be independent and he wanted out. It came as a real shock to me. You think things are fine and then you find out that they're only fine for you."

Marie's sense of loss was heightened when her daughter left Chicago. She had always assumed that her daughter would become a partner in her business, but her daughter had other ideas. "She went off to graduate school in New York, saying she'd only be there for a couple of years. She has always had a thing about New York though, and if there's a way for her to stay there, I know she will. I say that I want whatever she wants for herself—that's what my mother always said to me—but to be honest about it, I'm very disappointed."

After Marie told the group about these two enormous losses, she became somewhat self-conscious. "It's not a very interesting story," she said, "just typical menopause or middle age. Anyhow, I'm pleased that my eating has changed as much as it has."

Marie, who was living with a great deal of disappointment, did not really expect much from us either. But we did not want to leave Marie with a "that's just the way it's going to be for me" attitude. We told her that we could understand her pessimism with regard to eradicating mouth hunger. After all, most things in her life were disappointing these days, and her experience with mouth hunger fit right in that sad category. We urged her, however, to think about the day before and to recall those specific moments when she had eaten from mouth hunger.

"I know that one time I was at lunch with a client," she said easily. "I'd finished eating—I'd made a deliberate attempt to stop when I was full. We continued talking and, at some point, I started eating again and finished everything on my plate."

"What were the two of you talking about?" we asked.

"Actually, the client was talking about her family visiting the previous weekend," Marie replied and then started laughing. "I really didn't think about it at all, but you can imagine how I felt. There I am feeling like I've been given a bad break, and she's describing a scene out of the pages of *Good Housekeeping* in the fifties. It sounds like I'm envious, but I don't think it's that. I just pictured her domestic scene and I felt bad—mostly very disappointed."

When Marie thought about the circumstances surrounding the other times she had eaten from mouth hunger that particular day, they each fit the pattern. She had spoken to her daughter late in the afternoon and afterward had wandered mindlessly into the office kitchenette and eaten a few cookies. When she got home late at night after a movie with friends, she didn't feel hungry but she wanted ice cream.

Marie was unhappy. She was not in a major depression, but she did feel genuinely disappointed by how her life had turned out. When something happens that reminds her of her disappointment, she eats in an effort to sidestep that feeling. Why does she sidestep her feeling of disappointment? What might she do instead?

Throughout this chapter and the last, we have stressed the importance of good caretaking as you attempt to overcome mouth hunger. We have also mentioned how, whenever we talk about the need for self-caretaking, we encounter resistance. Our message about the importance of caretaking is not, in and of itself, a difficult one to hear. The underlying message, however, is that we must face up to our disappointments rather than deny them. And that can be very difficult to bear.

Marie feels disappointed. Her husband has left her, her daughter is gone, and there is nothing anyone can do to change things. Marie reaches for food in an attempt to make what is so, not so. She wants to obliterate a painful truth, but there is no way around it. We urge her to look the truth in the face and offer herself the comfort she deserves.

On some level, Marie knows that if she allows herself to be more in touch with her feelings, she will move through them faster and have more energy left over to pull her life back together. It is no secret that when you look directly at what is making you unhappy, you can make a decision either to do something about your situation or not to do anything about it. In either case, you will have more energy available if you approach your problem as an activist, with both eyes open. Marie, however, feels unable to do anything differently from the way she is doing it. Perhaps she fears being overwhelmed by pain or anger. Or, if she blames herself for what has happened, she may fear feeling unloved and alone. Rather then open her eyes, she feels compelled to look away.

How might caretaking see Marie through her fears? She could hold herself and reassure herself about her unconditional support. For example, she might say, "You can tolerate feeling disappointed. I'll support you through it." That would allow her to feel her feelings more deeply, which, in turn, would enable those feelings to change.

Marie could also question some of her ideas about what constitutes the "good" life and see which aspects she would genuinely like to keep in her life, which to change, and which to forgo. For example, she may or may not miss living with another person. If she does, she needs to think about how she could recreate that kind of a living situation. Does she want to launch a search for another intimate relationship? How would she feel about sharing her home with a friend or friends? After considering her options, she might realize that she has come to enjoy her privacy and would simply like some occasional weekend guests.

As you attempt to deal with mouth hunger, the underlying question is "How ready are you to assume the responsibility of caring for yourself?" Resistance to this self-caretaking can be formidable. All of us resist nurturing ourselves, just as we resist providing ourselves with the food we need, and just as we resist giving up our bad body thoughts.

Resistance Revisited

We have talked about the way in which situations that trigger our mouth hunger often tap into feelings that, consciously or unconsciously, bring us back to childhood. Ironically, we continue to fear those things we have already survived.

We have known what it is like, for example, to have no control over a person on whom we are utterly dependent. We know what it is like to have that person put us down for a nap and leave the room, when we want desperately to see her and have her hold us. We know what it is like to wish for total, absolute devotion from a parent, but have to share her love with her adult partner and with a brother or sister. We know what it is like to feel as if we are "not enough" when we have been excluded. We have felt gloriously elated and precipitously abandoned. We have felt sad, lost, alone, rageful, and envious. We experienced all of these difficult emotions at a time in our lives when we had very few coping skills. Yet, somehow, we all managed to survive.

Surviving these traumas, living through disappointments, is a part of the human experience and part of our individual development. It is how we learn to give and take and make trade-offs: We accept limitations on our powers in exchange for love, appreciation, and more privileges. We allow ourselves to be toilet-trained, for example, in exchange for big-girl status. And we make an effort to amuse ourselves while our mothers are busy in exchange for their approval. Under the best of circumstances, coming to terms with the major disappointments of our early lives is difficult. And many of us, unfortunately, had more than a tolerable share of disappointments. We accommodated them grudgingly and we continue to hold on to that grudge as adults. We want the unconditional love and support that we feel we deserved but never received. This residual resentment explains why some of us, as adults, are so bent on avoiding the feelings that we navigated as children. We are angry about having to caretake ourselves through them—again.

However you experienced your childhood, you have good reasons for not wanting to nurture yourself through your feelings, now. Why should you have such painful feelings in the first place? And why should you be the one to minister to hurts that were no fault of yours? Although the voice of the child within us all cries out, "It's an outrage!", the adults we have become must find a caring way to deal with this hurt and angry child.

If Marie allows herself the full depth of her feelings, she will have to mourn what she has lost, both in the present and in the past as well. Mourning, however, means acknowledging and accepting what has happened in one's life. Marie, like all of us, is reluctant to let life off the hook and move on. She wishes that what happened had not happened. We all wish that life would take care of us better; we are waiting for reparations.

We told Marie's story one evening in our weekly New York workshop. All of the women related to Marie's reluctance to experience her feelings of disappointment, mourn them, and then move on. They all understood how Marie's reluctance expressed itself in her resignation about her mouth hunger. In fact, they were eager to talk about the ways in which they experienced their reluctance to examine their feelings.

"I don't want to pay so much attention to myself."

"I've had the same trouble caretaking my feelings that I've had with all the parts of this approach," said a woman named Joyce. "Whenever I think about catering to my own needs, I feel like an overworked mom with a bratty kid who's always making demands. First, I have to fill the food bag and then I have to shop for all those clothes. Now I'm supposed to do all this work around my feelings. I can see, though, that my not wanting to be bothered is my way to avoid thinking through the problems that are really troubling me. It's my way of dismissing the validity of my feelings and putting myself down."

"I'm embarrassed."

"I have a similar reaction to Joyce," said Nancy, another member of the group, "except I feel infantile, not bratty. It makes me feel silly to go sit on the couch and talk to myself about what I'm feeling. I know that when I do it—when I think of myself as two people rather than one—I end up feeling reassured and I calm down, but the embarrassment gets in my way."

"There are no models for good caretaking."

"It's so automatic for me to eat when I'm upset," said Jill in response to both Joyce and Nancy, "that it takes everything I have to make myself pause. I've had some success getting myself to stop for a minute before reaching for food, but often, after I manage to do that, I don't know what to do next. There really are no models for eating in the way we're trying to eat, and there are no models for the kind of caretaking you're suggesting either. In my family, people ate when they were upset. It was all very predictable. I'd say, 'I'm angry,' and my mother would say, 'Eat something—you'll feel better.' And if that didn't work, she would dismiss my feelings with some flip remark. 'That's ridiculous,' she once told me when I told her I was depressed. 'What have you got to be depressed about? We give you everything you ask for.' "

Many of us, like Jill, do not have a clue about what constitutes attuned caretaking. It is hard for us to trust our instincts when it comes to "knowing" exactly what we need. It's reasonable to question how you can provide good caretaking for yourself if you've never experienced it. Unconditional self-regard cannot simply be invented. It is also true that some of our notions of what we need are exaggerated because they are based on childhood yearnings that have been greatly exacerbated by deprivation. Beginning to care for yourself requires a commitment to doing something different for yourself at this point in your life; after that, it involves learning by trial and error.

Becoming a self-caretaker is a daunting but richly rewarding project. It is helpful to keep in mind that you have made progress with your compulsive eating problem because you were willing to do three things: to stop condemning yourself, to question many popular ideas, and to start listening to your inner signals. These are basic guidelines for all good caretaking.

"I'll do it for my kids, but not for myself."

"What's interesting to me is that I often feel that I don't know how to care for myself, but I almost always seem to know how to care for my kids," said Betsy, another workshop participant. "So, my problem isn't so much a lack of knowledge as it is some reluctance to treat myself differently from the way I was treated as a child."

How does Betsy treat herself? "When I'm in trouble," she said, "I get terribly impatient and nasty with myself. But I notice that when I'm impatient with my kids, I'm very quick to apologize and I'm always thinking about better ways of responding to them." Betsy paused for a moment before adding, "I realize as I say it that I work at being patient with my kids. It doesn't just come naturally."

Betsy gave us an example that involved her daughter Shelly, who was very shy. "Shelly does very well in school, but she doesn't like to be singled out for it. She never wants to be the star of the play or center stage in any way."

Betsy had also been a very shy and talented child. "I sang quite well," she told us, "but if I tended to withdraw when people asked me to sing, my parents would say, 'Oh, come on, there's nothing to be bashful about.' I'd hesitate and hesitate but finally give in—but I was never doing it *for me.* I was always performing for my parents and whomever else had pressured me."

Based on her experience, Betsy made a conscious decision to respect her daughter's shy nature. "My husband and I talked about it a lot and we made a decision that we were not going to push her," Betsy explained. "I talked to each of Shelly's teachers about it and they've respected our wishes. They never single Shelly out in the ways that make her uncomfortable."

The other day Shelly came home from school and told Betsy that she was going to be the queen in a school pageant. Betsy was thrilled that her daughter was feeling so much more comfortable about getting attention and she also enjoyed this clear validation of her decision not to push her daughter in a way she had been pushed as a child. "But what dawned on me," Betsy told the group, "was that I need to give as much thought to how I treat myself as I do to how I treat my daughter. For my children, I really stop myself and think about what I'm going to say, what I'm going to do, what feelings are involved, and how I'm going to handle a situation. *I* deserve the same kind of treatment."

A few of the women had strong reactions to Betsy's story. "As Betsy was talking, I got anxious," said Ann. "I just can't imagine not pushing my child into the spotlight—even if the child was scared. I'd be too worried about my child missing out on things. I was really relieved to hear that it turned out all right."

Betsy was quick to point out that, for her, the happy ending involved her daughter feeling more comfortable with herself—not being the pageant queen. "I don't need her to be the queen. I just want her to feel comfortable in her own skin and to know that I respect who she is."

A group member named Karen said that as she listened to Betsy's story, she became worried that Betsy's approach would not help Shelly get over her shyness. "It's so hard to remember that acceptance—not criticism—is what leads to change," she said.

"I loved Betsy's story," said Nancy, "because she really thought about how she was going to handle this issue of shyness. I find her thoughtfulness deeply moving. It's clear that thinking things through is exactly what we all need to do for ourselves."

It was getting late and Becky, who had been quiet during most of the meeting, had a closing remark.

"Some days I feel like being a good mom to myself," she said, "and some days I don't. I'm the same way with my son. Some days, I love taking care of him and some days I don't. But, I know that he needs me every day, regardless of what kind of day I'm having, and I take care of him even when I'm not in the mood. I can't say the same for the way I care for myself. When I'm neglecting myself, I think it would help if I reminded myself of what I do for my son . . . even when I don't feel like it. Why do I think that when it comes to myself, good caretaking is optional?"

Holding Back On Letting Go

As we've said before, attuned caretaking combined with accumulating experiences of eating from stomach hunger will lead to a decrease in mouth hunger. Interestingly, however, many women report that as soon as they notice the decrease in their mouth hunger, it begins to recur with greater frequency. "It's as though there's something really threatening about acknowledging my progress," one woman commented. We mentioned earlier that fear of success can trigger mouth hunger. We recommended that you view such mouth hunger as a signal and check to see if you are moving too fast for your own comfort or if you are simple reacting to having broken an irrational taboo. Here, the loss of mouth hunger itself represents a success and evokes mouth hunger.

What is the fear of moving beyond mouth hunger? What is the fear of moving on? What is it about this progress that makes many people reach for food?

We explored these questions one night in our New York workshop. "I've been doing really well for several weeks," said Joelle. "I've been eating consistently in response to stomach hunger, and I've been feeling very good and strong. The other day, though, I mentioned this progress to a friend and, sure enough, that night I felt compelled to eat even though I wasn't hungry. This is not the first time I've noticed that sequence of events."

"I do the same thing, but with a twist," said Katherine. "I've hardly had any mouth hunger lately, but I've noticed that when I eat, I have trouble stopping when I've had enough. I know that eating beyond fullness is really the same thing as mouth hunger, so I've been concentrating on stopping when I've had enough. It feels great when I can do it, but usually, an hour or so later, I go and get something more to eat, even though I'm not hungry. It's as if I'm saying to myself, 'You think you're so great? I'll show you!' "

Everyone seemed to recognize the syndrome. Clearly, different people have different reasons for undoing their success, but the phenomenon of taking two steps forward and one step back is a common one.

Joelle began to explore what was behind this defeating pattern for her. "What frightens me most is the thought of not having food available for comfort," she said. "I sucked my thumb until I was nine and it was a real cause célèbre in my family. My parents put awful-tasting stuff on my thumb to force me to stop. It was humiliating to suck my thumb, but I just couldn't stop. I don't know exactly why I was sucking my thumb, but I'm sure it was soothing in exactly the way food became soothing when I got older."

Joelle was afraid that not eating from mouth hunger was the same as giving up her thumb, of giving up a source of comfort against her will. She needs to remind herself often that she is no longer eating from mouth hunger because her need to use food for comfort has faded. No one has taken food away from her; no one has even suggested that she should give it up. She is in no danger of becoming the "good," submissive girl she once thought she should be and never quite could be.

The more secure you feel as a result of eating from stomach hunger and being attentive to your needs, the less power food has to soothe. You know that it will always be there for you, should you need it, but increasingly you will find other kinds of comfort that are more effective.

Katherine, who no longer experiences mouth hunger but noticed that she has been eating beyond feeling full, has a different kind of problem. Katherine is uncomfortable with success. "My mother always made fun of people who acted self-confidently and felt good about themselves," she told us. "Now, whenever I start feeling proud about having freed myself from the tyranny of food, I get into trouble. I grew up in a family that regarded pride as a sin."

Katherine's pride about her progress feels to her like a particularly grievous sin because her mother and all three of her sisters have serious eating problems. "Whenever I allow myself to relish the fact that I've overcome this problem," Katherine explains, "I feel like I'm flaunting my success in front of my sisters and my mother. And as soon as I imagine their disapproval, I reach for food. It's as though I'm saying, 'Don't worry, I'm still a part of the family.' "

Katherine and her caretaker have some serious questioning to do. First of all, they need to question why pride in one's accomplishments should be regarded as a sin. Katherine has struggled long and hard to free herself from compulsive eating. Who says there's anything wrong with enjoying the fruits of that labor? Katherine and her caretaker also need to recognize some of the anger she feels about having been stifled as a child, and they need to mourn the fact that she was unable to take pleasure in her accomplishments.

With Pam, another member of the group who complained about sabotaging her progress with mouth hunger, we discovered that each time she stops having mouth hunger, she feels thin—and as soon as she feels thin, she starts to worry. We saw earlier that success with different aspects of this approach can provoke concerns about getting thinner. Pam thinks that if she loses weight, people will expect more of her. "I'll have to act more confidently," she said, "and I'll have to look for a new job. I think that people will view me as an achiever and then I'll have to produce."

We will discuss this commonly held idea that losing weight brings with it more demands for achievement in the following chapter. For now, it is enough to say that many people begin worrying about life as a thin person as soon as their mouth hunger lessens. If this happens to you, reassure yourself that you will never push yourself to go any further or faster than you feel comfortable. *You* set the pace. You can give up using food for comfort, and perhaps even lose some weight, yet not alter your life in any other way. If you choose never to take a step beyond that point, it will be fine. If you choose to head out into the unknown, that will be fine also. As long as you know you are in charge, you will feel safe.

Moving On

At the last session before our summer break, Bettina, a longtime participant in our New York weekly workshop, wanted to tell us about a dream she had.

"I dreamed it was our last meeting before the summer break," she said. "We were all waiting out in the hall when I noticed Joyce and a few others saying good-bye to a very large woman. The woman had no shape—she was just straight up and down and very, very large. Joyce told me that the woman had announced that she was going to be leaving the group and that now the time had come. I said to the woman, 'Why are you going? Don't leave.' But Joyce said, 'She got stuck in mouth hunger.' When Joyce spoke, the woman started crying and I felt really terrible. Then Joyce said to me, in a very comforting voice, 'Now, now. She has to leave.' And then the woman left."

The group listened quietly as Bettina talked about her dream. "I think," she said, "that the woman was my mouth hunger telling me that she had to leave and I felt upset about the loss. I think I had a last fling with mouth hunger this week. I knew exactly what was happening, but I said, 'Who cares?' and ate six oatmeal cookies."

When we asked Bettina what had been happening at the time she ate the cookies, she replied, "I just had one of those moments when I noticed that I hadn't had any mouth hunger for a very long time. I was also aware that my clothing felt loose and that, in general, I'd been feeling good. I got scared, the way I always do when I notice my progress. I felt like I was a long way from home. Even though I felt that way, I didn't really *have* to eat the cookies," Bettina said, "but I ate them anyway."

Bettina said that something about the dream reminded her of a brief relationship she had once had with a man. "Early on in the relationship I discovered that he was a womanizer," Bettina recalled. "I had a history of self-destructive relationships with men, but in this instance, I lost interest soon after I discovered what he was up to. Boy, was he surprised," Bettina continued. "Women always wanted more from him, but I realized that I was much more interested in pursuing the painting I was doing at the time than I was in seeing him. That's the way I feel now about my mouth hunger. I can take it or leave it. I have better things to do."

We all loved Bettina's dream and her association to this man in her past. We cautioned her, however, about this idea of a "last fling."

For most of you, mouth hunger is a well-established pattern. You may well get to a point where you do not eat unless you are physiologically hungry, but once you have reached that point, you should expect that there will be times your mouth hunger resurfaces. If and when you confront issues or feelings that are unfamiliar to you, a resurgence of mouth hunger may well signal that you feel in danger. When that happens, you may heed it's call and eat. If you do, you must simply regard it as a sign that both the mechanical and emotional aspects of your caretaking need reinforcing and that you must retrace the steps that freed you from mouth hunger in the first place:

- Stock your house with the foods you want.
- Take special care to speak gently to yourself about your mouth hunger.
- Dress comfortably in clothing that makes you feel attractive.
- Be on guard for bad body thoughts. When they occur, make sure to speak to yourself lovingly, and reassuringly.

Life Without Mouth Hunger

We sometimes ask people who no longer have much mouth hunger what life is like without it. In other words, "How is it going for you now that you no longer eat in response to your problems?" Their answers are quite consistent.

- "It's an incredible relief to no longer be obsessed with food and weight, but my life is my life. Sometimes it's fine and sometimes it's not so fine."
- "Once my eating let up, I saw how depressed I really was and I started going for help. I'm grateful to have solved the eating problem because now I feel I can make the changes I've always needed to make."
- "I often think about how I used to eat constantly. Now I feel anxious a lot more than I'd like to and I see all of the ways in which I'm stuck. I guess this is how ordinary people feel in their lives. I know I have more work to

do—I'm just resting. Solving the food thing, though, was a major accomplishment and I'm very proud of myself for doing it."

- "Working on my eating in this way has opened up a new world to me. You convinced me to get interested in all aspects of my eating and now, for the first time, I'm interested in myself. I never knew it was possible to make such big changes and I'm sure that I will now make other changes in my life as well. I feel I've learned an approach that will be very useful to me in the future."
- "Stress doesn't end. You just deal with it without food."
- "I let go of mouth hunger and, in exchange, I got myself back—with all my troubles and all my joys. What's really different is that I now approach my life with the same introspection, kindness, and acceptance that I used to solve my eating problem. I guess what I'm saying is, I feel much more empowered and it's had a very beneficial ripple effect."
- "I could say that I don't have much mouth hunger anymore and that would be accurate. I'm pleased about that. But I know that I eat more than I need each time I eat from stomach hunger and that's really a form of mouth hunger. I know that if I stopped as soon as I was full, I'd lose weight. I may not have mouth hunger anymore, but I'm quite fearful about losing weight."

There is an intimate link between mouth hunger and the concerns women have about losing weight. Until you understand these concerns, you can expect your mouth hunger to linger in one form or another. It is time, then, to discuss the issue of weight loss.

Chapter 15

If I Were Thin . . .

You may have been tempted to turn to this chapter about weight loss before reading the rest of this book. After all, most of you have spent the better part of your lives associating *eating problems* with *weight problems.* It takes time to see these two issues as separate. It also takes time to liberate yourself from your wish to conform to the culturally idealized notion of beauty.

We have made our position regarding this so-called ideal female shape very clear: The ideal needs to be changed, *not* our bodies. Although weight loss is not our focus, the fact remains that many women who cure their compulsive eating by feeding themselves on demand do lose weight. However, their weight loss is a by-product of curing their compulsive eating rather than a goal.

What happens to these women when they notice their weight loss? Interestingly, many of them head straight for the refrigerator. They have mouth hunger as soon as they notice that their clothes are loose, just as they did after they'd lost weight on diets.

It is easy to understand why women eat compulsively after they have lost weight by dieting. First, they have been deprived of numerous foods and, second, the diet did nothing to change their problem with compulsive eating. But why would women who have nurtured themselves, accepted themselves, and, in large measure, resolved their eating problems return to compulsive eating as soon as they notice they are losing weight?

Hard as it is to believe, our desire to be thin is actually fraught with ambivalence. We may long to have an "ideal" body, but when that ideal is itself problematic, its attainment leaves us caught in a bind.

We have said that as women cure their compulsive eating and begin to lose weight, they encounter a number of common pitfalls. Specifically there is the pitfall of celebrating weight loss; the pitfall of believing that no matter how thin you are, you should be thinner; and the biggest pitfall of all: the fears you associate with being thin.

You have spent years thinking about how wonderful life would be *if only you were thin.* Now it is time to explore some of your darker feelings about thinness, the feelings that make you run to food for safety. The more familiar you are with these feelings, the better prepared you will be to deal with the mouth hunger they engender.

The Danger of Celebrating Weight Loss

Letty, a participant in a Texas workshop, was feeling great about herself. She had been eating from stomach hunger with ever-increasing consistency and felt calmer and freer than she had in many years. Something happened, however, that warned her she was beginning to slip.

"The other day I felt thinner and decided to get out the box of clothing I'd put away because the clothes were too small," she told the group. "I tried on a pair of pants and, sure enough, they fit. So did everything else in the box. I was thrilled. That night I ate a quart of ice cream."

What makes Letty's story interesting is that she reports feeling pleased about her weight loss . . . and then she turned to food. Under ordinary circumstances, we enjoy feeling pleased. When it comes to weight loss, however, feeling pleased can engender the kind of anxiety that sends us running to the refrigerator.

When you swore off diets, you promised yourself that you would accept your body regardless of its size. When you then feel pleased about losing weight, that promise rings hollow. Why celebrate weight loss when you have declared all sizes worthy of celebration? Why is your new size "better" than your old size? If you celebrate your new size, aren't you really saying that there was something less acceptable about your old size?

The group was discussing this problem of acceptability when Letty asked, "Isn't it natural to be pleased?" It's a reasonable question and the answer is yes. In this culture it is almost impossible not to be pleased when you lose weight. Since self-rejection always triggers mouth hunger, however, it is important to find a way to feel pleased about your weight loss without rejecting who you were before you shed the pounds.

A woman in a San Francisco workshop offered an analogy that captures this point. "One year I went to Aruba on my vacation and had a very nice time," she said. "The next year, I decided to go to Mexico. Does that mean that Aruba was no good? No. They're different places and both were interesting to me. I think we have to have that same attitude toward our bodies. Fat is one place, thin is another. The culture may be screaming that thin is better, but we have to remain neutral."

You can best remain neutral after you have lost weight if you do the following:

1. Remind yourself that you are having a "diet" reaction if you start feeling thrilled about losing weight.
2. Remember your old body and remind yourself to be respectful of how nice it was.
3. Take a minute to think about your real achievement: that you no longer feel compelled to eat when you are not hungry.
4. Get back to your mirror work, always striving to inhabit your body out to the edges. If you keep up with the changes in your body, you will be prepared when others react to your appearance and you will not get carried away by their applause. No doubt they think that you look better when you are thin, but they have not challenged their prejudices the way you have.

If Thin Is Good, Thinner Is Better

Donna, a participant in a California workshop, told us that as soon as she notices that she has lost some weight, she begins to have fantasies of losing more. "I begin to think about how long it will take to get even thinner. I think about what events I have coming up and flip into that old diet mentality of wondering how thin I'll be for them and how great I'll look. Before you know it, I'm eating up a storm and feeling totally out of control again."

Many of us have fallen into this trap. No sooner do we notice our weight loss than our fantasies take over. Before we know it, we're walking down the runway in a bathing suit, a crown on our head, a dozen roses in our arms, and tears streaking our mascara.

In order to understand the flaw in this future-directed thinking, it is important to grasp a very fundamental principle which applies to the part of your weight that is the result of eating compulsively: *If you could tolerate being any thinner than you are right now, you would be that thin.*

What are you actually imagining when you project a thinner you into your future? For starters, you are imagining a *different you,* a you who has less of a need to eat in response to mouth hunger. This "future you" is a person who is capable of sitting with many more feelings than you are right now. Is it any wonder that when you imagine yourself living without the comfort of food, you end up yearning for precisely that comfort? Talk to a child who is strongly attached to a "lovie" about how someday, when she is a grown-up, she won't need her "lovie" anymore, and the chances are that her grip will tighten. Talk to yourself about a time in the future when you will no longer need food for comfort—and watch yourself head for the refrigerator.

What can you do if you start imagining yourself getting even thinner the moment you notice that you have lost some weight? We urge you to summon yourself back to the here and now. Yes, you might say to yourself, it would be nice to have less mouth hunger, but for the moment, I still need to turn to food when I confront certain issues. Depending upon all the other factors that determine my size, it is possible that when I have less need to turn to food for comfort, I may lose more weight as a by-product of being able to sit with more feelings. But for the moment, I am where I am with stomach hunger and mouth hunger—*and that's just fine.*

The Many and Varied Fears of Weight Loss

Many of us have fears associated with becoming thinner or smaller which may produce mouth hunger or may cause us to eat beyond fullness in an attempt to maintain ourselves at a weight that is larger than we were "designed" to be. Compulsive eaters have used food either to numb themselves or to make themselves feel "big enough" to deal with whatever felt threatening to them. Sometimes, when a compulsive eater becomes thinner or "smaller," she imagines that she is more vulnerable. She forgets that, as a result of handling her feelings in a direct way—without using food as a buffer—she has actually become bigger and more capable emotionally.

Our definition of thinness has nothing to do with actual body size. Thinness is you minus your mouth hunger—whatever size your body becomes once you no longer need food for comfort. Consciously investigating your fears of becoming thin helps you learn more about those concerns which trigger your mouth hunger. Although this investigation may result in your becoming thinner, that is not its purpose. Let us say at the outset that we have no interest in promoting weight loss per se. Investigating your fears of thinness helps you know yourself better and makes it possible for you to work through certain problems that, at the moment, you sidestep by reaching for food.

Fantasy Exercise

In order to help you learn more about why weight loss triggers your mouth hunger, we invite you to join us on the following fantasy excursion that begins with imagining that you no longer eat from mouth hunger and that, in fact, you are thin. Close your eyes, take some deep breaths, and get as comfortable as possible. Then, move through this fantasy slowly, one part at a time.

Part 1

Imagine yourself getting considerably thinner. Try to really feel thin. Work from that feeling of thinness and let an image come to your mind of yourself, thinner. Picture yourself. Where are you? What are you doing? What is happening around you? How are you feeling?

Hold on to that image as you move into Part 2 of this exercise.

Part 2

What sort of scene have you projected your thinner self into? Is the scene you are picturing an idyllic one—something you would like to see happen? Or are you imagining yourself in a situation that makes you uncomfortable? In either case, stay in your fantasy long enough to imagine what problems you might have if your fantasy somehow became a reality. Think about it carefully. What might you *not* like about being in this situation? Once you have answered this question, hold onto your fantasy and move on to Part 3.

Part 3

Think about the following statement: In the unconscious, a thin body often symbolizes the body of a child. Go back to your fantasy and reconnect with the problem you think you might have if you were thin. Now, consider the possibility that the feelings you are having in your "thin fantasy" reflect feelings you had as a child. Perhaps what is causing you anxiety in your thin fantasy also caused you anxiety when you were young. If you are feeling self-conscious in your thin fantasy, perhaps you also felt self-conscious as a child.

Now consider the following: If you lose weight as an adult, you will be thinner, but you will not be more childlike. You may have unresolved problems and feelings that are rooted in your childhood, but the fact is, you are no longer a child trying to cope with these unresolved feelings. You are an adult, with an entirely different set of coping skills and you are, at present, trying to come to grips with these problems. Does reminding yourself of your current adult status lessen the anxiety in your fantasy of becoming thin?

Promise yourself that you will remember the feelings you encountered in this fantasy and that you will think about them over the next few days. Then, in a slow and gentle way, bring your attention back to your body in the present moment.

It is helpful to touch base with the "thin you" of your fantasy as often as possible. A brief, daily visit into a thin fantasy gives you practice in experiencing the feelings that have been difficult for you in the past. Remember, the goal of these fantasies is to discover the thoughts and feelings that were unmanageable for you as a child and that may well be the source of your mouth hunger as an adult.

We each have fantasies of being thin; we each have core feelings or problems that need our attention. Despite the fact that we are all different from each other, several common themes emerge when women begin to share their fantasies of being thin. Indeed, when we talk about our thin fantasies, the feelings and fears that we share about being thin are the very same feelings and fears that we experienced growing up as girls in a male-dominated world. These gender-specific problems include feeling looked at, feeling powerless and "less than," fearing our own sexual desires, feeling the pressure to be perfect, fearing envy, fearing our own anger, and feeling invisible. All of these feelings are associated with weight loss and need to be examined more closely in order to move beyond them.

In order to explore your associations to weight loss, you must remember that, by definition, fantasies, like dreams, are free from the constraints of logic. For example, you may *know* that, should you lose weight, you will simply be a smaller version of yourself; in your fantasies, however, you may *believe* that you will be a child again, vulnerable and dependent. Or you may *know* that fat does not make you stronger or more adult, but you may *believe* that being larger makes you more powerful.

The Problem of Being Looked At

The thin fantasy women most often share involves some variation of being looked at. The women in our groups imagine that if they were thin, they would attract attention. Some of these fantasies involve being admired or desired and are pleasant. The women who report these pleasant feelings sometimes picture themselves walking along the beach in a bikini while onlookers watch with admiration. Other fantasies, however, turn frightening and elicit fears of being preyed upon and harmed. The setting and action of the fantasy may be the same as in the pleasant version, but the women experience themselves as being vulnerable to sexual assault.

These contradictory variations of the same scene are not surprising given the fact that when we imagine ourselves thin, we are imagining ourselves confronting the concerns we have had since childhood. No matter how varied our childhoods, our individual experiences contained the contradictions inherent in being a girl-woman in contemporary culture. Our thin fantasies connect to our ideas about the culturally ideal woman.

Who is this ideal woman? Clearly, she is powerful enough to galvanize the attention of everyone who sees her. But what does all that attention mean? Does it make her powerful, or does it make her vulnerable? Is the power in the eye of the beholder or the beheld? Are you in control when men look at you, or are they? And, if you work hard at creating yourself so that you will be looked at and desired, how much of you is left at the end of the day?

Owning Yourself

Gail, a New Yorker, struggled with these issues in her fantasies of becoming thinner. One evening, she told us what she had discovered.

"For a long time I had enormous resistance to these thin fantasies," she said. "I would leave our meetings resolved to do them regularly, but I never followed through. Finally, I made a decision that, more than anything, I wanted to break the back of my 'addiction,' so I did a thin fantasy every day for a month. I gradually began to identify one of the central issues in my life.

"In my fantasy, I would see myself walking down a street wearing new clothes. I felt thin. As soon as I noticed that I felt thin, I would get scared and stop the fantasy. I'd tell myself that the fantasy was crazy and remind myself of how huge I really was. But I pushed myself gently and, little by little, I was able to go further.

"What I kept feeling was that if I were thin, I would not own my body," Gail explained. "The thin body simply didn't belong to me. When I asked myself to whom it did belong, I suddenly realized that it belonged to my mother, and it belonged to men, and in a more general way, it belonged to society."

Gail told the group that as a child, she had always felt like a piece of property. "My mother was preoccupied with my appearance. She'd put me on diets and the moment I lost weight, she'd buy new clothes for me and push me to show off my new clothes and my new body to my father." Gail felt she had no allies in this situation. Eventually, she got bigger and bigger.

After a month of doing the thin fantasies, however, Gail was able to reassure herself that as an adult, she was her own boss. "I keep reminding myself that I own myself. I decide how I want to be. It's no different than if I own a vase," she pointed out. "Anybody can look at it, but I own it. And anybody can wish they owned it, but they can't have it because it's mine."

Gail's sense that she can make her own rules and protect herself is still fragile. But this idea that she owns her body has given her a new feeling of confidence. In fact, she has even allowed herself to lose a little weight. Gail's experience is not unusual. She wants the attention, but when she imagines getting it, she feels invaded and overwhelmed.

In response to Gail's story, Mary said, "I have a fantasy of being thin that's related to Gail's. Each time I imagine myself getting thinner, I feel like a deer caught in the headlights." Everyone in the group agreed that a deer caught in the headlights was a poignant image of the perfect little girl, dressed for everyone to admire, yet frozen into immobility by the invasive glare of the spotlight.

This "good girl" training involves learning to groom our bodies for the pleasure of others. Ironically, when we do this and "succeed" in attracting attention and pleasing those who are looking at us, many of us not only feel frozen but naughty as well. Which brings us to the topic of guilt.

The Burden of Guilt

"When I imagine myself thin," said Linda during a California workshop, "I see myself in a bikini. In my fantasy, I enjoy wearing the suit. In fact, whenever I lose weight, I wear revealing clothes. I've always thought I enjoyed showing off my body, but it's odd that I've never managed to stay thin for very long. Obviously, something about showing off my body must make me feel uneasy." Linda decided to revisit her fantasy and pay closer attention to her feelings. "Sure enough," she said when she wrote to us a few weeks later, "while I was parading around in my bikini, I definitely had the sense that I was doing something wrong."

Women are taught to desire male attention, but when they

succeed in capturing that attention, they usually experience a confusing mixture of pride, guilt, and fear. In an essay about the effects of the adult's look upon the subjectivity of the girl, Dr. Emilce Dio Bleichmar, a psychoanalyst, comments on this mix of feelings.

> The girl—like all women as reflected in the myth of Eve—at once possesses a provocative body while at the same time she must feel guilty for possessing a body which attracts looks. . . . Under the male's sexual undressing gaze, her body is exposed and open to observation. It becomes the object of the look, a look which goes through her and "inhabits" the body, creating a constant feeling of being looked at. This sensation persists even in private when there is no one else around. When the woman looks in the mirror or when she bathes, there is always another detached pair of eyes looking at her body through her own "sexualized" eyes. And so, whether she is alone or takes special caution, there is still no safe space to keep secrets. No matter how much she hides and covers up, her body is still there to be looked at and undressed. From this arises the need to avoid the eyes that are looking, since meeting the look would be tantamount to returning the look in an act of provocation that acknowledges the sexual significance of the interchange and is understood by both protagonists as a tacit agreement. . . . The result is a peculiar subjective situation for the girl: she finds herself in a position of rousing the man's desire without having assumed the active role. . . . The girl learns to turn away her eyes, to avoid meeting the eye, to not look at men, to walk with her head down.

Bleichmar emphasizes that a girl's body is eroticized by the culture early in life and that a young girl carries a sense of guilt with her because she knows the effect her body has on others. Indeed, she is so keenly aware of being observed, that she has difficulty developing independent self-observations as well as her own sense of desire. Often, being looked at becomes a substitute for true sexual desire and activity.

Is it any wonder that we return to this central problem of our girlhoods—to the fact that our bodies elicit attention and, at the same time, we both like and dislike it. We crave the attention, even as we fear it and feel guilty about it.

Fear and Vulnerability

Many women report that when they fantasize being looked at, they feel frightened of being attacked sexually. While the vulnerability we often feel in our thin fantasies is a reflection of the vulnerability we experienced as children, it is also true that this vulnerability continues to be a factor in our lives as mature women. Our fantasies of sexual danger are all too often grounded in harsh social realities.

Our childhood anxieties about sex are another part of this matrix. When we discussed situations that prompted mouth hunger earlier, we noted how sexual feelings and fantasies can make little girls feel guilty. This same guilt can persist into adulthood and trigger mouth hunger.

Children have all sorts of anxiety-provoking fantasies about sex. They often assume that the sexual activity they imagine taking place between adults is like a fight in which someone is in physical danger. Or, it is possible for them to imagine themselves "married to Daddy" and get frightened about being a lot smaller than he is. Consider Christine, for example, who said that when she imagined herself thin, she suddenly felt very small all over. "I had the strangest idea," she confided to the group. "I had the thought that even my vagina would get smaller and that as a result, intercourse would be painful. If it's true that in these fantasies, the thin body can symbolize the child's body, perhaps I think that if I got thin, I'd be a child's size but having sex with an adult."

As she became more aware of the connection between her fantasy of thinness and the size she was as a child, Christine was able to laugh about the equation she had made between being thin and being childlike. Her fantasy of thinness had tapped into a childhood fantasy that must have caused her fear at the time. Someone in the group commented that considering the popularity of "waif" fashion models, the thinness/childlike connection is not really so far-fetched.

Childhood fantasies are an essential part of development. Fantasizing allows the child to safely explore her wishes and fears. Unfortunately, not all children are safe to explore in this way and, as adults, their fears of thinness are based on memories of incest.

The incest victim is robbed of a fantasy life; incest invades the protective shield of fantasy, totally overwhelming the child with forced sexual activity. She is not only looked at in the sexual way that is part of normal cultural life, but she is taken as a sexual object by an adult, often by the father who is supposed to protect her. It is no wonder that many incest survivors develop eating problems. Food symbolizes the early, safer part of their lives and, on a deep level, they believe that getting larger will protect them against assault.

When an incest survivor who is large imagines herself becoming thinner, she reexperiences the vulnerability she felt as a child when she was overtaken by a trusted adult. Before such a woman can reach a point at which she no longer feels that she needs the protection of extra food and extra weight, she has a great deal of emotional work to do.

Although the experience of an incest survivor is extreme, it has its place on one end of the continuum of experiences that all women share. All children have guilt and anxiety as a result of their sexual wishes and fantasies; beyond their fantasies, however, all girls have guilt and anxiety that are the products of their position in the world.

A recent discussion among members of our New York workshop illustrates how the fear and guilt about being looked at sexually play themselves out in the fantasies women have about becoming thin.

"As I was trying to imagine myself thinner, I remembered something I witnessed the other day," said Bea. "I saw a thin woman walking down the street and I watched the reaction of the men around her. Their heads kept turning, staring at her rear as she walked past them. I wondered if she knew what kind of attention she was getting. I wondered if she was afraid. If I were thin, like her, I'd be afraid of being attacked."

"I have a friend who men look at a lot," said a fellow group member named Rebecca. "I'm so aware of their eyes when the two of us are together. She walks into a restaurant and heads turn. On the street it's the same thing. I used to think I envied her, but I'm no longer so sure. It seems too silly. I'm not sure that these men even know what they're looking at or why. Sometimes I think it's as simple as 'Oh, there's an ass. I probably should whistle at it.' I have one male friend who told me that he feels obligated to look."

At this point the discussion took an interesting turn. Although everyone was still relating to the theme of sexual vulnerability, the women began to talk about their difficulties in saying no.

Rachel said that, on the one hand, she felt that if she were thinner, more men would be attracted to her and she would have a better social life. "But I really experience a lot of conflict about it," she added, "because even though I want the attention, there's a part of me that also fears it." Rachel recalled that this past summer her social life picked up without her having lost any weight. "That feels safer to me," she said. "The other day a man asked me out, but he's married and I turned him down. At this weight, I feel in control. I worry that if I'm thinner, I won't be in control. If some man wants me, I'll just acquiesce. It occurred to me the other day, though, that saying no does not have to be a function of size. Maybe I could retain a sense of my own authority even if I'm smaller."

"I can remember getting interested in boys when I was a teenager and really enjoying their attention," said Cynthia, another participant. "But they were always pushing for sex, and when I'd refuse, they'd call me a tease. Being fat is a way for me to avoid all of that."

Lisa, a married member of the group, had a similiar experience. "When I was thin, I couldn't say no to my husband if he wanted sex," she said. "If I looked gorgeous—which meant thin—I assumed my body belonged to him. Somehow when I'm fat, I'm not 'Daddy's little girl' in the same way. I worry that if I lose weight, I'll lose myself again. It's so hard to disconnect these ideas about thinness from feelings of being childlike, girlish, and subservient to men. Women of my generation were raised to believe that our bodies existed for the pleasure of men."

As we talked, it became clear that most of the women in the group felt stymied by the sexual vulnerability they imagined would be the result of getting thinner. Some of the women feared being looked at; others feared being unable to say no; still others feared being attacked. As women, many of us end up experiencing sexuality as something that is forced on us but for which we bear the burden of guilt.

The group discussion was productive. One woman, Lois, told us that she had found a way of dealing with the sexually aggressive looks she received from men and with her own feelings of vulnerability. Lois had always attracted attention from male onlookers because she has very large breasts. "I think all of the attention I got when I was young was a source of my eating problem," Lois explained, "but when I got older, I decided to deal with it by going on the offensive. In short, I just refuse to be an object. When men look at me sexually, I look them right in the eye and say hello in an assertive, friendly, nonsexual way. Their eyes may say, 'I've got you in bed right now,' but my voice says, 'No, you don't. We're just two people passing each other in the street.' "

Lois found that as long as she made the overture, she didn't feel threatened. "Men who come on to women in this way want to depersonalize the situation," she explained. "They may want to see me as nothing more than two big breasts, but I don't allow it—which pleases me enormously and gives me the upper hand."

Joan, another member of the group, said she was too shy to take control the way Lois did, but was inspired to think about not taking the rap for the attention she thought she'd attract if she were thin. "If I could just stay clear about the fact that I'm not asking for the attention by being thinner, maybe I wouldn't feel like I was the bad one. I might even begin to enjoy my body more," she said.

Ruth, a grandmother in the group, reacted to this discussion with a story. She told us that she had recently been visiting her granddaughter and had asked the little girl for a hug. "My granddaughter said, 'No,' and my son said, 'Be a good girl and give Grandma a hug.' I know he didn't mean any harm, but for the first time, I heard what those words meant and I was horrified by what he was really asking my granddaughter to do," Ruth said. "Hugs should be given freely . . . because you *want* to give them. They shouldn't be equated with being a 'good' girl." Ruth apologized to her granddaughter and told her that she understood not wanting to give hugs on command.

When she got home that night, Ruth thought about what had happened. "I realized," she told us, "that being a good girl has always meant giving in to what others want. If our fears of being thin are connected to the problems we had when we were children, it's no wonder that we fear becoming good, passive little girls who acquiesce to the demands of others."

How do you overcome the fear and guilt you feel about losing weight and attracting attention? The best place to start is with a reality check. The fear women feel about the implied threat in the looks and catcalls from men is not unreasonable. Some men look at women in an aggressive way in order to assert their dominance. Their attention feels intrusive because it *is* intrusive, and these intrusions are disconcerting and even frightening.

While acknowledging the reality of male aggression, it is also important to recognize that even though imagining ourselves being thin evokes memories of childhood, thin bodies do not transform us into vulnerable children. We are adults and we can say no. If we have difficulty doing so, we can seek help in overcoming passive acquiescence. We can take courses in assertiveness, talk about the issue with friends and develop support networks. To deal with our concerns about physical vulnerability, we can take courses in self-defense.

Many of us have a great deal of work to do before we overcome the passivity that has limited us since childhood, a passivity that leaves us feeling especially vulnerable to the leers of male onlookers. The fact is, however, that *passivity is as much a problem when we are fat as it is when we are thin.* Some women say that they can avoid the kinds of encounters that frighten them by staying large, by not resembling the culture's stereotype of desirability. Other women, though, are angry about having to eat more food than they need to compensate for their inability to deal with this problem directly.

All of us who were trained to be "good girls" as children have suffered as a result of that training. That suffering is evident when we equate being thin with being admired but threatened and defenseless. We can begin to be less afraid of thinness when we recognize that our fantasies resonate with our earliest lessons in being female, and we can begin to counter those lessons by reclaiming our bodies for ourselves.

The Problem of Feeling "Less Than"

Think about the female image that our culture has idealized for the past three decades. It is a thin image—straight up and down, no curves. This idealized body is in sharp contrast to the soft, rounded female body as it was idealized in the past. The distinction is an important one. Today, women idealize and aspire to have the body of a preadolescent girl or boy. In our view, this idealization is an expression of cultural misogyny. Indeed, the very curves that mark the onset of a girl's puberty—breasts, buttocks, and hips—have no place on the female body to which we aspire because femaleness is considered "less than" in the culture.

It makes perfect sense that women who live in a culture in which men hold power would long to be more "boylike." The body of a young boy holds the promise of a powerful male future. The pleasurable aspects of this fantasy are quickly soured, however, by the realization that *no matter how thin we become, we will still be "only" girls.* When push comes to shove, boylike does not have the same potential as boy. The idealized version of thinness promoted in our culture—if you are thin you will be powerful—turns out to be the wished-for power that most girls assume is out of their reach.

The fantasies that follow poignantly reveal how these women felt about growing up in a world in which boys were privileged. They also reveal another inherent property of fantasies: that one thing can, at the same time, represent its opposite. In other words, on one level fatness represents femaleness, and on another it stands for the "power" of masculinity. Similarly, thinness symbolizes the "ideal" of masculinity but also represents girlhood vulnerability.

"I've always been concerned about being taken seriously," said Janet in a workshop at Lake Austin Spa Resort. "I hated when adults treated me dismissively just because I was a child and I hated it even more when the fact that I was a girl led to the same kind of dismissal. In my family, my father was powerful and my mother wasn't. It was always clear to me that he wished I had been a son rather than a daughter, so I tried to do my best for him. He believed that boys were ruled by intellect and girls were ruled by emotions, so I was determined to be as intellectual and unemotional as any boy. My weight makes me feel more powerful, more masculine. When I fantasize myself thin, I see myself as a girl and I assume that I won't be taken seriously."

"When I imagine myself thin, I see myself riding my bike down a hill in white shorts," said Lucille, a participant in an advanced workshop in San Francisco. "I go into a coffee shop that I often frequent, a place in which I feel very much at home. Then, in my fantasy, the men whom I generally have a good time with begin to focus on me sexually and I suddenly feel like

I'm nothing. When I'm fat, we're peers. When I'm thin, they're the powerful men and I'm the powerless girl."

"I'm embarrassed to say this because I recognize that it's such a put-down of women and I hate the fact that I feel this way," said Julie in the same workshop. "But when I fantasize about becoming thin, I see myself becoming just like my mother. She was totally caught up in what she wore and what she looked like. My father was the one who did the 'serious' work and who had the power. I've always prided myself on being like him. I know, intellectually, that if I lost weight, I'd be the same person I am today, but on an entirely different level I'm afraid that losing weight would transform me into a stereotypical 'girl.' What if all I want to do is shop and be taken care of? What if I start spending hours in front of the mirror? It's awful, but I worry that if I lose weight and allow myself to be female, I won't be as good as the average man."

The fantasies on the East Coast sound very much the same. "When I imagine myself thin, I'm usually at a singles' event, feeling ashamed and inadequate," said Rita in New York. "I can't stand being in a situation where I'm waiting passively to be chosen. It makes me furious. Despite the women's movement, when you go to a singles' gathering, it seems to me that it's still the men who do the choosing."

"When I imagine myself thin, my stomach is flat and it's quite clear that I'm a woman," said Sophie in Boston. "When my stomach hangs down over my genital area, I feel more blurred—like, am I male or am I female?"

Laura, also in that Boston workshop, told us that she's always shocked when she is shopping and someone says, "Can I help you, ma'am?" Laura explained, "I'm convinced that I look more like a man than a woman with this excess weight and I think I want it that way. I even walk like my father when I'm heavy. So I'm surprised when strangers respond to me as a woman. In my fantasies of being thin, I feel exposed and weak, the way I did as a girl."

What can we do about the fear that underneath the ideal of thinness lurks the reality of the "insignificance" of girls? We must remind ourselves, just as we did when we feared being looked at, that we do not return to a childhood state of feeling or being "less than" when we become thinner. If you have such fantasies, however, they reveal that, as an adult woman, you are still struggling with the feelings of insignificance you learned to associate with being "just a girl." As women, this struggle exists within each of us regardless of our size.

We may feel more substantial, more adult, or even more like a man when we are large, but, paradoxically, our size reflects our feelings of inadequacy rather than our feelings of strength. As compulsive eaters, when we had uncomfortable feelings of being "less than," we "added" the symbolic strength of food to ourselves and thus made ourselves larger.

In order to feel substantial regardless of our size, we need to comfort the little girl within us when she feels "less than." We need to challenge the ideas that led her to feel that way, help her to speak up, and encourage her to enjoy her female body, whatever its size. Her conclusion that she *is* "less than" is a falsehood, an untruth, based upon her experience that men have it better. It is up to us to help her correct the distortion and *feel* the truth of her equality.

Sexual Fears

One of the most prevalent themes in thin fantasies we have encountered over the years involves associating thinness with promiscuity.

"If I imagine myself thin, I see myself at a party and I see my husband's friends coming on to me."

"If I'm thin, I'm afraid I'll want to sleep around."

"When I imagine myself thin, I see myself being unfaithful to my partner. It's as if my weight keeps me safely anchored in my relationship."

Many women from diverse backgrounds struggle with their sexual feelings in general, and with their sexual feelings within their primary relationships in particular. Deborah, a participant in an advanced workshop in California, helped us all gain some insight into our fears of thinness and sexual promiscuity when she explored her fantasy with the group.

"Sex with my husband has always been nice," Deborah told us, "but it pales in comparison to an incredibly intense sexual relationship I had when I was in college. I find myself thinking about that early relationship when I have fantasies of being thin and it frightens me. I think I worry that if I were thinner, I'd go looking for that kind of passion again."

We reminded Deborah that although she may be frightened by some of her desires, she always has the choice of whether or not to act on them. We were so intrigued by the prevalence of fantasies like Deborah's, however, that we wanted to explore further.

We asked Deborah to think about how this fantasy of having an extramarital affair might relate to an issue from her childhood. She was silent for a while. "I can't think of anything that relates to this directly," she finally said, "but I remember feeling cooped up. You know," she added in an almost offhanded way, "I'm an only child. My father was adopted, so I'm his only blood relative. His love for me is extremely intense."

As we talked, it became clear that Deborah's fantasy of seeking sexual intensity outside of her marriage if she lost weight stemmed from her fears of being intensely sexual within her marriage. For Deborah, intimate intensity of any kind evoked memories of her relationship with her father—and there were aspects of that relationship that felt both stifling and taboo to her.

Given that so many women express concerns about promiscuity in their thin fantasies, it is possible that many of us are struggling with similar issues about sexual intensity within our primary relationships. A girl's body may be looked at, admired, even desired. Her sexual desire, however, has always been subject to approbation and the regulation of men. It is no small coincidence that a society that worries about women's sexual appetites raging out of control also worries about women's unrestrained appetite for food. After all, it is easier for all of us to focus on our hunger for food than it is to contemplate our hunger for sex.

Striving for Perfection

Women who were expected to be great achievers when they were children often worry about what kinds of expectations will be placed on them if they lose weight. These concerns, like the others we have been discussing, show up in their fantasies of what life would be like as a thin person.

"As soon as I imagine myself thinner, I think about how I won't be able to maintain it."

"Whenever I think about being thin, I begin to worry about what people will expect of me."

"I always think that if I'm thin, people will assume that I have it all together and, as a result, will ignore or avoid me."

These fantasies are rooted in childhood environments in which great emphasis was placed on the importance of accomplishments. Many women grew up believing that they had to do great things in order to be considered worthwhile.

A number of different circumstances can lead to this drive for perfection. For some women, it is the legacy of their mothers' unfulfilled desires. "My mother never had a career," one woman said, "but all of her daughters are professionals. She lived through us. *We* were her great achievement—and we're still paying dearly for our accomplishments."

Other women equate thinness with the drive for perfection because they believe they must compensate for being "just a girl." Still others see a connection between fearing thinness as a source of added expectations and what "good girl" training felt like to them as children—endless demands to conform, restrict, and satisfy the desires of others.

How do you counter this fantasy? Once again, the solution requires rethinking your "good girl" training and learning to challenge it with a strong and resounding "Who says?" Implicit in that challenge is the kind of unconditional self-acceptance we have discussed throughout this book. It is you who must decide that losing weight as a result of feeding yourself on demand has no strings attached. And it is you who no longer measures your worth by the number of your accomplishments.

The Problem of Envy

"I always have the same fantasy of being thin," said Eileen, a woman in a San Francisco group. "When other women comment on my weight loss, their voices always sound nasty and resentful to me. I know that I've always envied thin women, and I expect that others will feel the same way toward me if I make it into the thin 'in' group."

Eileen had no trouble making the connection between her fantasy and her childhood. She and her sister, who is two years younger, had always been extremely competitive with each other.

Women express this concern about envy so often, however, that we were interested in exploring its roots beyond sibling rivalry.

Some say that envy is an inevitable component of childhood. All children envy the power of their parents. If a child is made to feel special, her good feeling about herself will soften this inevitable envy; if she is ignored or treated badly, her envy will be intensified.

A woman named Luisa told us that in her thin fantasy she invariably feels inadequate and envious. "I've envied thin women for years and years," she said, "so it came as a big surprise to me that, when I imagine myself thin, I still feel inadequate in comparison to them." Luisa went on to tell us that, as a girl, her mother seemed incredibly glamorous to her. "I know that my mother was obsessed with her body, but to me, she was the ideal. I can remember men looking at her when she walked into a room," Luisa explained, "and she certainly had the attention of my father. Their relationship seemed very romantic to me. As it turns out, my mother and I are built very differently—I think I have the same body type as my grandmother—and it's a real struggle for me to believe that my body could ever be as attractive as my mother's. Needless to say, I've never felt that I could win with men."

Elizabeth had a different variation on the theme of envy in her thin fantasy. "I never articulated this before," she said, "but in my fantasy, my mother was looking at me in an angry way. I've always worried about her being jealous that my dad and I can talk for hours about our common interests. Now we're both lawyers. As long as I'm fat, I think she sees me as having a problem. If I get thin, will it seem to her that I have it all?"

The issue of envy is clearly very complicated for girls. Not only do girls experience envy in relation to their mothers, but envy as a "normal" response gets reinforced as they move out into the world. The culture in which we live is an ideal growth medium for the envy so many women feel. How can we help but feel envy when only one body type is admired, when the system has room for so few of us to succeed, and when men decide who among us is worthy of attention? The effects of envy are circular: The more envious we feel, the more we fear envy from others.

We cannot begin to acknowledge our own envy and the envy of others as a form of admiration until we have granted ourselves permission to go after whatever it is that we want. Envy is a by-product of passivity. When we believe that we can really go for it, regardless of what that "it" may be, then we can look at those who already have "it" as role models rather than as roadblocks.

The Problem of Anger

Many women who eat from mouth hunger are stuffing their anger down with their food. As soon as they move beyond mouth hunger, they have to confront their anger by owning it and dealing with it. This anger shows up in their thin fantasies.

"In my thin fantasies, I become incredibly bitchy. I say whatever I want to anyone who crosses my path."

"I can't even begin to imagine myself thin without imagining myself as being mean. My fantasy of thinness involves flaunting my new body to make other women feel uncomfortable and threatened."

If you fear becoming mean-spirited once you are thin, anger probably fuels much of your mouth hunger. It may be that you were treated cruelly as a child, particularly with respect to your eating and your weight, and you have spent years being cruel to yourself. You worry that if you do not turn this anger against yourself, you will direct it at others. What you neglect to consider, is that you have begun to treat yourself with a great deal of kindness and, as a result, you are becoming less angry.

When women lose weight on a diet, they are much more likely to become self-righteous and downright snide about large women who represent their loathed former selves than if they lose weight as a result of demand feeding. Demand feeding, which is a direct result of self-love and self-care, is much more likely to inspire compassion than reproach.

Many women who feed themselves on demand and treat themselves with love and respect are no longer willing to be passive and to be treated disrespectfully by others. As a rule, they become considerably more comfortable about speaking their minds. Given our "good girl" training in passive acquiescence, we often confuse speaking our minds with taking an angry stance. (Indeed, people who are invested in keeping women "in their place" will often call an assertive woman a bitch.) It takes some practice to know and feel the difference.

Feeling Invisible

A survey commissioned by the American Association of University Women, *Shortchanging Girls, Shortchanging America,* documented that girls emerge from adolescence with poor self-images, relatively low expectations from life, and much less confidence in themselves and their abilities than do boys. It is no wonder that many girls grow into women who struggle with feeling unseen.

"When I imagine myself thin, I imagine myself disappearing. Poof! I just vanish," said one woman, echoing the sentiments of thousands of others. Sometimes this fantasy of disappearing represents a solution to the conflict that many women feel about being seen, which we discussed earlier. The idea of being looked at and being vulnerable to scrutiny or attack is so frightening that "disappearing" seems like a preferable alternative.

The sensation of not being seen is also an accurate reflection of the way many women experienced themselves during their childhoods. "I never felt like anything I said counted," one woman reported, as several others nodded in agreement. "I always felt invisible when I was around my brothers," someone else in the group added. "I realize that my brothers didn't choose to be boys and therefore privileged, but the more they acted as if they were special, the more I felt unseen."

One woman in a Texas workshop, who felt invisible in her thin fantasy, recalled an interaction she'd had with her mother when she was ten or eleven. "I remember saying to my mother that I felt a power within myself, which I assumed I had gotten from her, but that I didn't see her using it. My mother looked me in the eye and in the most confident and knowing way said, 'When you start getting interested in boys, you'll learn to tone yourself down.' "

Many women have pointed out that for women who are short, this problem of invisibility has a particular edge. "In my fantasies of being thin, I *really* disappear from view," one of these women said. "It's bad enough that women are encouraged—like children—to be seen but not heard, but short women have a particular problem being taken seriously."

Other women whose weight as children was a major focus of family attention also have special problems equating thinness with invisibility. "It's true that my weight has always attracted negative attention," said Alma in Texas, "but when I think about being thin, I imagine myself disappearing into the woodwork."

Losing weight as an adult will not turn anyone into an invisible little girl and, on some level, we all know that we do not need to maintain extra weight in order to be seen. But on another level, we are not so sure of this. One woman who equated weight loss with invisibility told us that she had started doing simple stretches and exercises to remind herself of her substantiality. Others in the group liked her idea. We all need lots of reminders about our right to be present in the world.

How do we reconcile the thin, happy, confident women in magazines who are surrounded by admirers with the frightened, ashamed, invisible thin women we encounter in our fantasies? In our strivings to be thin, we are striving to be the quintessential good girl: smiling, inviting, subtly tempting, clean, and admired (like the women in the magazines). Above all, the good girl is thin enough to be hardly there. She is a whisper, a shadow. "I will make myself powerful by conquering all of my needs and ultimately disappearing," says the anorexic to herself, as she starves her way to "perfection."

We all worship the thin girl—the thin body—because we are told that she is flawless, without any problems. And to the extent that the thin body symbolically represents our childhood, the thin woman embodies the problem-free past we wish that we'd had. The truth is, our childhood was not perfect and this truth is reflected in our thin fantasies:

"If I'm thin, I'll be hurt."

"If I'm thin, I'll be worthless."

"If I'm thin, I'll be promiscuous."

"If I'm thin, I'll disappear."

We all feel good for a few minutes when we manage to reach our "ideal" weight because, for those few minutes, we feel in synch with a cultural ideal. The cultural ideal we worked so hard to attain, however, feels empty once we attain it. Even in the safety of our fantasies, once we get beyond the moment of triumph we discover that our thin bodies house the same anxieties our large bodies did—plus some.

Is it any wonder we experience mouth hunger when we lose weight? Is it any wonder that we no longer want to be good girls, when good girls consistently feel that they're missing out on important experiences and opportunities? The prison of dieting is the very same prison we inhabit when we strive to be good girls. Being restricted in what we can eat, think, feel, say, and do is antilife. And the so-called reward for being "good"—being looked at—can never substitute for real living. Our fantasies of being thin are filled with information about the problems we could not solve as girls, but that we must solve now.

How can we move beyond our restrictions? The answer lies in self-care. You must promise yourself that if you lose weight, you will protect yourself against cultural expectations, your own and those of others. If being looked at makes you uncomfortable, you can make it a point to wear loose clothing. If you are frightened by sex, you need not pursue encounters that might lead to sex until you are ready for them. And if you are worried about pressuring yourself to accomplish more and more, you can promise yourself that you will ease up.

This kind of protection is important. It is, however, only a first step. Our fantasies make it clear that the concerns we have about being thin are related to much more than our body size and shape. They are, in fact, the very same issues that consistently trigger our mouth hunger. These are profound issues that have been part of us for most of our lives and can no longer be sidestepped.

There is a little girl inside you who very much wants your help. She is delighted that you are feeding her so well and treating her so much better than you have in the past. Now, however, she wants you to attend to these problems and she wants you to start working on them at your present size. These problems have no easy solutions. They are, after all, the problems that girls have growing up in a patriarchal world. However, working on these problems rather than eating about them constitutes a big leap forward.

Chapter

16

SPEAKING UP

IMAGINE THIS: YOU GET UP IN THE MORNING, TURN ON THE TV AND AS you dress for work, you listen to the news being reported by an anchorwoman who wears a size twenty. On the bus to work, you flip through your favorite magazine, which this month, miraculously, contains no ads that use women's bodies to sell products. During your coffee break, you enjoy the company of the other women in your office, and not one of you, even for a moment, talks about dieting or weight.

After work, you have a doctor's appointment and, for once, the issue of your body size is not a subject for discussion. Later that evening, you have a dinner date with old friends whom you haven't seen for years. And guess what? No one mentions or even thinks about what you're eating or what you weigh.

Does all this sound improbable, even impossible? Improbable, perhaps. Impossible? *No.* This scenario is a potential that may have to wait for our daughter's daughter's daughter's time, but it *is* a possibility and it *can* happen—if we lay the groundwork. Until that time arrives, all of us have to figure out how to handle what comes flying at us in all directions from a misogynistic culture that tells women to shrink their bodies and curb their appetites.

All of us frequently encounter friends, coworkers, family

members, doctors, exercise/fitness personnel, and all sorts of other people who feel free to comment on our eating habits and our size. In fact, when it comes to bodies and eating, no comment, however rude or hurtful, is off-limits. Whether they are overt or subliminal, intrusive remarks about weight and food are culturally sanctioned—and rampant.

How do you handle the wayward wounding comment? Generally, there are two main points to keep in mind. First, remind yourself that whatever people are saying to you is no different from what you have said to yourself about fat and food for so many years. Like you, everyone else in this society has learned their lessons all too well. But that is changing, which brings us to our second point. Now, when others direct their comments at you, you can begin to deal with them in a productive rather than self-denigrating way. This is not easy, but the rewards are all yours. Think of it in this way: Each time someone makes a comment, you have the opportunity to firm up your newfound views about eating and weight. These views may still be somewhat shaky, but speaking up will help you anchor your new perspective securely within yourself.

Body Talk

Asserting, Not Defending

You're walking down the street, thinking what a beautiful day this is, when a band of construction workers suddenly breaks into a chorus of elephantine "ba-boom, ba-booms" as you approach them.

You're standing in line at a checkout counter. Not having had the time to shop for the past two weeks, you've got a very full cart. The person behind you gives you and your shopping cart the once-over. "Ever hear of world hunger?" he sneers. "Think how many people you could feed with all that."

You're standing in a movie line with your six-year-old daughter and the woman behind you murmurs in a soft, sympathetic voice, "She's got such a pretty face. You should help her lose weight before it's too late."

Can you think of any other group of people who are the targets of such freely offered comments and unsolicited advice? Racial minorities? Not a chance in this day and age. The physically challenged? Most average people view themselves as far too sensitive to make such transgressions. Yet women of large size are targets for the kind of wholesale derision, cruelty, and insensitivity that we have cited above. The question is, what do we do about it?

When we hear comments of this nature, many of us want to disappear down a big hole or rise up and smash whoever is responsible. While both responses are understandable, they are also both defensive and counterproductive.

When you shrink in shame in the face of hostile remarks, you collude with your insulters. You feel too humiliated to reply, because part of you still agrees with the insults. As difficult as this may sound, it is important for you to challenge that voice within that agrees you shouldn't eat so much, shouldn't buy so much food, shouldn't take up space, . . . shouldn't, shouldn't, shouldn't.

Margot, an office manager in Jacksonville, Florida, admitted to us just how hard it is for her to speak up. "The other day my brother-in-law asked me why hadn't I lost weight yet with this antidiet program," she reported. "He went so far as to say that it must be because I've been too busy eating all those Oreo cookies. I didn't say anything but, boy, was I angry! A few hours later, the incident was still bothering me so I decided that, instead of turning his words against myself and having bad body thoughts, I'd think about why I didn't respond to him and what I could have said."

This process proved quite useful to Margot. "I figured out that I didn't respond because I had the very same question. Why wasn't I losing weight? Was I eating all the wrong foods? Apparently I felt shaky about having legalized Oreos, along with everything else. I also forgot, under pressure, that it's not food per se that makes compulsive eaters gain weight. I realize now that even if I can't speak up at the moment, I can use my discomfort to zero in on what I need to challenge in myself and how best to speak up the next time."

The more Margot reflected, the more she got a handle on her experience. "I could have pointed out to my brother-in-law that even though I haven't lost weight, for the first time in my life I'm not afraid of food and I'm not obsessing about the size of my hips. I could even have said, 'The fact is, I may never lose

any weight. But that's okay with me because I'm feeling great.' Next time, I might even ask him how he would feel about me if I never lost an ounce. Would it make any difference in our relationship? I hope I will speak up the next time, but even if I don't, I know that some day I will."

Sometimes it's hard for people to speak up, not only because the comments of others mirror our old ways of thinking, but because at times we actually use such comments to bolster internal resistance to our new point of view.

Emily, for example, told us, "I was speechless when my roommate asked me how I could possibly eat foods high in fat when I was struggling with my weight." The reason Emily was speechless was because she had not resolved this issue within herself. Emily was having a hard time legalizing foods and was not able to feel free about her food choices. In fact, in the not-so-distant past, she had told her roommate that it would be better if they bought only low-fat foods for the house because she was watching her weight. Although she was trying to change this line of thinking, she had not yet done so fully and therefore did not have much to say in response to her roommate's intrusive comment.

What can you do when the time for quiet suffering has passed? What if you are rightfully angered by other people's comments and want to lash out? After all, when people invade your space, unrestrained anger seems like a perfectly appropriate response. We have learned, however, that lashing out actually underscores a defensive position. Consider the following two responses to the same situation.

Marion, who weighs 280 pounds and is five feet tall, was shopping in a mall one Sunday afternoon. A little girl pointed at her and said repeatedly, "Mommy, look at the fat lady." The girl's mother unsuccessfully tried to hush her. Finally, Marion walked over and said, "You'd better teach that little brat some manners."

A woman named Helaine had exactly the same thing happen to her. However, she walked over to the child and said, "You know, you're right. I'm probably one of the fattest women you've ever seen. And do you know what? I'm also a mommy and I teach school and I love to swim. What do you like to do in your free time?" Helaine then assured the mother that she needn't bother to silence her daughter; the child was not being impolite but simply making an observation. "Furthermore, by hushing up children," she said, "you give them the impression that there is something unspeakable about fat."

Helaine was on sure ground. She felt very accepting of her size and was able to respond from a position of power and strength. She asserted herself and in the process was actually able to educate others. Marion's angry response, on the other hand, just pushed people away and did nothing for Marion herself. In fact, she became very defensive and walked away feeling ashamed and powerless.

When speaking up for yourself, you must first think about how to state your case in a way that will help you. But before you begin, bear in mind that you will never be able to convince everyone of your perspective. In fact, convincing others is not the point of speaking up.

Presumably you have already made up your mind to stop dieting, to legalize food, to feed yourself on demand, and to become a loving caretaker of your body, whatever size it may be. Whether others agree or disagree is immaterial; you, and you alone, have decided on an approach. Still, we recommend an assertive response to situations such as the above, as long as you understand the difference between what is genuinely *assertive* and what is unproductively *aggressive.*

If your new way of thinking still feels shaky, you probably still feel vulnerable, defensive, and edgy. When your partner says, "Do you really need to eat that? You just had dinner," you might be tempted to snap, "Yes, and why is it any of your business?" But that would mark the end of a very nice evening.

Instead you might say something like the following: "I know you find it hard to watch me eat when you think I shouldn't. You have watched me diet for years and I have always insisted that you keep certain foods out of sight. Now I've given up ideas of abstinence and I'm learning to eat on demand. I really think this way of eating is best for me, even if it makes no sense to you. I hope you can hold back on your comments, but when you can't, I'll remind you." Do you hear the difference? We're sure you do. Again, bear in mind that you can arrive at this stage of assertion only when *you* believe that it is totally fine for you to be eating.

Let's look at some guidelines for making these kinds of assertions. The best assertion is one that acknowledges the fact that you were once of the same mind as the person commenting on your size and/or your eating. In other words, you let them know that you understand where they are coming from. Once you have established this, you can move on to explain that you now see things differently and you can explain as much about your new point of view as feels comfortable for you. You genuinely do not feel defensive, and you genuinely hope that others can hear what you have to say. Let's look at another example.

You and your mother-in-law are going out to lunch. Suddenly she says, "Darling, why do you tuck in that shirt when you wear those pants? You have such beautiful clothes and I know how much you want to look good. It would be much more flattering if you wore it out." Your response might be, "I know that we were all taught that tucking in our shirts was too revealing and made fat women look even fatter, but now I see it differently. I feel better and prefer how I look when I'm more defined; it's really how I want to dress now. I know this will sound strange to you, but I really like my body just the way it is. In fact, I may be this size forever, so I don't want to wait until I'm thinner to tuck in my shirts." With that, you head for lunch, your dignity and your relationship with your mother-in-law intact.

Speaking Up at Gatherings

"I don't want to go to my high school reunion. What will people think when they see how fat I've gotten?" Sound familiar? The first step toward resolving this kind of conflict is to realize that you fear public opinion because you were once part of that public. You know what people might say about your weight because you have had all the thoughts one could possibly have on this topic. Indeed, you have probably vilified yourself much more thoroughly than anyone else ever could. Consequently, an entire litany of imagined indictments plays through your mind when you imagine what might be going through the minds of your reunited schoolmates. "How could she have let herself go like that?" "I remember her as being thin and beautiful. What could have happened?" "Look at her. She must be in real trouble."

In fact, some of your best friends from high school may be thinking just what your worst fears suggest they are thinking. The question is, how are you going to deal with that? For starters, you can remind yourself of your new thinking on the subject of fat. The fundamental tenet of this new thinking is that fat is not a moral violation nor is it a measure of intellect, popularity, sensitivity, leadership, or character. Your body size reflects your genetics, metabolism, years of dieting, age, and history of using food to allay anxiety. Furthermore, you could not possibly weigh what you weighed twenty years ago and, for that matter, no one else attending the reunion will weigh the same either. Your weight reflects not only your aging process but also your years of living. You may have had . . . a difficult divorce . . . money problems . . . pregnancies . . . a career change. Today, those challenges are behind you. After years of dieting, however, you were left with an eating problem, and now you are resolving that.

Others may still be filled with the usual misconceptions about fat, but the stronger you are in your new views, the less upsetting their misconceptions will be. Although you yourself were once a card-carrying member of this fat-phobic public, remember that you have gone on to challenge these notions and have changed your mind about many things. Perhaps others can do the same.

Another angle to consider: It is likely that other factors are making it difficult for you to contemplate going to this reunion—perhaps disappointment in your career or in your marriage. Instead of coming to grips with the real conflicts you are experiencing, you have targeted your weight as the focal point of your concern. Once you feel entitled to go where you want to go, at whatever size you are, you will have a far better chance of getting in touch with the real issues that have been troubling you.

One night, in one of our New York workshops, Mirella tried to figure out what was really troubling her about her upcoming high-school reunion. The group pushed her to go beyond her initial thought: They will see how fat I've gotten. It took awhile, but her expression finally changed and she said quietly, "I know what I think they will really see. Twenty years ago I was voted most likely to succeed. I'm afraid I haven't lived up to that title. I guess I haven't made up my mind about whether I'm satisfied with myself." Once this insight surfaced, Mirella felt relieved. "It doesn't have to do with my weight at all," she realized, "and I feel much more relaxed about going."

Let's say that you, like Mirella, go to a reunion, office party, wedding, or baby shower and someone says to you, "My, you've gained some weight since I last saw you." What should your response be? In one of our workshops, members tossed around a few possibilities. "Oh, I hadn't noticed," someone suggested. "Thanks for sharing." We would categorize this response as somewhat aggressive, but then again, sometimes you just can't resist being a little snide when you know the other person really doesn't have your best interest at heart and simply wants to get a dig in.

If you would like to go beyond aggressive reactions to more constructive behavior, an alternative response might be something like this: "You're observant. I *have* gained some weight. Unfortunately, I spent many years on diets, and as you may have heard, diets make you fatter and are generally unhealthy. I'm out of that trap now and feeling much better." Or consider this response: "Yes, I have put on weight. This has been a hard time for me and food has helped me get through it." Yet another tack: "Yes, I'm bigger now, and even though we live in a culture that thinks fat is bad, I've learned to like my body just the way it is."

Sometimes intrusions can be deflected before you even reach the point where you have to address the unsolicited comment. Susan wanted to join a health club to swim, but was afraid of how others would react to her size. Specifically, she was afraid that they would weigh and measure her. She had heard many stories about such practices. When Susan brought these anxieties to one of our weekly workshops, Arianna, another member of the group, told her, "If you were going to buy a vacuum cleaner, you wouldn't let them measure your arm, would you?"

With that in mind, Susan went to the health club and, before even filling out the application, informed them that if she had to be weighed and measured to gain entry into this club, she would not pursue a membership. They assured her that being weighed and measured was not a requirement, even though it was a routine practice. Susan joined the club, was never measured, and now swims forty laps a day.

Speaking Up at the Doctor's

How many of you put off going to the doctor for fear of what he or she will say about your weight? Your expectations about what you will be told are probably correct. We forget, or perhaps were never taught, that doctors are our consultants. We *hire* them for their opinions and guidance about our health. You may need to go to more than one consultant but, ultimately, it is you who must make the decisions about your body.

Often, when a large woman goes to a doctor for a sore throat, she ends up getting a lecture about her weight, as if the sore throat has something to do with her size. The lecture may be kindly or stern, encouraging or fear-provoking. Regardless of the packaging, the bottom line is that, in many and perhaps most cases, this sort of lecturing is unwanted and unnecessary. How can you best handle this and other situations like it?

You might bluntly tell your physician that you do not want to discuss your weight unless he or she can document how it directly affects the condition that brings you into the office for a visit. And when you go for a check-up and are told to get on the scale, you can ask if this is really necessary.

One workshop participant did just that. Told to step up on the scale, Lily said to her new internist, "I don't want to come here if I have to be weighed. Can you explain your rationale for putting me on a scale, when *I* can tell you my weight within ounces?" The doctor replied, "We need to know your weight in case anything happens to you. If you got sick and started losing weight, I would need to know how much weight you had lost. Or, if I needed to prescribe medicine for you, I would need to know your weight." Lily answered, "First off, if I started to lose weight precipitously, don't you think we would both see that by using our eyes? We wouldn't need the scale as an indicator. Furthermore, if I should need a prescription in the future, my weight today wouldn't be very significant." He thought about what she said and agreed that weighing-in was more a habit than a necessity.

Of course, weighing-in is a habit that carries with it a lot of implications about power, authority, and value. Lily was able to get what she needed and, in doing so, shifted the balance of power—no mean feat when dealing with the medical establishment. In many doctors' offices, it is the nurse who insists that you get on the scale before the doctor attends to you. It is her job and she may be insistent about it. What do you do? You have options. You could ask to speak to the doctor about it, or you could decide to allow her to weigh you, but make it clear that you do not want to know the numbers and turn your back to the scale.

Carrie, five months pregnant, told us that when she visited her obstetrician, he only commented on her weight gain and never once mentioned how the baby was doing. She felt like a naughty child each time she went for one of these visits. This infuriated her because it robbed her of the pleasure of her pregnancy. She took action and wrote the following letter to her doctor.

> If we are to continue our doctor/patient relationship, you need to know something about me. I have been a compulsive eater/dieter ever since a well-meaning pediatrician put me on my first diet at the age of twelve. I have spent years of my life obsessed with weight. I can get on a bathroom scale, find out that I've gained a pound, and scream at myself about it all day. Believe me, I can yell at myself a lot better than you can. I don't need to pay a doctor for that.
>
> Over the last year or two, I've read a lot on the subject of compulsive eating and I have made several permanent changes in my life in relation to food.
>
> Change #1: I will never diet again. Every diet is followed by a period of regaining at least the weight that was lost, usually more.
>
> Change #2: I will not focus on my weight. It is too easy to become obsessed with the numbers that appear on the scale. I refuse to buy into the myth that if the numbers are low, I'm a good girl and I can have a good day. If the numbers are high, I'm a bad girl and a day of self-loathing follows.
>
> I have decided to approach my problem by focusing on physical hunger instead of weight. I will eat each time that my body tells me it needs food, and I will try to eat only the amount that my body requires to satisfy the hunger. If all goes as planned, I will gradually begin to eliminate the times that I eat when I am not hungry. This will not work overnight. However, I am convinced that this approach offers the only permanent solution to my eating problems.
>
> I need your help.
>
> First, I do not want to be weighed each time I come to your

> office. I will not spend the remaining four months of this pregnancy obsessed with weight and food. I am larger than I'm designed to be because I eat for reasons other than physical hunger. If it were possible for me to control that, I would have done so by now. Keeping a monthly record of my weight is not going to help me. If you must know my weight for some medical reason (and I really hope that you decide you don't), I do not want you to discuss it with me. Please understand that I do not want to gain more than the recommended weight; but if I do gain forty or even fifty pounds, the world will not end.
>
> Second, weight and body size are painful issues for most women in this society. You are in a business where all your customers are women. It would help if you were a little more understanding of our problems.
>
> If I don't hear from you within a week or two, I will assume that what I have said is acceptable to you and that we can continue our relationship. Thank you.

As it turned out, Carrie's doctor was apologetic and continued to treat her without any mention of weight. Instead, they discussed her concerns about the baby and her upcoming delivery.

One evening a group member named Anya told us how inspired she had been by Carrie's letter. In fact, it motivated Anya to speak up to her orthopedic surgeon. She had been going to him for a back problem and he had made a joke about not finding a pulse in her legs because they were so heavy. Recently, when she went back for a checkup, she told him that the comment he had made was not funny to her, even if he intended it to be. She went on to say that women are very sensitive about their bodies and do not like these unsolicited comments. Since he treats women of all shapes and sizes, he should try to be more sensitive about this issue.

To Anya's surprise, this doctor was appreciative that she had spoken up. He said that he was unaware that his jokes, which were meant to relax the patient, had quite the opposite effect. He also said that he would try to be more sensitive in the future and actually thanked her for raising his consciousness.

Another evening, a group member named Ruth expressed concern that at her next appointment, her doctor would tell her that losing weight would improve her medical condition. She asked us what she could say in response. We suggested the following:

"I know you are convinced that my medical problems are weight-related, although I have read opinions to the contrary. Be that as it may, the advice I've been given all these years about losing weight has resulted only in weight gain and an even greater obsession with food and body size. We all know now that dieting makes you fatter and is dangerous. I believe that ninety-eight percent of people who lose weight regain that weight, plus some. Therefore, I have decided never to diet again. I need to get good medical treatment at this size. Do you think you can provide that?"

Another woman whom we met at Lake Austin Spa raised a different though related concern. "Forget about doctors for the moment," Kira said. "The worst people to confront are your friends and family who are concerned about your health. What do you do when a dear friend says, 'Why aren't you doing something about your weight? You can hardly walk anymore. You know your knee pain would diminish if you weren't carrying so much weight around.' "

The answer the group formulated went something like this:

"You know better than anyone else that if I could do something to lessen my agony, I would have done it by now. Unfortunately, I listened to my doctors all these years and dieted. Look where it got me . . . fatter with each successive try. I now know that I must do something radically different. I may not lose much weight at first, but at least I won't put any more on. That would be a big relief. As far as my knee problems go, I'm thinking about strengthening my thigh muscles and doing exercises that will help me while I'm at this size. I need relief now and I can't wait until I have a different body. I'm angry that for so many years, I yelled at myself and thought that I had caused this problem when, in fact, the medical community advised me poorly. Now I have to take this into my own hands and I will need all the support I can get from you."

Whose Bad Body Thought Is This, Anyhow?

"My husband says he doesn't find me attractive anymore."

"My lover wants sex less often since I've gained all this weight."

"My coworker looked at me the other day and told me that she was concerned about all the weight I've put on."

"My mother worries about what I eat because she's afraid I won't be able to fit into my wedding gown."

The comments never stop. Like Ole Man River, they just keep rolling along and we are expected to roll along with them. The fact is, we no longer want to.

We talked extensively about bad body thoughts in Chapter 3. We hope we convinced you that each time you comment on the size of your body, no matter what you weigh, you are actually commenting on something else that is disturbing you at that moment. Bad body thoughts are a way of speaking in code. Just as you used to speak in code, other people have also learned to translate their concerns into fat talk—we are all products of our culture.

When others make comments about your body, they are actually having bad body thoughts of their own. They are disguising some private, personal, painful feeling. Let's look at some examples, starting with the most common one: the disgruntled lover or mate who cites your weight as the reason he or she no longer feels as attracted to you sexually.

Let's not mince words here. Having the person you love tell you that he or she does not want to sleep with you because you have put on weight is devastating. You feel that your world is collapsing and that you are to blame. Your old tapes start to play. "Of course I am much less desirable and attractive at this size—in fact, I'm disgusting."

No matter how hard you have been trying to question these assumptions, or how diligently you have tried to break your body-bashing habit, these tapes trigger an old response that makes it extremely difficult to hold your ground and to recognize that what you are dealing with is simply another bad body thought situation.

What you must come to understand is that, this time, it is your partner who is having the bad body thought. He or she is using your body to communicate his or her own issue. This issue may have nothing whatsoever to do with you or it may involve you in some tangential way, but rest assured, it is *not* about the shape of your body. Perhaps your lover has difficulty with intimacy or is having a hard time at work and feels powerless. Somehow, your body has become the target. If, however, you do not allow yourself to succumb to the slings and arrows, and if, instead of caving in, you hold your ground, you may be able to find out what is really going on.

A group member named Harriet told us about her experience. "My husband said he couldn't stand how fat I've gotten. Fat, to him, is a sign of weakness and he can't stand weak people. I was so hurt and so angry. At first I told him that the size of my body was none of his business and that I didn't want him making any comments about it. I reminded him that I don't comment on his baldness. But then I realized we were just getting into name-calling, so I took a deep breath and remembered the group's discussion about other peoples' bad body thoughts. An hour later, away from the heat of the moment, I approached him and said, 'We need to talk.' I told him what I had learned about all the yelling I do at myself and how I use my body as a target for all of my unspoken thoughts and feelings. I then asked if he would think about what was going on in him at the moment he told me that my fat represented a weakness that he found repulsive. What was going on at that moment *inside of him* that he was repulsed by?"

The group waited to hear how Harriet's husband responded. "At first he insisted that his concern was my weight," Harriet continued. "I told him that I, too, had always assumed that my bad body thoughts were about my body but had learned otherwise. I pointed out to him that I had been the same size for months before he raised the issue. I kept pushing and finally he was able to say that during a staff meeting that day, he felt he had not come across with his point of view strongly enough and, in fact, he was voted down on a very important issue. So it was *his* weakness that was bothering him and that provoked the bad body thought he directed at me."

Natalie, who teaches aerobics in Portland, Maine, told us this story. "I started a new class last week and in walked a trim-looking man," she recounted. "He took one look at me and came hurrying over before the class began. He asked me how I could be teaching this class when I myself was heavy. He had expected a thinner instructor. At first I was taken off-guard. In fact, I suddenly felt a bit inadequate and started to question my own abilities. Then this little voice reminded me that this was *his* bad body thought and I should not allow myself to be taken in by it. Instead, I asked him if there was anything else upsetting him other than my size. He offhandedly mentioned that he was surprised to see that he was the only man in the class. Then I understood the comment. He felt overpowered by all these women. What better way to assert control and put me in my place than to talk about my fat? It was a good thing that I got a grip on myself, because the fact is, I am one hell of a good aerobics instructor."

Friends, coworkers, or family members may raise the question of your weight in more benign ways. They are "concerned about you" or "worried about your health" or "just thinking about how wonderful you looked after your last diet." In fact, they mean well. Why is it, then, that their comments feel unbearably oppressive to you? For a very good reason: They are making *you* the dumping ground for *their* bad body thoughts.

At the moment your friend or colleague brings up *your* size, there is something on *her* mind, and we can assure you that the "something" is not the size of your thighs. Your friend may think it is and you may think so, too, but it's much more complicated than that. Two days ago you weighed the same as you do now, but did she feel compelled to say anything then? No.

This other person in your life operates the same way you do. You have the same body every day. On certain days, however, you *feel* fat, and on certain days, she *feels like drawing attention* to your weight. She chooses to say something at a given moment because something is bothering her, something she cannot name directly or, perhaps, even acknowledge. Maybe she just got off the phone, having lost an account to a competitor in another firm. You stop by to talk; she looks at you; she says that she is worried about you because you have gotten so much bigger. Who's too big? You? Or the competitor?

When people make these kind of remarks, we are quick to take them personally and at face value. It's hard not to. Remember, however, that a bad body thought is never about your body *even when it's someone else's.* If you keep that in mind, you will be able to figure out how to respond. Don't forget that you have options and that these options should be tailor-made for the situation at hand. Sometimes you may want to address the other person's bad body thought very simply. "I know you're concerned about my size, but I'm actually quite pleased with how I'm handling my eating and my weight," you might say. "I've stopped dieting and I'm feeling great."

With others, you may decide to engage in a more elaborate exchange. For example, Wanda told us that she got to a point where she could no longer listen to the concerns that her lover Joan had been voicing about her body. So one morning, when Joan launched into another discussion of Wanda's weight, Wanda decided it was time to take the matter in hand.

"I know that, at this moment, you believe that the problem is my fat, but I don't see it that way," Wanda stated squarely. "I've come to realize that when any of us focus on fat, it has to do with some discomfort we're feeling but are unable to name. I talk fat language too, but now I know that it is a signal that something is bothering me—and it's *not* my body. I know it's tempting to believe that the problem at the moment is my size, but I assure you, it's not."

Another group member, Suzanne, told us how she handled a recent interaction with her mother. They had gone out to eat and, as soon as Suzanne placed her order, her mother had said, "You know, dear, don't you think you should order something less fattening? Remember that your wedding is in six weeks and you want to make sure you'll still fit into your wedding gown."

Suzanne responded by saying, "Mom, I know you have my best interests at heart, but I've spent my life focusing on my eating and my weight, and I'm not willing to do that anymore. I want to enjoy the preparations for the wedding. Whatever my weight is, it will be just fine. I've already spoken to a seamstress in my neighborhood. If my gown needs to be let out at the last minute, she can do it without much cost or hassle. I know you want everything to be perfect and I'm sure I'll look terrific. So let's enjoy our meal."

There are times when an examination of the other person's bad body thought can illuminate the sometimes murky depths of a relationship. Take the case of a group member named Barbara, who had put on some weight before visiting her elderly aunt. After Barbara's third square of her aunt's famous shortbread, which Barbara hadn't been lucky enough to taste in several years, her aunt said, "You know, you're starting to look like your sisters. You used to be the thin one."

Although her aunt's remark stung a bit, Barbara resolved not to let it bother her unduly. Instead, she realized that something must be bothering her aunt and it certainly wasn't her weight. She thought about her aunt's comments in the same way she would think about her own bad body thoughts and she asked her aunt, "In what ways—besides my weight—am I beginning to resemble my sisters?"

With that seemingly innocent question, an important story unfolded. Because she was straightforward and spoke her mind, Barbara had always been this aunt's favorite niece. The two of them had enjoyed a very honest relationship over the years.

Recently, however, Barbara's aunt felt she was being lied to—and, in fact, she was. Barbara's mother, her aunt's sister, had long been in a nursing home with Alzheimer's disease. The aunt, who herself was growing increasingly enfeebled, had the uneasy feeling that her sister had died and that no one had told her the truth, not even Barbara. So when the aunt told Barbara she was getting heavy like her sisters, what she really wanted to say was, "You're getting to be like your sisters—who always lie to me."

In an emotional moment, Barbara admitted to her aunt that her mother had died a month earlier. Painful as the exchange was for them, it was still a relief to both Barbara and her aunt that Barbara had been able to decode bad body thoughts, *even when they belonged to someone else.*

You never know who will voice a bad body thought, but you should always be prepared. Often in our workshops large women report being asked if they are pregnant. Different people ask the question—coworkers, friends, family, even strangers on the street. It's a touchy situation that needs a sophisticated reply.

Sheila works in a conservative law firm. Her boss, who is a woman, said to her, "People in the office have been too embarrassed to ask you, but they've noticed that you're wearing loose-fitting clothes. Are you pregnant?" Sheila told our group that she was mortified by this question. She was particularly upset because she felt it was a hostile question, since her boss knows how she struggles with her weight.

When asked to provide some background on what had happened, Sheila told the group that she had taken to wearing a new style of clothing to work in order to feel more comfortable. "Is this the price I have to pay for comfort?" Sheila asked the group. The women in the group agreed that as long as she was subscribing to the firm's informal dress code, which she was, Sheila should certainly not have to pay a price for her newly found comfort. They went on to point out that Sheila's new, more relaxed look might be threatening to her boss, who is fairly uptight. Sheila agreed, although she still wasn't clear about how she might have handled the situation.

Wanda had a suggestion. "Perhaps you could have said: 'No, I'm not pregnant. If I were, I would have told you. What I think you're referring to is my being large and, specifically, the fact that I've taken to wearing a different style of clothing. You're seeing my stomach. All women have stomachs, even when they're not pregnant. It comes with being female.' "

Carla, in our New York workshop, told us about a time a younger woman offered her a seat on a crowded bus. She knew that the woman mistook her for being pregnant and she was incredibly embarrassed. "I didn't know what to do," she told the group. "I was so tongue-tied I just said, 'Thank you,' and sat down. I felt mortified. I spent days thinking about how else I could have handled the situation. I would love to get to a point where I could just smile and say, 'Thanks a lot. I know I look pregnant, but I'm not. Thanks anyway.' I know I have a ways to go in the acceptance department before I'll be able to do that, but I felt better after I came up with a possible reply."

"Positive" Fat Talk

When people you love are not commenting on how bad you look, how much weight you've gained, or how much you've eaten, they are often commenting positively about these very same issues. "Oh, you look so great. You've lost so much weight."

In the past, you sought out or welcomed these positive comments about your eating and your weight. You received them as compliments. Underneath your momentary thrill, however, was an angry feeling that you may or may not have experienced consciously. Your anger was connected to the unspoken question, "What was wrong with me before?"

It may seem strange to consider that these positive remarks could be anything less than positive. But in our experience, and in the experience of people who have been doing this work for any length of time, positive comments like these are jarring. First of all, they are intrusive. Your body belongs to you. It should not be up for inspection at every turn. Furthermore, there is much more to you than the size of your body and you deserve to be related to as a person.

At its core, the problem of "positive" comments is very complicated. Many group members are surprised by how negatively they react to such remarks. As you step yourself in this work, however, you begin to react differently than you did in the past. When your friends used to say, "You're looking great, how much weight have you lost?" you replied, "Thanks. I've lost about ten pounds." Now that same kind of exchange creates conflict.

Saying "thank you" when someone compliments you for losing weight implies that you agree that weight loss is a good thing, deserving of compliments, and that the reason you look good is *because* you have lost weight. The real story, however, is that you felt good about yourself and the way you looked long before you ever lost an ounce. Moreover, if you had not felt good about yourself, you would never have lost any weight. You liked the way you looked before and you like the way you look now. The person giving you the "compliment," however, has a different point of view. She thought you were too fat before and that you look better now because you are thinner.

You are correct to think that if you simply say, "Thank you," you are acquiescing to the traditional view of weight loss. It is important to recognize, however, that people who make "positive" comments about your body sometimes do so when they don't know how else to express themselves. Someone might say, "Gee, you look great," to a friend who has just recovered from knee surgery, when what she means to say is, "I'm so relieved that you're not still suffering—I was worried about you." Few of us would reject the decent impulses behind such comments, and we may be inclined to ascribe similar impulses to "positive" comments about weight.

Indeed, many people with a great deal of experience using our approach still grapple with this issue. Positive comments about their weight and appearance throw them off; they don't know what to do with them. Here are some of the different ways women have solved this particular problem.

Addie, a medical technician, said the following to a friend who had "complimented" her on her weight loss. "I'm glad you think I look good," she said. "I also used to believe that losing weight makes people look better, but I've come to the conclusion that looking good has little to do with weight loss. What you're noticing is how much better I feel because I no longer obsess about my food and my weight."

Another approach was suggested by Tessa. "A friend told me how terrific I looked and assumed it was because I was dieting. Since she is such a dear friend, I explained to her that my looking good had to do more with the feeling of being entitled to dress, shop, eat, and go wherever I want, regardless of my size. I told her that she probably had picked up on my new attitude."

Janet told us that she had more trouble with "compliments" about her weight loss when they were made by casual acquaintances or distant relatives. "I really don't want to give long explanations," she said. "It's true that I've lost a lot of weight, but I don't actually look so different to myself because I've been working in front of the mirror the whole time. I can understand, though, that I look quite different to someone who hasn't seen me for a while. Invariably they say, 'Oh, you look so great. I can't believe how much weight you've lost.' I make it a point never to say thank you. Instead, I say, 'Yes, I have lost weight, but I think what you're reacting to is that I'm feeling good at the moment.' Often, they go on and want to know how I did *it.* I say very simply, 'I gave up dieting and made weight a nonissue in my life.' "

Rachel, who attends our weekly workshops, got straight to the point. "Sooner or later we have to challenge this business of discussing our weight all the time. The other day an old friend said, 'God, you look so different. How much weight have you lost?' I answered her by saying, 'I know you mean well and that you are happy for me, but I see the question of weight differently now than I used to. Women have a way of greeting each other by focusing on what we look like. But I would love for us not to talk about each other's weight and try to say what's on our minds.' "

Food Talk

Food is an integral part of our social lives and many of us who are working on overcoming compulsive eating feel anxious about situations that come up in the context of shared dining. How do you remain true to your own appetite and still break bread with loved ones? To answer this, it is useful to remember that eating is supposed to be an entirely natural function. It makes as little sense to eat when your stomach isn't empty as it does to go to the bathroom when your bladder isn't full.

Relating to others, even when food is present, has to do with a hunger for companionship. Eating, even when others are present, has to do with a hunger for food. With this idea in mind, you can choose from one of many options. If it is important to you to eat with a friend, you can plan your day so that you are likely to be hungry at around the time you have arranged to get together. Or, as we discussed in Chapter 7, you can arrange to meet your friend but not eat if you are not hungry. Deciding to eat or not may have an impact on the people with whom you are dining. Your independence around food may evoke questions and remarks, and you will want to be ready to respond.

I'm Not Hungry

"My new boyfriend is a wonderful cook, and one of the ways he shows that he cares for me is by inviting me over for elaborate dinners," said Ruthie. "I just don't know how to tell him that I may not be hungry when I'm at his house or, if I am, I may want something other than what he has prepared."

Someone in the workshop that night suggested the following. "The next time he calls to ask you over for dinner, tell him how much you appreciate all the trouble he goes to, but then explain that you are trying to eat only when you are hungry and you are trying to match your body's hunger signal with the specific food it needs at any given moment."

Ruthie picked up on this suggestion and decided to talk to her boyfriend about it. "I'm going to say, 'Sometimes I'm just not that hungry when I come over. Do you think we can get together and have food be optional? I know you love to cook, and some of the time I'm prepared to make sure I'm hungry at a specific time, but not every time we see each other. Or if you want to cook on a day we're getting together, how about letting me take some food home with me if I'm not hungry when I'm there? That way I won't miss out but at the same time I won't sabotage my eating needs.' "

Holly, a computer programmer, had a problem related to eating in the workplace. "My staff takes a lunch break together at the same time every day," she told the group. "It's a very social time for us during an otherwise hectic day. They would feel very hurt if I didn't eat with them."

We asked Holly to think about saying that she just wasn't hungry but would love to share their company if not their food. She felt that this response would not work. Others chimed in, saying that they too have trouble not eating at lunch and dinner, especially when that is the social agenda.

Judy told the group that when she was out the other night and didn't eat, her friend said to her, "There you go again. What kind of crazy diet are you on now?" Judy spoke up for herself by saying, "I'm not on any kind of diet. It may sound nuts to you, but from now on I'm only going to eat when my body needs fuel and I'm going to stop when I'm full. Not eating with you is not any reflection on you or on our friendship. It's not meant to make you feel uncomfortable. But I have to tell you that, ever since I started listening to my body, I've never felt better. I wish you could be happy for me."

Louise had yet another story. "I visited my brother for two weeks," she told us. "I really like going there, but I was in a quandary about bringing my own foods and not eating when they do. My sister-in-law is incredibly uptight. You've never seen a kitchen as well organized as hers; she absolutely insists on everything being in its place. I've had trouble with her in the past when I needed to eat differently from them because I was on a diet. Meals and mealtimes are very rigid in that household."

This year, before Louise arrived at her brother's house, she decided to call ahead and pave the way. She reported her conversation with her sister-in-law, Janis, to us:

Louise: I can't wait to see all of you. It's been such a long time. I'm calling you ahead of time to tell you that I'm no longer dieting. . .

Janis: [tsking] Oh, Louise.

Louise: No, listen. Instead of dieting, I'm trying to listen to what my body needs. I eat only when I'm hungry and only what I'm hungry for. I know you want what's best for me and I'm going to need your help while I'm visiting.

Janis: What do you want us to do?

Louise: I'm bringing some food with me that I'm used to eating and I'll need to put some of it in your refrigerator. I will absolutely respect your eating schedule and will be very happy to sit with all of you at meals, but I may choose not to eat at those times if I'm not hungry. I'll be fine just preparing what I need when I'm hungry. This may sound disruptive and weird, but it's quite simple and easy. I've been doing this for some time now and I've never felt better.

Janis: Oh, Louise, why do you always have to make such a big deal about eating? Honestly, if it's not one diet, it's another. People eat meals because that's what they're supposed to do. Is it so hard for you to do that?

Louise: I know after all my years of dieting and restrictions, this sounds like just another crazy solution. But trust me, it isn't. Eating on demand is the most natural process possible. And I finally feel like I'm on the way to resolving my eating problems.

Janis: Well, have you lost any weight yet?

Louise: No, but I'm a lot less obsessed and certainly less miserable. You'll find me much easier to be around and more at peace with myself. I'll tell you more when I see you.

Out of Sight, Out of Mind

There are times when what works for you does not work for someone close to you. For example, when you live with people who have food restrictions due to medical problems, what happens when you want to bring in foods that they cannot tolerate? And what do you do when they have expressed a need to keep certain "forbidden" foods out of the house?

Obviously, part of living with others involves negotiation. Food and eating are areas to think through and discuss. You no longer live in fear of food. As a matter of fact, you know now that you eat less whenever you are surrounded by food. But your spouse or partner may have different needs, and all of it can be talked about.

Martha told us how she handled her situation. "My husband has had several heart attacks and is now on the Pritikin diet. I feel like I've been sneaking around, eating all those foods that he's not allowed to eat and that we're not supposed to keep in the house. Of course, I want to help him take good care of himself, but in the process, I see what's happening to me.

"It became clear to me that I needed to pay as much attention to myself as my husband does to himself," Martha continued. "He has a heart problem and I have an eating problem. He is quite aware of what he needs to do about his food. But what about me? I thought it was time that I talk with him openly about what I needed to do for my problem. We had to come to terms about our different dietary needs."

Making the decision to talk with her husband was not easy for Martha. "I feared that if I brought in my foods, he would be tempted to eat them and then go off Pritikin," she said. "That thought made me feel too guilty for words. In fact, he has told me that seeing foods around that he can't eat is extremely difficult for him. But I pushed myself to discuss this with him at a time when we both were relaxed and not on the run. Together we came up with some possible solutions.

"First, we came up with the idea of labeling my foods and agreeing that he wasn't allowed to take from my supply. This seemed like a good idea, because I remember your saying in *Overcoming Overeating* that we need to protect our supply so that we know it's always there. We tried this out for a while, but he had too much trouble seeing these goodies of mine around. So we tried another approach. I put my food in a separate place, a place where it wouldn't be in his face. I don't feel like I'm hiding the food, because whenever I want some, I eat it openly, just like he eats his Pritikin food openly."

Although the process was a difficult one for Martha, it has paid off. "I realize now that the mechanics of what to do about this problem are workable as long as I don't defer my needs to his," she told us. "His problem may be life-threatening, but I'm dealing with a problem that has consumed my life."

A Family Affair

Many women are concerned about how our approach to food will impact their children. We believe that there is no healthier way to raise children than to feed them on demand. But we also know that old ways die hard. Parents are under enormous pressure to "control" their children's eating behavior. Even if you remember how much chaos this kind of control created in your own life, it is difficult to feel secure enough to let your children eat when, what, and how much they want. Do not be surprised if your community—relatives, friends, teachers—does not understand or approve of what you are doing. After all, you once shared their point of view and you may still have your own doubts about demand feeding. Your insecurity, however, should not hold you captive to their beliefs.

It may be unusual for children to grow up seeing their mother eat an ice cream sandwich for dinner, but we believe that you are setting a very good example by eating on demand and not yelling at yourself about your eating or your weight. We encourage you to read *Preventing Childhood Eating Problems* by Jane R. Hirschmann and Lela Zaphiropoulos. This book teaches you how to set up a demand-feeding approach with your children.

At this point, the best thing you can do for your children's eating is to get this approach under way for yourself. Explain what you are doing to your children, and make certain that you do *not* apologize for it. You might educate them by saying something like the following:

"You have heard me yell about how fat I am and how I should eat less and diet more. Well, I've changed my mind about all of that. I know now that dieting is a bad thing and instead, I'm going to feed myself much the same way I fed you when you were a baby—when, what, and how much your body needed. That's the way we all should eat. My food choices and eating patterns may look strange to you at first, particularly because I will be eating in a way that I used to tell you not to do. I know now that I made a mistake when I tried to control your eating. If this works well for me, and if you're interested, we can all eat on this system.

"For now, I will need to bring in a lot of food and have it around at all times. I'm going to put my name on my foods. If they're foods you like, I'll get you your own supply. I think we'll try to keep dinnertime at six o'clock, but I'll check with everyone to see who's hungry and for what before I start cooking. From now on, no one will be forced to eat at mealtimes, even though I may still want us to sit down and be together."

You may feel that before you can embark on a new way of living in the world with food, you have to organize everyone in your family to do the same. A word of caution: You cannot possibly put everyone in your family on this system until you have figured out what the system is and where you encounter roadblocks. In speaking to your family about this approach, remember that the goal is to pave the way for you to focus on *your* process. It should not be your intention to convince everyone that this is the approach they need to follow. Studies done on children and eating show that kids, in the long run, end up eating much like their parents. No surprise. Parents have a huge influence on their youngsters. Once you have become comfortable with this approach, your children will follow by example.

Speaking up is a process that needs your continual fine-tuning. Remember that each time someone comments on your weight or your eating it is an opportunity for you to strengthen your new views by voicing them out loud. As we said earlier, you must first let people know that you hear them and understand where they are coming from. Second, state that you see things differently and move on to express your point of view. There is no need to be defensive and no need to convert anyone to your position. You are simply stating and restating your point of view whenever it is necessary. Above all, remember that this is *your* body and *your* eating.

A Final Word

We are often asked for "good, hard data" to validate our work. "How do we know that your approach really works?" professional and laypeople alike ask. "We know all about the evidence against diets," they say, "but where is the evidence that you are any more successful?" And the inevitable one: "How about some statistics to show that your approach really does cure compulsive eating?"

More interesting than these questions (or our answers to them) is the bigger question of what people are really asking for when they ask for "good, hard data." The fact is, the information they really want in order to determine whether or not we are successful is information about weight. Do people who use our approach lose weight? Do they keep their weight off? Do they gain weight?

Questions like these are reasonable when asking whether or not a diet is successful, because the promise of a diet is that you will lose weight. Indeed, most diets fulfill that promise for a while, but most women who "succeed" at traditional diets never touch upon their painful obsession with food and weight.

The goal of our program is to liberate those of you who have spent a lifetime hating your bodies and feeling tortured by your compulsive relationship with food. We do not judge our success by the numbers on your scale, but by *the extent to which you accept yourself.* We do not judge our success by the willpower you call into play in your efforts to avoid the foods you crave, but by the degree of comfort you feel around food and by the extent to which you are able to think about your problems rather than eat about them. Many of the women who meet our standards of success lose weight as well. Their weight loss, however, is a byproduct of our approach—it is not the goal.

When a participant in an Overcoming Overeating workshop tells us that our approach is working, she is referring to the fact that she feels less afraid of food, less hateful toward her body, less driven to eat in response to anxiety, and more driven to eat in response to hunger. In our view, these accomplishments are much more significant and lasting than weight loss. Still, many people cannot imagine what success feels like in a context that does not focus on weight. According to Jackie, a woman in Florida, the kind of success we aim for feels like this:

> I just had to write you personally to thank you for giving my life back to me! I realize now that for the past twenty-five years it has felt like I've been in prison, and you just walked up to my prison door, unlocked it and said, "You're free—go out and enjoy your life!" This may sound exaggerated, but it's really *exactly* how I feel. Never before have I felt so *calm* around food. For the first time in my life, I actually even forgot about foods that are in my house.
>
> I can't begin to tell you how good it feels to be a part of the "real" world now—to have *regular* Coke in my refrigerator for company or even for myself; to bake birthday cakes for people, rather than avoiding that pleasure out of fear; to go to weddings and feel genuinely satisfied (a word I never knew before!) with a piece of cake. I am now able to *live free* in a world of food, without feeling deprived, self-conscious, or uncomfortably restrained!!
>
> My sense of freedom has had an impact on my family as well. This past Valentine's Day, for example, was the first time since I was a child that I got a box of chocolates as a valentine. My husband gave them to me and said that it was really a pleasure to be able to buy me whatever he wanted—instead of worrying about what diet I was on. He gave me the candies in the morning and I ate three pieces. Then something truly *amazing* happened: I *forgot* about them. In the past, the box would have been empty

within an hour, but now they remained right beside my chair all day, and I didn't think about them.

After working for nearly four months at legalizing food, demand feeding seems like a natural next step. I really don't like feeling too full anymore, and I actually enjoy eating when I'm hungry more than when I'm not. But if I'd have told myself when I first started this that I *had* to wait till I was hungry and stop eating when I was full, I think I would have rebelled. It feels good to nurture my hunger instead of fighting against it. I think this is how we were meant to eat in the first place. I'm just going through a healing process to return to that natural state.

Overcoming body hatred and dieting are formidable tasks, and women often lament how much work it takes to free themselves. It *is* true that freeing yourself from Bad Body Fever requires considerable persistence, patience, and courage. You are challenging cultural beliefs that are strongly reinforced as well as battling your own built-in safeguards against change. We have proposed nothing less than a radical, life-changing transformation. We cannot emphasize enough that it is a gradual process, one that requires that you work with yourself gently and compassionately.

Each of us approaches this work with a unique history, a particular style of making changes and individual requirements for outside help. For many, having the support of others making the same struggle is invaluable. We hope that increasing numbers of women will form groups to discuss these issues. Some women prefer to do this work with a professional. They seek out therapists, dietitians or other health providers who embrace the Overcoming Overeating philosophy. What's important is that you get started and that you give yourself permission to do it your way.

Although this is the end of the book, we hope that, for you and for all of us, it is only the beginning of a new chapter. As you know, we sincerely believe that it is crucial for women to move beyond body hatred and dieting. To that end, we have started the Overcoming Overeating Newsletter as a vehicle for women to talk with one another about this process of change. In addition, with the publication of this book, the National Center for Overcoming Overeating is launching the Women's Campaign to End Body Hatred and Dieting. We hope you will join us in these efforts and that together we will find ways to reclaim our bodies, our appetites, and ourselves.

Appendix

A WORD ABOUT THE RESEARCH

WITH THE PUBLICATION OF *OVERCOMING OVEREATING* IN 1988, WE HAD a unique opportunity to reach a large sample of compulsive eaters beyond our private practices. With the help of Linda Nagel, Ph.D., we designed the questionnaires that appear in all editions of the book. Those questionnaires form the basis of our research.

We asked readers to fill out one questionnaire before reading the book and another three months later. Approximately five percent of the 200,000 people who bought our book responded to these questionnaires. We began to code and analyze the information from our readers with the help of a grant from *American Health* magazine, then edited by Joel Gurin.

What were we after? First, we wanted to find out whether women's need to eat in a driven way was changed by the Overcoming Overeating approach. Second, we wanted to see if our approach had an impact on the way women felt about their bodies.

The results delighted us. It was clear that our respondents made some very significant changes in three short months. We realized, however, that our results could be discounted because of problems with our sampling and our time frame. It could be argued, for example, that only those readers who were successful with our approach would bother to send in the second questionnaire. And, with regard to our three-month time frame between questionnaires, many people who go on diets feel that they are successful after three months as well. We decided to extend our research to include a two-year follow-up study.

Dr. Mary Steinhardt, a professor in the Department of Kinesiology and Health Education at the University of Texas at Austin joined our project. We sent the two-year follow-up questionnaire only to women who had responded to the first questionnaire but had not sent in the second one. From a sample of 750 women, 656 were still at the same address two years later. Of these 656, 420 returned our second questionnaire and became part of our study. We assumed that this sample would yield different results from those who sent back the three-month follow-up report. We were wrong.

We developed several scales, the first of which was an eating preoccupation scale, which measured how much time people spent obsessing about food and eating. As part of this scale, respondents were asked to rate statements such as "I feel ashamed of my eating habits," "I feel controlled by food," and "I think about food much of the time."

A body preoccupation scale measured the extent to which our respondents were preoccupied by thoughts about their weight and appearance. For example, statements on this scale included "I'm ashamed of how I look," "My weight makes me feel bad about myself," and "I feel that I am overweight."

A third scale—an emotional eating scale—measured how often certain emotions sent a respondent in search of food. We asked readers whether they reached for food when they felt anxious, lonely, tired, angry, unloved, worried, and so on. All of these responses were compared with the responses given by the same readers two years earlier, before reading the book for the first time.

What we found was a confirmation of our work. There were significant decreases in body preoccupation, eating preoccupation, and the need to eat compulsively in response to a variety of emotional states. The results are recorded in the research report that follows.

By way of summary, however, it is significant to note that 90.2 percent of our respondents felt some degree of shame about their appearance before reading *Overcoming Overeating* and two years later, only 66 percent felt this way; 94.6 percent felt controlled by food before reading the book, and only 65.4 percent felt that way two years later; 88.6 percent ate when they were angry before reading the book, compared to 72.3 percent two years later.

Colleagues in related fields are now studying our approach. These studied, which support our premise that you can begin to cure your compulsive need to eat only once you have stopped dieting, will add to the burgeoning body of antidiet research.

EFFECTIVENESS OF THE OVERCOMING OVEREATING APPROACH TO THE PROBLEM OF COMPULSIVE EATING

Mary A. Steinhardt, Ed.D.,
and Linda Nagel, Ph.D.*

Abstract

The purpose of this study was to examine the effectiveness of a nondiet approach, described in the book *Overcoming Overeating*, in reducing eating preoccupation, body preoccupation, and emotional eating over a 2-year period. 750 subjects who had purchased *Overcoming Overeating* were used to investigate the efficacy of this nondiet approach. Repeated measures ANOVAs revealed significant decreases in eating preoccupation, body preoccupation, and emotional eating over the 2-year period. Using multivariate analysis that controlled for entry level measures, we found positive associations between the mechanics of the curriculum and eating preoccupation, body preoccupation, and emotional eating (R^2 values increased from 8% to 15%). Given the poor outcomes of current weight-loss treatments, the public health implications of encouraging individuals to stop dieting and adopt a non-restrained, internally directed eating style called demand feeding should be evaluated further.

Effectiveness of the Overcoming Overeating Approach to the Problem of Compulsive Eating

It has been argued that the prevalence of dieting among women in our society has more to do with physical appearance and social mobility than with health (Berman, 1975; Ernsberber & Haskew, 1987; Rodin, Silberstein, & Striegel-Moore, 1985; Rothblum, 1990, 1992; Wooley & Wooley, 1984). Current socie-

*Mary A. Steinhardt, Ed.D., is Associate Professor, Department of Kinesiology and Health Education, The University of Texas, Austin, TX 78712. Linda Nagel, Ph.D., is with the Columbia-Presbyterian Medical Center, New York, New York.

tal preference for a thin physique has lead to a preoccupation with food and body size such that "normal" eating is now characterized by dieting (Polivy & Herman, 1987). Weight-loss treatments, the cultural prescription for the body size problem, are generally ineffective (Brownell & Kramer, 1989; Goodrick and Foreyt, 1991; Kramer, Jeffrey, & Forster, 1989; Wadden, Stunkard, & Liebschutz, 1988; Wooley & Garner, 1991; Wooley & Wooley, 1984) and in fact create more problems than they solve (Polivy & Herman, 1983, 1985a, 1985b). Even the few who manage to lose weight may not be much better off; their lives are often characterized by constant preoccupation with weight and body size, semi-starvation, and symptoms produced by chronic hunger (Vincent, 1979).

Diets are ineffective because, physiologically and psychologically, people fight back against food restrictions. Numerous investigations have demonstrated that the body responds to dieting by a metabolic slowdown (Brownell, 1987; Dullo & Calokatisa, 1990; Dullo & Girardier, 1990; Pavlou, Hoefer, & Blackburn, 1986; Steen, Opplinger, & Brownell, 1988), which may contribute to weight regain after a period of dietary restriction. The majority of people who lose weight return to baseline levels after one year (Goodrick & Foreyt, 1991). Lasting weight loss occurs only in approximately 5% of individuals trained in behavioral self-management of obesity (Kramer, Jeffrey, & Forster, 1989), and 10% of individuals who combine behavioral training with very low-calorie diets (Wadden et al., 1988). Chronic dieting is a testimony to the failure of diets to resolve eating problems. Given the rarity of long-term success, most dieters experience frequent weight fluctuations, which have been associated with a greater risk for coronary heart disease and death (Lissner et al., 1991).

On a psychological level, people respond to the deprivation of dieting with the desperation of binging (Polivy & Herman, 1985, 1987). "Binge eating" or "compulsive eating" is both a consequence and a precipitant of dietary restraint (Wardle, 1987). Compulsive eating, which is increasingly prevalent in the population (Conners & Johnson, 1987; Heatherton & Baumeister, 1991; Katzman, Wolchik, & Braver, 1984; Pyle, Mitchell, & Eckert, 1993), reflects the conflict between a biological drive for food and a cultural drive for thinness. The authors of *Overcoming Overeating* view the compulsive reach for food both as a natural response to the restriction of dieting and as an attempt at self-soothing that ultimately fails. When individuals eat compulsively, they are using food to evoke feelings of comfort and caretaking, because at that moment they are unable to perform those functions intrapsychically (Hirschmann & Munter, 1988).

Emotional distress can produce increases or decreases in eating behavior. In dieters, it appears that the distress of ego threats or personal failures disinhibits otherwise inhibited eating behaviors. In contrast, nondieters experience physiological suppression of eating following ego threats or personal failures (Heatherton, Herman, & Polivy, 1991).

Disinhibition in dieters is associated with low self-esteem. Compulsive eating is almost invariably followed by self-recrimination about eating and body size (Heatherton & Baumeister, 1991; Polivy, Heatherton, & Herman, 1988). The subsequent self-hatred, which mimics cultural attitudes toward overeating and overweight, serves to punish the individual for needing to go to food for help. Compulsive eating also serves to block self-awareness and meaningful thought about identity and the implications of life events (Heatherton & Baumeister, 1991). In the end it disguises the true nature of the problem (Hirschmann & Munter, 1988). People spend lifetimes thinking they have eating and weight problems, when, in fact they have calming problems.

Given the negative outcomes of weight loss treatments, many frustrated dieters are beginning to consider alternative approaches (Ciliska, 1990; Polivy & Herman, 1992). One nondiet alternative is presented in the book *Overcoming Overeating* (Hirschmann & Munter, 1988). The book is based on 20 years of clinical experience working with compulsive eaters in individual and group settings. The purpose of this study was to evaluate the effectiveness of this nondiet approach in reducing eating preoccupation, body preoccupation, and emotional eating over a two-year period.

METHODS

Subjects for the study were a convenience sample (N=750) randomly selected from the population of approximately 2,700 individuals who in 1989 had independently obtained the book *Overcoming Overeating* and completed and returned a questionnaire in the back of the book before they started reading. Each of these 750 individuals was mailed a follow-up questionnaire a minimum of two years after receipt of the first questionnaire ($X=26.77 \pm 2.97$ months). Ninety-four of these subjects had changed addresses and could not be contacted. Of the remaining 656 subjects, 420 questionnaires were returned following two reminder letters, for a return response of 64%. All subjects were women and represented all 50 states across the United States. The study was approved by the review board for research with human subjects at the first author's university.

Overcoming Overeating Approach

PROGRAM PREMISE. A compulsive eater is defined as anyone whose hand or mind reaches for food although she is not physiologically hungry. This symptom occurs in people of all sizes and not all overweight individuals are overeaters.

The compulsive reach for food can be caused by the cultural mandate to be "thin" with its handmaiden, dieting, and/or by anxiety. Whether the compulsion results from efforts to diet or developmental failure and intra-psychic conflict, the result is the same. Overeaters have disconnected eating from physiological hunger.

A cure for overeating must first help a person challenge cultural attitudes toward body size and cultural pressure to diet. Second, a cure must help people eliminate the need to use food as a tranquilizer rather than as a fuel. This is accomplished by reconnecting food with physiological hunger (i.e., feeding oneself on demand). When a person begins to eat on demand, anxiety is reduced and the need to reach for food compulsively is greatly diminished.

PROGRAM DESCRIPTION. In the initial phase of this work, people are encouraged to challenge attitudes about eating and weight that they have previously taken for granted. Although body hatred feels like an inherited characteristic, it is important to demonstrate that it is acquired, and functions as a displacement for other concerns. People are encouraged to accept their body size as evidence of their genetic heritage as well as their history with food and eating, neither deserving of contempt. It is stressed that accepting one's body whatever its size is a precondition for losing weight; that criticism and contempt produce anxiety and compulsive eating rather than change. Various tasks are suggested (e.g., mirror work, eliminating scales and clothes that do not fit, etc.) to foster self-acceptance. Emphasis is placed on the way in which one talks to oneself about one's body and eating. An accepting attitude, as opposed to a punitive or pseudo-loving one, is presented. This work leads to a decrease in anxiety.

The next part of the work involves stopping dieting and "legalizing" foods—making all foods equal in a psychological sense (i.e., no longer thinking in terms of fattening or nonfattening). As previously stated, dieting, the cultural response to the idealization of slenderness, leads to binging or compulsive eating. "I shouldn't eat that" leads to increased desire. But dieting mistakenly assumes that food itself is the problem, and must be carefully regulated.

In fact, the compulsive eater's problem is not food itself, but how she uses food: to calm herself down when she feels anxious. In the Overcoming Overeating approach, the inability to stay on a diet is viewed as an appropriate response to inappropriate restrictions. External regulation is not viewed as helpful because it will never foster the internal regulation that optimally underlies eating. Only when people live freely in the world of food can they begin the process of internal regulation.

Not dieting and legalizing foods also greatly reduce anxiety. One no longer has to worry about scarcity or famine; if there are no restrictions, rebellion is unnecessary. In addition, once food is no longer forbidden, the displacement involved in compulsive eating no longer functions. Typically, when compulsive eaters have a forbidden wish or idea, they eat a "forbidden food" and then accuse themselves of being "bad" for having done so. If food is not forbidden, compulsive eating becomes less effective as a disguise for other problems.

Central to the approach is the reconnection of food and hunger, which is called demand feeding for adults. The first task is for clients to note the difference between "stomach" or physiological hunger and "mouth" or psychological hunger. Then compulsive eaters are taught to eat when they are hungry, to choose exactly what their bodies crave at that moment, and to stop eating as soon as they have had enough. In the process of becoming attuned feeders, they are demonstrating that they can responsibly care for themselves. This reworking of the earliest experience of need and the satisfaction of need diminishes anxiety and provides a model of attuned caretaking that can be generalized to needs other than hunger. The emphasis on discovering who one is as an "eater" fosters individuation.

Statistical Analyses

Scales were constructed from the questionnaire items to measure eating preoccupation, body preoccupation, and emotional eating. The Eating Preoccupation Scale included 14 items and had an internal consistency of (alpha=.81). Sample items included: "I think about food much of the time," "I feel controlled by food," "I feel guilty about eating certain foods," and "I'm critical of myself if I eat when I'm not hungry." The Body Preoccupation Scale included 4 items and had an internal consistency of (alpha=.73). These items included: "I feel that I am overweight," "I'm ashamed of how I look," "My weight makes me feel bad about myself," and "My proportions make me feel bad about myself." Subjects responded to both the Eating Preoccupation and Body Preoccupation Scales using a (0=false), (1=somewhat true), and (2=very true) response format. The Emotional Eating Scale included 16 items and had an internal consistency of (alpha=.83). Subjects were asked, "When you are feeling the following emotions or moods, how often do you react by eating?" Sample emotions or moods included: anxious, lonely, tired, depressed, angry, unloved, worried, rebellious, disappointed, and sorry for myself. Subjects responded using a (1=rarely/never), (2=sometimes), or (3=very often) response format.

All analyses were limited to those subjects (N=420) who completed and returned a 2-year follow-up questionnaire. Paired t-tests were performed to test for mean differences between subjects who completed both questionnaires (N=420) and those who only completed the initial questionnaire (N=330). Mean scores for both groups were not significantly different for eating preoccupation ($t=.32$; $p>.05$) or emotional eating ($t=1.38$; $p>.05$). However, subjects who did not return the 2-year follow-up questionnaire had lower body preoccupation scores than subjects returning the 2-year follow-up questionnaire ($t=2.19$; $p<.05$).

Subjects were grouped based on a "yes" or "no" response to the question, "Have you stopped dieting?" at follow-up. One hundred and five subjects reported they were still dieting at the 2-year follow-up and 315 subjects reported they had stopped dieting. Three repeated measures analysis of variance (ANOVA) tests were performed using a 2 (group) by 2 (times) design with eating preoccupation, body preoccupation, and emotional eating as the dependent variables.

Multiple regression was used to assess the convergent validity of the three dependent variables as indicators of subjects' overall satisfaction with eating at the 2-year follow-up, as measured by the question, "How satisfied are you about your eating?" Responses were coded as follows: (1=slightly/not at all), (2=somewhat), or (3=very). The validity of the dependent variables was supported in that the regression equation accounted for 55% of the variance in subjects' overall satisfaction with their eating at follow-up ($p<.001$).

Finally, three multiple regression analyses were used to determine if mastery of six curriculum mechanics presented in *Overcoming Overeating* predicted changes in eating preoccupation, body preoccupation, and emotional eating at 2-year follow-up, after controlling for each of these measures at time one. For each mechanic of the curriculum subjects were asked, "How hard was it for you to implement the following?": legalizing food, stopping the yelling about your body and/or your eating behavior, identifying hunger, identifying what you want to eat when you're hungry, stopping eating when full, and accepting your body as it is now. Responses for each curriculum mechanic were coded as follows: (0=didn't implement), (1=very hard), (2=not too hard), and (3=easy). Standardized regression coefficients (β) are reported for each regression equation.

Results

Demographic characteristics indicated that subjects (N=420) ranged in age from 14 to 65 years, with a mean age of 36±10.6 years. Only 1.6% of subjects had not completed high school. Twenty-seven percent had attended some college, 32% had college degrees, and 21% were enrolled in or had completed postgraduate work. Most subjects were white (97%); a small proportion were Black (1.6%), Hispanic (.3%), and Other (.9%).

Repeated Measures ANOVA Results

The 2 (group) by 2 (time) ANOVA with eating preoccupation as the dependent variable had a significant interaction ($F=42.45$; $p<.001$). While both groups displayed a downward trend in eating preoccupation across time, the group that stopped dieting decreased significantly more than the group that continued to diet (Figure 1). The ANOVA with body preoccupation as the dependent variable also had a significant group by time interaction ($F=8.52$; $p<.01$). Again, both groups displayed a downward trend in body preoccupation, and the group that stopped dieting decreased significantly more than the group that continued to diet (Figure 2). Finally, the ANOVA with emotional eating as the dependent variable also had a significant group by time interaction ($F=7.81$; $p<.01$). Both groups again displayed a downward trend in emotional eating, with the group that stopped dieting decreasing their emotional eating significantly more than the group that continued to diet (Figure 3).

Effectiveness of the Curriculum Mechanics

Descriptive statistics revealed that *Overcoming Overeating* was helpful to respondents (Table 1). Mastery of the curriculum mechanics were effective in predicting eating preoccupation, body preoccupation, and emotional eating. Results of the multiple regression analysis with eating preoccupation as the criterion accounted for 27% of the variance. After controlling for eating preoccupation at time 1 ($R^2=.12$; $p<.001$), mastery of the curriculum mechanics increased the R^2 value by 15%. The curriculum components that accounted for the increased variance were "stopping eating when full" ($\beta=-.19$; $p<.001$), "accepting your body as it is now" ($\beta=-.16$; $p<.05$), and "legalizing food" ($\beta=-.10$; $p<.05$).

Results of the multiple regression analysis with body preoccupation as the criterion accounted for 35% of the variance. After controlling for body preoccupation at time 1 ($R^2=.24$; $p<.001$), mastery of the curriculum mechanics increased the R^2 value by 11%. The curriculum components that accounted for the increased variance were "accepting your body as it is now" ($\beta=-.25$; $p<.001$), and "identifying what you want to eat when you're hungry" ($\beta=-.09$; $p<05$).

Figure 1. Cell Means for Eating Preoccupation Measured Across Time by Dieting Behavior

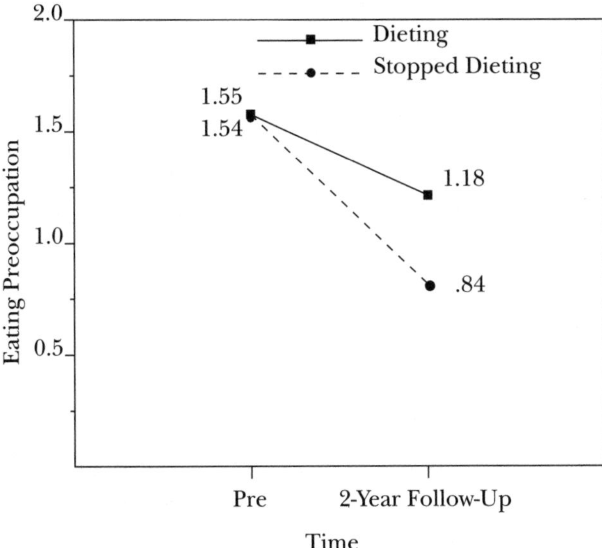

Figure 2. Cell Means for Body Preoccupation Measured Across Time by Dieting Behavior

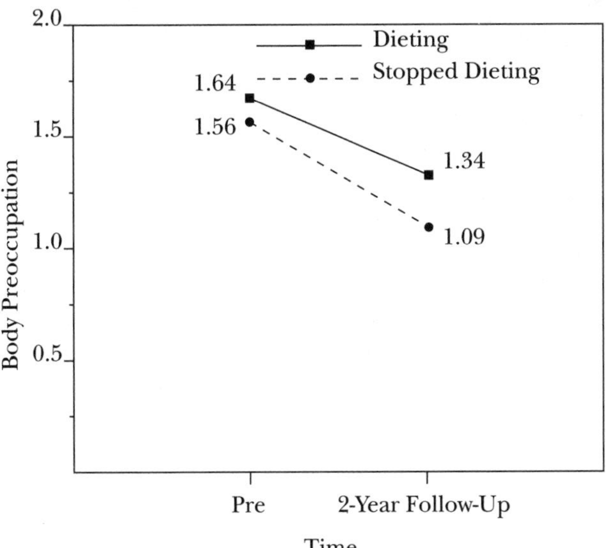

Figure 3. Cell Means for Emotional Eating Measured Across Time by Dieting Behavior

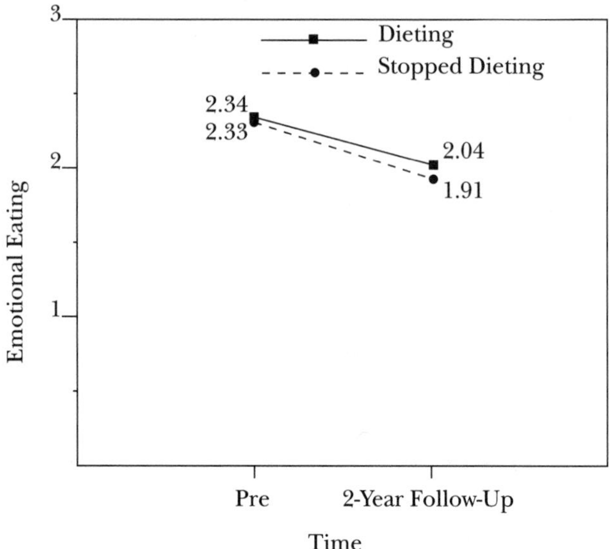

Table I. *Descriptive Data for Sample Questionnaire Items*

	PRE	2-YEAR FOLLOW-UP
	(percentage responding very true)	
My weight fluctuates	34.1%	17.8%
I feel "controlled by food"	72.7%	27.2%
I take laxatives or vomit to eliminate food I've eaten	8.1%	1.7%
I eat when I don't feel hungry	84.0%	31.6%
I feel ashamed of my eating habits	69.6%	25.4%
When you are feeling the following emotions or moods, how often do you react by eating?	PRE	2-YEAR FOLLOW-UP
	(percentage responding very often)	
anxious	64.2%	37.4%
depressed	72.3%	42.0%
disappointed	63.1%	29.7%
sorry for myself	75.9%	41.4%
unloved	66.1%	35.2%

Results of the final multiple regression analysis with emotional eating as the criterion accounted for 28% of the variance. After controlling for emotional eating at time 1 (R^2=.20; p<.001), mastery of the curriculum mechanics increased the R^2 value by 8%. The curriculum components that accounted for the increased variance were "stopping eating when full" (β=-.12; p<.01), "identifying what you want to eat when you're hungry" (β=-.10; p<.05), "accepting your body as it is now" (β=-.10; p<.05), and "identifying hunger" (β=-.09; p=.056).

Discussion

Although there is general agreement about the poor outcomes of current weight-loss treatments (Goodrick & Foreyt, 1991; Kirkley & Burge, 1989; Wooley & Garner, 1991; Wooley & Wooley, 1984), exploring nondiet alternatives is difficult because of the powerful cultural context in Western society which shapes biomedical thinking (Ernsberger & Haskew, 1987; Ritenbaugh, 1982). Our weight-obsessed society continues its efforts to prevent or eradicate fatness (Wooley & Wooley, 1984); as a result, researchers continue to search for the program or technique that will minimize the dieting failure rate (Rothblum, 1990). Faced with persistent high recidivism, rather than turning to nondiet alternatives, researchers have increasingly focused on weight loss maintenance skills and relapse prevention (Lissner et al., 1991). The Overcoming Overeating program is radically different in that it encourages individuals to stop dieting and adopt a non-restrained, internally directed eating style called demand feeding.

Results of this study indicate that the Overcoming Overeating approach to the problem of compulsive eating is effective in decreasing eating preoccupation, body preoccupation, and emotional eating over a two-year period, particularly for individuals who implemented the mechanics of the curriculum.

Eating Preoccupation

All of our subjects initially scored high on the eating preoccupation scale. They typically felt controlled by food, thought about it a great deal of the time, struggled not to eat it, and felt guilty and critical of themselves after eating. The techniques that significantly contributed to decreases in eating preoccupation were stopping eating when full, accepting one's body as it is now, and legalizing food.

Stopping when full is one of the most difficult parts of the curriculum to master because, for the compulsive eater, food is highly symbolic. Those who are able to stop eating when they are full no longer use food to move from an anxious to a calm place. They have in effect learned to use food as the fuel it was intended to be.

Those who are more readily able to accept their body at its current weight will no longer be obsessively preoccupied with how to lose weight. As a result, they will feel much more relaxed around food. In addition, because they have ceased to compare themselves to societal ideals, they will be less motivated to escape from self-awareness through compulsive eating (Heatherton & Baumeister, 1991).

The concept of legalizing food goes right to the heart of eating preoccupation. Food is a preoccupation for so many people because it has been considered off-limits. The more one feels one should not eat a particular food, the more focused on that food one will be. When foods are no longer regarded as either fattening or nonfattening, (i.e., when one is "living freely in a world of food"), one will no longer feel controlled by food.

Body Preoccupation

The compulsive eater, in addition to being preoccupied with food, is preoccupied with the size and shape of her body (Heatherton & Baumeister, 1991; Polivy & Herman, 1985; Vincent, 1979). The mechanics of the curriculum that significantly contributed to decreases in body preoccupation were accepting your body as it is now and identifying what you want to eat when you are hungry. It is always a struggle for someone who has spent many years trying to alter the size of her body to come to terms with the fact that she may have to live at her current size for some time, if not forever. Those individuals who are able to challenge the notion that we should all inhabit one body type and who are able to develop a comfortable relationship with their body in its present form, no longer are continuously unhappy with their bodies. Many techniques for living comfortably in one's body are presented in *Overcoming Overeating*, including mirror exercises, eliminating scales and clothes that do not fit, and dressing in new ways (Hirschmann & Munter, 1988).

It is interesting to note that the ability to identify what you want to eat when hungry had a significant effect on body preoccupation. One can hypothesize that someone who is able to know and to state clearly what her body is craving at any particular moment of hunger has a certain amount of respect and esteem for herself. These individuals are able to know and to state who they are, and would thus find it easier to accept the unique configurations of their own bodies. The person who is able to state the particular food she is hungry for is reshaping her intrapsychic cognitive responses (Heatherton & Baumeister, 1991). In other words, she is able to say, "This is my body. It may not be the body that is currently accepted by the culture but it is mine, and I can accept its unique needs for food." These individuals are able to trust and accept their unique needs and, in so doing, break the cycle of negative body thoughts.

Emotional Eating

Compulsive eaters come in a variety of shapes and sizes and with a variety of personality types and psychopathology. The characteristics that they all share is that, after years of dieting and/or compulsive eating, they have disconnected food from physiological hunger and use it instead as an antidote for anxiety. By working with the Overcoming Overeating approach, a compulsive eater should reach the point where it does not occur to her to eat unless physiologically hungry. In other words, she develops the ability to think about her problems, rather than to "eat about them." For this reason, perhaps the most significant finding is that study participants reported a significant decrease in the need to use food for emotional reasons.

The assumption underlying the Overcoming Overeating approach is that reconnecting food with physiological hunger and increasing self-acceptance are the two major factors in curing compulsive eating. The experience of getting hungry and feeling fed is at the heart of the interactions between the infant and her environment, and ultimately leads to a sense of security (Mahler, Pine, & Bergman, 1975). When compulsive eaters begin to respond to their physiological hunger signals in an attuned way, they are in a sense reparenting themselves. They are showing themselves that they can adequately provide for themselves. These experiences of need and need satisfaction (i.e., responding to stomach hunger) once again become the building blocks in developing a sense of security. The more secure someone feels, the less anxious she is, and therefore, the less need she has to reach out to food for caretaking.

It is noteworthy that all the elements of demand feeding (e.g., identifying hunger, identifying what you want to eat when you're hungry, stopping eating when full, along with accepting your body as it is now) significantly predicted a decrease in the need to use food for emotional reasons. In essence, demand feeding cured compulsive eating.

Limitations and Conclusions

Possible limitations of this study warrant consideration. Our sample was a convenience sample of those individuals who obtained the book *Overcoming Overeating* and mailed in a questionnaire in the back of the book. Although we reported the internal consistency of the psychometric scales used in this study and addressed the convergent validity of these scales, further psychometric properties should be evaluated. Unfortunately, physiological changes in body composition were not collected. Given the health risks associated with weight cycling and obesity, future research examining the effectiveness of nondiet approaches should include physiological measures. Research conducted in Australia supports the notion that nondiet approaches do not cause individuals to gain excessive amounts of weight. A mean weight loss of 3.1 kg was reported for subjects (N=56) at 2 years following completion of a 10 session group program designed to discourage dieting behavior and reduce preoccupation with body weight, food and eating (Roughan, Seddon, & Vernon-Roberts, 1990).

The response rate to the 2-year follow-up survey was 64%. Although nonrespondents at the 2-year follow-up scored similarly to respondents at pretest, nonrespondents were less preoccupied with thoughts of body size and shape than respondents. Thus, the women in our study may be more preoccupied with thoughts of physical appearance when compared to the general female population. Finally, further research is needed to determine if these findings, based on women across the United States who purchased the book *Overcoming Overeating*, can be generalized to the population at large.

Despite these limitations, the study is distinctive because it evaluates the effectiveness of a nondiet approach to the problem of compulsive eating. Our findings are strengthened by their consistency with research conducted in Canada (Ciliska, 1990; Polivy & Herman, 1992) and Australia (Roughan, Seddon, & Vernon-Roberts, 1990) which evaluates similar alternatives to strenuous weight loss efforts. This approach to eating is also supported by numerous investigations showing that young children are capable of adequately regulating their food intake, making coercive feeding strategies unnecessary (Birch, Johnson, Andresen, Peters, & Schulte, 1991; Davis, 1939). Together these results suggest that stopping dieting and implementing the process of internal regulation (i.e., demand feeding) lead to improvements in compulsive eating.

References

Berman, E. M. (1975). Factors influencing motivations in dieting. *Journal of Nutrition Education, 7*, 155–159.

Birch, L. L., Johnson, S. L., Andresen, G., Peters, J. C., & Schulte, M. C. (1991). The variability of young children's energy intake. *The New England Journal of Medicine, 324*, 232–235.

Brownell, K. D. (1987). Obesity and weight control: The good and bad of dieting. *Nutrition Today, 22(3)*, 4–9.

Brownell, K. D., & Kramer, F. M. (1989). Behavioral management of obesity. *Medical Clinics of North America, 73*, 185–201.

Ciliska, D. (1990). *Beyond Dieting.* New York: Brunner/Mazel.

Connors, M., & Johnson, C. L. (1987). Epidemiology of bulimia and bulimic behaviors. *Addictive Behaviors, 12*, 165–179.

Davis, C. M. (1939). Results of the self selection of diets of young children. *Canadian Medical Journal Association, 41*, 257–261.

Dulloo, A. G., & Calokatisa, R. (1990). Adaptation to low calorie intake in obese mice: contribution of a metabolic component to diminished energy expenditures during and after weight loss. *International Journal of Obesity, 15*, 7–16.

Dulloo, A. G., & Girardier, L. (1990). Adaptive changes in energy expenditure during refeeding following low-calorie intake: evidence for a specific metabolic component favoring fat storage. *American Journal of Clinical Nutrition, 52,* 415–420.

Ernsberger, P., & Haskew, P. (1987). Rethinking obesity: An alternative view of its health implications. *The Journal of Obesity and Weight Regulation, 6,* 58–137.

Goodrick, G. K., & Foreyt, J. P. (1991). The business of weight loss: Why treatments for obesity don't last. *Journal of the American Dietetic Association, 91,* 1243–1247.

Heatherton, T. F., & Baumeister, R. F. (1991). Binge eating as escape from self-awareness. *Psychological Bulletin, 110,* 86–108.

Heatherton, T. F., Herman, C. P., & Polivy, J. (1991). Effects of physical threat and ego threat on eating behavior. *Journal of Personality and Social Psychology, 60,* 138-143.

Hirschmann, J. R., & Munter, C. H. (1988). *Overcoming Overeating: Living Free in a World of Food.* New York: Fawcett Columbine.

Katzman, M. A., Wolchik, S. A., & Braver, T. (1984). The prevalence of frequent binge eating and bulimia in a non-clinical college sample. *International Journal of Eating Disorders, 3,* 53–62.

Kirkley, B. G., & Burge, J. C. (1989). Dietary restriction in young women: issues and concerns. *Annals of Behavioral Medicine, 11,* 66–72.

Kramer, F. M., Jeffrey, R. W., & Forster, J. L. (1989). Long-term follow-up of behavioral treatment of obesity: Patterns of regain among men and women. *International Journal of Obesity, 13,* 123–126.

Lissner, L., Odell, P. M., D'Agostino, R. B., Stokes, J., Kreger, B. E., Belanger, A. J., & Brownell, K. D. (1991). Variability of body weight and health outcomes in the Framingham population. *The New England Journal of Medicine, 324,* 1839–1844.

Mahler, M. S., Pine, F., & Bergman, A. (1975). *The Psychological Birth of the Human Infant.* New York: Basic Books.

Pavlou, K. N., Hoefer, M. A., & Blackburn, G. L. (1986). Resting energy expenditure in moderate obesity. *Annals of Surgery, 203,* 136–141.

Polivy, J., Heatherton, T. F., & Herman, C. P. (1988). Self-esteem, restraint, and eating behavior. *Journal of Abnormal Psychology, 97,* 354–356.

Polivy, J., & Herman, C. P. (1983). *Breaking the Diet Habit: The Natural Weight Alternative.* New York: Basic Books.

Polivy, J., & Herman, C. P. (1985a). Dieting and binging: A causal analysis. *American Psychologist, 40,* 193–201.

Polivy, J., & Herman, C. P. (1985b). Dieting as a problem in behavioral medicine. In E. S. Katkin & S. B. Manuck (Eds.), *Advances in Behavioral Medicine* (pp. 1–39). New York: JAI Press.

Polivy, J., & Herman, C. P. (1987). Diagnosis and treatment of normal eating. *Journal of Consulting and Clinical Psychology, 55,* 635–644.

Polivy, J., & Herman, C. P. (1992). Undieting: A program to help people stop dieting. *International Journal of Eating Disorders, 11,* 261–268.

Pyle, R. L., Mitchell, J. E., & Eckert, E. D. (1993). The incidence of bulimia in freshman college students. *International Journal of Eating Disorders, 2,* 75–85.

Ritenbaugh, C. (1982). Obesity as a culture-bound syndrome. *Culture, Medicine and Psychiatry, 6,* 347–361.

Rodin, J., Silberstein, L. R., & Striegel-Moore, R. H. (1985). Women and weight: a normative discontent. In T. B. Sonderegger (Ed.), Nebraska Symposium On Motivation: Psychology and Gender (pp. 267–307). Lincoln: University of Nebraska Press.

Rothblum, E. D. (1990). Women and weight: fad and fiction. *Journal of Psychology, 124,* 5–24.

Rothblum, E. D. (1992). The stigma of women's weight: social and economic realities. *Feminist Psychology, 2,* 61–73.

Roughan, P., Seddon, E., & Vernon-Roberts, J. (1990). Long-term effects of a psychologically based group programme for women preoccupied with body weight and eating behaviour. *International Journal of Obesity, 14,* 135–147.

Steen, S. N., Oppliger, R. A., & Brownell, K. D. (1988). Metabolic effects of repeated weight loss and regain in adolescent wrestlers. *Journal of the American Medical Association, 260,* 47–50.

Vincent, L. M. (1979). *Competing with the Sylph: The Quest for the Perfect Dance Body.* Princeton: Princeton Book Company.

Wadden, T. A., Stunkard, A. J., & Liebschutz, J. (1988). Three-year follow-up of the treatment of obesity by very low calorie diet, behavior therapy, and their combination. *Journal of Consulting and Clinical Psychology, 56,* 925–928.

Wardle, J. (1987). Compulsive eating and dietary restraint. *British Journal of Clinical Psychology, 26,* 47–55.

Wooley, S. C., & Garner, D. M. (1991). Obesity treatment: The high cost of false hope. *Journal of the American Dietetic Association, 91,* 1248–1251.

Wooley, S. C., & Wooley, O. W. (1984). Should obesity be treated at all? In A. J. Stunkard & E. Stellar (Eds.), *Eating and Its Disorders* (pp. 185–192). New York: Raven Press.

Bibliography

American Association of University Women (1991). *Shortchanging Girls, Shortchanging America.* Washington, D.C.

BLEICHMAR, EMILCE DIO (1993). "La femme provocatrice: une théorie sexuelle infantile (les effects du regard sexuel de l'adulte sur la subjetivié de la petite fille)" in Jean Laplanche et Collaborateurs, *Colloque International de Psychanalyse.* Paris: Presses Universitaires de France.

CHERNIN, KIM (1982). *The Obsession: Reflections on the Tyranny of Slenderness.* New York: Harper & Row.

DINNERSTEIN, DOROTHY (1977). *The Mermaid and the Minotaur.* New York: Harper & Row.

PINKOLA ESTÉS, CLARISSA (1992). *Women Who Run with the Wolves.* New York: Ballantine.

FALUDI, SUSAN (1991). *Backlash.* New York: Random House.

FROMM, ERICH (1965). *Escape from Freedom.* New York: Avon.

HIRSCHMANN, JANE R., & MUNTER, Carol H. (1988). *Overcoming Overeating.* New York: Fawcett Columbine.

HIRSCHMANN, JANE R., & ZAPHIROPOULOS, LELA (1993). *Preventing Childhood Eating Problems* (originally, *Are You Hungry?*). California: Gürze Press.

HUTCHINSON, MARCIA GERMAINE (1985). *Transforming Body Image.* California: The Crossing Press.

La Rouche, Janice, & Ryan, Regina (1984). *Janice LaRouche's Strategies for Women at Work.* New York: Avon.

Lerner, Harriet Goldhor (1986). *The Dance of Anger.* New York: Harper & Row.

Lewis, Helen Block (1971). *Shame and Guilt in Neurosis.* New York: International Universities Press.

Lyons, Pat, & Burgard, Debbie (1990). *Great Shape.* California: Bull Publishing Company.

Orbach, Susie (1982). *Fat Is a Feminist Issue II.* New York: Berkley.

Seid, Roberta Pollack (1989). *Never Too Thin: Why Women Are at War with Their Bodies.* New York: Prentice-Hall.

Sharpe, Ella Freeman (1968). *Collected Papers on Psychoanalysis.* London: The Hogarth Press.

Wolf, Naomi (1991). *The Beauty Myth.* New York: William Morrow.

Resources

Freda's Secrets
c/o Freda Rosenberg
4113 Barberry Drive
Lafayette Hill, PA 19444
Check for $15 payable to Freda Rosenberg*

Lake Austin Spa Resort
1705 Quinlan Park Road
Austin, TX 78732
1-800-847-5637

NAAFA
P.O. Box 188620
Sacramento, CA 95818
916-558-6880

The Overcoming Overeating Newsletter
c/o Jade Publishing
935 W. Chestnut Suite 420
Chicago, IL 60622
1-800-299-0577

*Prices subject to change.

Radiance Magazine
P.O. Box 30246
Oakland, CA 94604-9937
510-482-0680

Rememberings and Celebrations Cards
(gentle words for self-care)
Robyn Posin
Box 725
Ojai, CA 93024
805-646-4518
Check for $15.50 payable to For the Little Ones Inside*

*Prices subject to change.

General Information

The National Center for Overcoming Overeating
Directors, Carol H. Munter, C.E.D.S.,
and Jane R. Hirschmann, C.S.W.
P.O. Box 1257
Old Chelsea Station
New York, NY 10113-0920
Phone: 212-875-0442

The Chicago Center for Overcoming Overeating
Directors, Carol Coven Grannick, LCSW,
and Judith Matz, LCSW
P.O. Box 48
Deerfield, IL 60015
Phone: 708-853-1200

The Houston Center for Overcoming Overeating
Directors, Karen Carrier, M. Ed., and Kathy White
12609 Memorial Drive
Houston, TX 77024
Phone: 713-464-6152

The New England Center for Overcoming Overeating
Directors:

Barbara Ganzer, LICSW
27 Glen Street, Suite 12B
Stoughton, MA 02072
Phone: 617-341-4885

Cheryl Juba, M.A.
733 Turnpike Street, Suite 214
North Andover, MA 01845
508-686-4432

A Full-Day Introductory Workshop on Overcoming Overeating

Carol and Jane have recorded a live, five-hour introductory workshop based on the Overcoming Overeating approach. Available on audiocassette tapes by calling 1-800-299-0577

The Overcoming Overeating Newsletter

This quarterly newsletter provides a forum for readers who want to put an end to body hatred and dieting.
To subscribe call 1-800-299-0577

TO JOIN THE WOMEN'S CAMPAIGN TO END BODY HATRED AND DIETING CALL 1-800-299-0577

INDEX

About the Authors

CAROL H. MUNTER is a psychotherapist and Certified Eating Disorders Specialist in private practice in New York City. She started the first anti-dieting group for women in 1970. She was a member of the faculty of the New School for Social Research. Currently, she is the codirector of the National Center for Overcoming Overeating.

JANE R. HIRSCHMANN, M.S.W., is a psychotherapist in private practice who specializes in treating women and children with eating problems. She was on the faculty of the New School for Social Research for more than a decade. She is the codirector of the National Center for Overcoming Overeating, and coauthor of *Preventing Childhood Eating Problems* (Gürze Books).